Robert Cormier

Daring to Disturb the Universe

Robert Cormier

Daring to Disturb the Universe

PATTY CAMPBELL

Delacorte Press

Published by Delacorte Press
an imprint of Random House Children's Books
a division of Random House, Inc.
New York

www.randomhouse.com/teens

Educators and librarians, for a variety of teaching tools, visit us at
www.randomhouse.com/teachers

Library of Congress Cataloging-in-Publication Data

Campbell, Patricia J.
Robert Cormier : daring to disturb the universe / Patricia
Campbell.—1st ed.
p. cm.
Includes bibliographical references and index.
ISBN-13: 978-0-385-73046-4 (pbk.) —
ISBN-13: 978-0-385-90074-4 (Gibraltar lib. bdg.)
ISBN-10: 0-385-73046-2 (pbk.) — ISBN-10: 0-385-90074-0
(Gibraltar lib. bdg.) 1. Cormier, Robert—Criticism and
interpretation. 2. Young adult fiction, American—History and
criticism.   I. Title.
PS3553.O653Z625 2006
813'.54—dc22
2005023595

The text of this book is set in 11-point Times.

Printed in the United States of America

10 9 8 7 6 5 4 3 2 1

First Edition

Robert Cormier

Daring to Disturb the Universe

Contents

Acknowledgments.................................... ix

Foreword... xi

Chapter One
A Disturbing Master and Mentor 1

Chapter Two
A Life with a Sweet Bonus............................ 11

Chapter Three
At the Typewriter.................................... 35

Chapter Four
The Chocolate War 53

Chapter Five
The Dark Chocolate Controversy...................... 67

Chapter Six
Beyond the Chocolate War 81

Chapter Seven
I Am the Cheese 99

Chapter Eight
After the First Death...............................119

Chapter Nine
The Bumblebee Flies Anyway 137

Chapter Ten
Fade...149

Chapter Eleven
The Younger Novellas:
Other Bells for Us to Ring,
Tunes for Bears to Dance To,
and *Heroes*. 169

Chapter Twelve
The Middle Novels:
We All Fall Down
and *In the Middle of the Night* 195

Chapter Thirteen
Tenderness 213

Chapter Fourteen
Last Words: *Frenchtown Summer* and *The Rag
and Bone Shop* 231

Selected Bibliography 249

Appendix I
Robert Cormier's Awards and Honors 273

Appendix II
Films Based on Robert Cormier's Novels 279

Index 283

Acknowledgments

The largest debt of gratitude for the creation of this book is owed to Robert Cormier himself, of course, for his friendship and generosity over the years, and for many good conversations, letters, and e-mails about his writing and his life. His wife, Constance, too, has been a good friend, a gracious presence, and a major help in getting the facts right about the Cormier family. Gratitude is also due the Cormier archives of Fitchburg State College, under the leadership of library director Robert Foley, with special thanks to him and archivist Janice Ouellette for their prompt and complete answers to even the most esoteric questions. Appreciation is also offered to Craig Virden, who first saw the importance of this book as a tribute to the memory of our mutual friend; to Beverly Horowitz, who carried on that conviction; to Karen Wojtyla, who shared stories of her time as Cormier's editor; to Joan Slattery and other staff at Random House Books for Young Readers, who scoured their memories and their files in response to my questions. And finally, many thanks to my editor, Krista Marino, for her respect for Robert Cormier and her help and guidance.

Foreword

The first time I saw Robert Cormier he was standing in a for-
est behind a pine tree branch. *Skulking,* I thought. For who
but a reclusive, brooding skulker could have written the ter-
rifyingly paranoid *I Am the Cheese,* a book that I had just
finished and that would haunt me for weeks. So there he was
on the back flap of the book jacket, just as I pictured him.
Later we laughed together at my first suspicions. Because
Robert Cormier was a kindly, cheerful, decent sort of person, something I found out in the first five minutes after
meeting him when he came to speak to the librarians of the
Los Angeles Public Library in 1978.

In the next few years he wrote three more magnificent
young adult novels after *The Chocolate War* and *I Am the
Cheese,* and my admiration for his work grew and grew. So
when I got a letter from Ron Brown, the editor of a new series titled Twayne's Young Adult Authors, asking if I would
like to write one of the first volumes, I stubbed my toe in my
haste to get to the phone and cry, "Dibs on Robert Cormier!"

The assignment entailed, as I had hoped it would, a trip
to Massachusetts to interview him in January 1984. The
Cormiers graciously invited me to stay with them for two

days. Bob picked me up in Boston, and as we went over the hill to Leominster I had the thrill of a first look at the town where he spent his life and set his stories. Later that night, as I lay in bed in the upstairs guest room, I could hear the clickety-clack of his typewriter below, as he wrote—I imagined—yet another great novel.

During the next two days he shared his life, his thoughts, his unpublished manuscripts almost nonstop, often with Connie's help and witty comments. He led me on a tour of the streets of Leominster, where he pointed out landmarks in his fictional town of Monument. We visited the public library where he was a trustee and where Adam Farmer fell in love with Amy; drove past the tenements where he grew up and Paul Moreaux faded; smelled the incense and enjoyed the hush in the cathedral that is St. Cecilia's in Leominster and St. Jude's in Monument; and even went around the back way through the woods to look down at dusk on the football field of the school where Cormier's son Peter refused to sell chocolates and *The Chocolate War*'s Jerry Renault met the pain of disturbing the universe. The next afternoon while Bob was busy writing, I spent happy hours shuffling through the piles of documents in the Cormier archives at Fitchburg State College, reading letters from editors and fans, and unpublished scenes and unfinished novels. The trip was the beginning of a lifelong friendship, with many visits and long letters and conversations.

Gradually his editors began to trust me with early galleys and even corrected manuscripts of his novels well before they were published. The first reading was for plot, simple abandonment to the pull of the good story. The second reading was better—discovering the structure, the hidden meanings and secrets, the underlying themes and shifts in voices that made his work so powerful. Then, after I had let my reactions jell for a few days, would come the best part, the phone call to discuss the new book with its author.

With characteristic modesty, Bob was always delighted to hear my praise, intrigued by my questions, good about criticism. He always said, "I know I can believe you when you tell me you think something is terrific, because you don't hesitate to say so when you feel something isn't."

One of the greatest joys of my life has been to be Robert Cormier's biographer—and his friend. I had the privilege of being one of his confidants about many things in his work, so I know how he struggled with the hard questions in his books; I know how tired he was of the constant censorship attacks; I know how very much he loved his work, his family, and his town; and I know how he cared profoundly about goodness. But most of all I know—and anyone who ever came in contact with him knows—that Bob Cormier was a great man as well as a great writer. If this book makes even a beginning at giving readers a sense of that beautiful human being and inspiring them to read his books for themselves, I will be content.

It should be noted that because of variation in pagination among the many editions of Robert Cormier's works, page citations to quotes from his novels are not given. Any other unattributed quotes are from interviews and conversations with him from 1978 to 2000.

—*Patty Campbell, January 2006*
Fallbrook, California

Chapter One

A Disturbing Master and Mentor

Robert Cormier was, and remains, the consummate master of young adult literary fiction. He was the first to show the literary world that YA novels could be not only realistic about adolescent concerns but also unflinchingly honest about the big questions like the abuse of power, the roles of courage and forgiveness and redemption, and the struggle to stay human in the face of evil. While the daring of his subjects has often drawn censorship attack, the brilliance of his writing earned him many literary prizes and places on honor lists. He was the recipient of the American Library Association's Margaret A. Edwards Award and the ALAN Award of the National Council of Teachers of English, both given for lifetime achievement in young adult literature, as well as many other honors, both national and international. His books have been translated into more than a dozen languages, among them French, German, Italian, Swedish, Chinese, and Japanese, and three of his novels were made into motion pictures.

The publication in 1974 of Cormier's first YA novel, *The Chocolate War,* initiated a new level of literary excellence in the fledgling genre of young adult fiction and also unleashed a storm of controversy about the darkness and hard truth-saying of his work that continues to this day. The stunned critical reception of *The Chocolate War* led to the realization that fiction for teens could be great literature, and eventually made possible the recognition of the young adult novel by the literary establishment with such honors as the National Book Award and the Los Angeles Times Book Prize, as well as the American Library Association's Michael L. Printz Award. Consequently the door was opened for many other young adult writers to find their own way to honesty and excellence.

Noted critic and author Michael Cart says, "As a writer of young adult novels, Robert Cormier is without peer. He is, simply, the single most important writer in a field that is made distinguished by his contributions to it."[1] Throughout the twenty-six years of his time as a young adult author Cormier continued to raise the stakes as to *what* could be said in a book for teens and *how* it could be said. He repeatedly surprised his readers with the originality of each new novel, while maintaining a continuity of recognizable style and themes that came to be called "Cormieresque"—short, cinematic scenes, taut dialogue, a deceptively straightforward story undergirded by intricate structure and layers of tricky allusion and metaphor, an intense focus on the emotion of the situation, doubling and parallels, an ironic interactivity with the reader that has only recently been recognized as postmodern, and a dark awareness of evil as an implacable obstacle in human affairs. But the crucial point about his importance in the development of young adult literature is that by being faithful to his vision, he freed other writers to follow their own. His work has inspired and given courage to many of the other greats in the field.

Contemporary YA writers have been quick to pay him tribute for that example:

Chris Crutcher offers heartfelt homage: "It's as simple as this . . . had there been no Bob Cormier . . . there certainly would be no Chris Crutcher."[2]

Chris Lynch, author of many powerful YA novels such as *Iceman* and *Freewill,* has credited Cormier with providing an epiphany in his own work: "*I Am the Cheese* was without question the most important YA title in my development as a writer. It was the book that made me say, 'Hot damn, you can *do* that? You can write a story that raw and real without translating it for the reader?' I cannot tell you how liberating that was for me."[3]

Gail Giles, whose *Shattering Glass* critics have related to *The Chocolate War,* says simply, "He's the master. That's all there is."[4]

Virginia Euwer Wolff, a National Book Award winner for *True Believer,* also credits Cormier with her own genesis as a writer: "I probably wouldn't be writing today if I hadn't read *The Chocolate War,* which had to live in the back of my mind for at least a decade before I put fingers to keyboard to try my own YA fiction. What a gift he was to our field, what a consciousness."[5]

Cormier was not only a literary example but also a counselor and friend to many young writers at the beginnings of their careers. Michael Cadnum, who nowadays writes unusual YA historical novels but whose early realistic titles like *Calling Home* were often referred to as Cormieresque, remembers that "Bob's manner to a younger writer was one of matter-of-fact graciousness, of intellectual hospitality. . . . No writer could meet Bob and feel that his life, and his relationship with his profession, was anything but gilded by the contact. We come away from this author and friend, and from his work, with a renewed faith in life. We have been told that we matter."[6]

Cormier's editors, too, were aware of his stature from the first. George Nicholson, who published several of his books for Delacorte Press, remembers that when Cormier's first novels appeared, "all of us who were editors in this [then] new thing called YA saw that here was a level of achievement that we had to go out and fill."[7]

One can measure Robert Cormier's influence on young adult literature by tracing the position his works hold in the history of the genre—what came before and after his groundbreaking books. The prototype of the form is, of course, J. D. Salinger's *The Catcher in the Rye,* a book Cormier admired. In *Catcher* we first hear that self-absorbed, angry, and touchingly vulnerable voice of the One True Outsider and see the adult world through his limited but judgmental perception, a point of view that became definitive for the form. Published in 1951, it was more than a decade ahead of its time. As Cormier himself has observed, if it had appeared later it would undoubtedly have been categorized as a young adult novel. But in the fifties, and for most of the sixties, fiction written for teens was a very different matter. Saccharine, heavily didactic, and careful to avoid taboo subjects, these "junior novels" dealt with trivial adolescent concerns like boyfriends and the senior prom, with an all-wise adult on hand to straighten things out in the end.

In the magic year of 1967 young adult literature was born with the publication of S. E. Hinton's *The Outsiders,* a tale of gang warfare and social class that captured something real. In the same year Robert Lipsyte's *The Contender* appeared, and the next year saw the publication of Paul Zindel's *The Pigman.* Critics soon began to see a pattern, to refer to this group of novels as the New Realism, but for the next five years there were actually very few books in the wake of these that fit that pattern squarely. Although several other writers of this so-called New Realism in the YA canon were already at work—Richard Peck, M. E. Kerr, Harry and

Norma Fox Mazer, Norma Klein—almost none of their books from this early period have survived as memorable.

Subgenres began to emerge during this period: Ann Head's *Mr. and Mrs. Bo Jo Jones,* an indisputably YA novel although published as an adult book, was followed by Zindel's *My Darling, My Hamburger* in 1969, and then by a trail of novels and nonfiction books about the dangers of teen sex and pregnancy. With the encouragement of publishers, new African American writers like Rosa Guy, Sharon Bell Mathis, June Jordan, and Alice Childress based young adult novels on the problems of growing up black in America. And John Donovan, Isabelle Holland, and Lynn Hall started a trend with stories of gay teens who suffered for their sexual identity.

Then *The Chocolate War* burst on the scene in 1974, and Robert Cormier, as Michael Cart has said, put the *literature* in young adult literature.[8] At first no one knew what to do with this astonishing and infuriating book. Almost immediately, though, a few YA writers were inspired to reach higher. The very next year S. E. Hinton wrote what some critics feel is her most literary book, the strangely mythic *Rumblefish;* Richard Peck tackled some serious social issues in *Representing Super Doll;* M. E. Kerr looked hard at religious hypocrisy in *Is That You, Miss Blue?;* and Judy Blume caught the nation's attention with her wise and realistic depiction of young love and sex in *Forever.* When *I Am the Cheese* was published three years later, in 1977, it became apparent that *The Chocolate War* was not an anomaly but the beginning of an unprecedented body of work for teens by an extraordinary writer. It was obvious that the genre was here to stay, and with Cormier's example there were almost no limits to how high it could fly.

Although Cormier had originally been surprised to find that he was writing YA novels, he felt warmly welcomed to that fellowship: "I was caught up in a world illuminated by intelligence, wit, and enthusiasm, was introduced to the works of wonderful writers like Norma Klein . . . Robert Lipsyte . . . and M. E. Kerr. . . . These and other writers I would read with such pleasure in the years ahead made me realize I had joined a caravan of stunningly talented people."[9]

Critics and students continue to evaluate and comment on Cormier's writing today because his work is timeless. Cormier's greatness lies in his universality, his focus not just on adolescent concerns but also on the basic moral and spiritual issues of the larger human condition—something that never truly changes.

When Cormier died, there was an outpouring of tribute, not only from writers, editors, and dignitaries of the literary world but also from teachers, librarians, parents, and teens who had been touched and changed by an encounter with Cormier or his books. Perhaps the one he would have liked best was the "Bouquet for Bob" published in *Voice of Youth Advocates,* a magazine aimed at young adult librarians and their teen readers. This collection of short personal testimonials expresses love and gratitude in many voices.

The most stunning flower from this bouquet, and one that epitomizes Cormier's effect on troubled teens, is a double tribute from a mother and daughter. Kelly Milner Halls tells of her concern for her teenage daughter Kerry, who was failing at school and "carving her arms like a block of cheddar" in her anger at the world. Her mother remembers "Kerry was not a reader. She said all YA books were 'stupid.' " But Kelly, a professional book reviewer, began to search for a book that would let her daughter know she was not alone, and found it in *Tenderness*. "She swallowed it whole—read it in two days."

Kerry found the validation she needed in Cormier's book. Her mom had said, " 'This one is gonna make you think, kid,' and *man,* was she right," says Kerry. "Robert Cormier understood what it felt like to be on the outside.

And he knew that even 'bad' kids were human. That meant a
lot to me, because at the time, a lot of teachers seemed to
think I was 'bad.' It may sound strange, but I always felt
Robert Cormier could see me when he wrote. Maybe he
didn't know *me*—but he knew kids like me."[10]

This respect and admiration between Cormier and his
young readers is memorialized in the Robert Cormier Center for Young Adults at his own Leominster Public Library.
The lively teen room and book discussion sessions noisily
presided over by young adult librarian Diane Sanabria were
close to Cormier's heart, and he often "just happened to
drop in" when they were talking about one of his novels.
After his death, a new center was proposed in his memory,
and Sanabria and the town jumped at the chance to make it
a real tribute to Leominster's most famous citizen. There
were new bookshelves and tables and chairs, new paint, a
brilliant neon sign of Cormier's signature. The art club at
the high school created a long mural showing a young
Cormier at his typewriter, his stories moving across the wall
in collage and acrylic. A maxim inscribed on the wall and
chosen by the teens was taken from one of Cormier's newspaper columns:

```
Never believe the people who tell
you that dreams don't come true.
Don't pay attention to those who
say that it's not worth the trou-
ble and nobody cares and why try
and there must be a catch some-
where. Don't succumb to the phi-
losophy that says it can't happen
here, the odds are too high, and
it's much too late and why take
the risk, because they might laugh
if you fail. But the people who
```

```
count don't laugh. And if you
don't fail, they cheer.¹¹
```

It is often said that Robert Cormier, like Jerry Renault in
The Chocolate War, dared to disturb his own universe, the
universe of young adult literature—but he also illuminated it
with the light of simple goodness. Michael Cart sees his influence pointing on into the future: "We need to encourage a
new generation of young adult writers to follow the risk-
taking and transformative example of Robert Cormier, who
single-handedly changed young adult literature forever
when he 'set free the subject of despair.' I'm not sure that
'despair' is quite the right word, though. What Cormier
really set free was the acknowledgment of the very real presence of evil in young lives. . . . Cormier took his . . . readers
into the heart of darkness and turned the lights on there—
showing them, and us, a place that, until he tested the bound-
aries, had been securely off-limits."¹²

Notes

1. Introduction to "Probing the Dark Cellars of a
Young Adult Writer's Heart," Frances Clark Sayers
Lecture, University of California, Los Angeles,
1999.

2. "A Bouquet for Bob," *Voice of Youth Advocates,* February 2001, 390.

3. Fraustino, Lisa Rowe, "The Age of Cheese:
Readers Respond to Cormier," in *The Phoenix
Award of the Children's Literature Association
1995–1999,* edited by Alethea Helbig and Agnes
Perkins, Lanham, MD, Scarecrow Press, 2001, 115.

4. Campbell, Patty, *"Shattering Glass:* A
Reader's Guide," New Milford, CT, Roaring Brook
Press, 2002.

5. Wolff, Virginia Euwer, e-mail to the author January 9, 2002.

6. "Robert Cormier Remembered," *Publishers Weekly,* January 1, 2001, 28.

7. Glick, Andrea, "Robert Cormier Dead at 75," *School Library Journal online,* December 1, 2000.

8. Cart, Michael, "Carte Blanche," *Booklist,* November 15, 2002, 587.

9. Cormier, Robert, "The Gradual Education of a YA Novelist," introduction to *Twentieth-Century Young Adult Writers,* Farmington Hills, MI, St. James Press, edited by Laura Standley Berger, 1994.

10. Halls, Kelly Milner, e-mail to the author, November 18, 2003.

11. Cormier, Robert, "The Cheers Were Like an Embrace," *(And So On . . . ,* John Fitch IV column), *Fitchburg-Leominster Sentinel and Enterprise,* May 10, 1983, B2.

12. Cart, Michael, *From Romance to Realism: 50 Years of Growth and Change in Young Adult Literature,* New York, HarperCollins, 1996, 270.

Chapter Two

A Life with a Sweet Bonus

The New York Times Book Review described Robert Cormier in his fifties quite accurately as "the picture of a small-city newspaperman—slight, sort of wispy, gray; a man who's reported the fires and Lions Club meetings and courthouse corruption. He's also a nice man, a family man. . . ."[1] His appearance had nothing about it that might have suggested he was a man who wrote novels of stunning impact about the monstrous and inexorable power of evil.

He himself recognized the paradox. He wrote: "Look at me: I cry at sad novels, long for happy endings, delight in atrocious puns, pause to gather branches of bittersweet at the side of a highway. I am shamelessly sentimental—I always make a wish when I blow out the candles on my birthday cake, and I dread the day when there may be no one there to say 'Bless you' when I sneeze. . . . I hesitate to kill a fly, but people die horrible deaths in my novels."[2]

His sunny compassion showed up in innumerable small ways. If you asked how to pronounce his name (Is it

Cor-*meer*? Cor-mee-*ay*?) he would assure you that the version you had just used was fine, and the way most people said it. But overheard speaking on the phone, he would introduce himself as Bob Cor-mee-*eh,* a pronunciation that might have had more to do with his New England background than his French Canadian origins.

Cormier confessed that Adam Farmer in *I Am the Cheese* is a character who comes close to being autobiographical, not in the events of the story but in the fears and phobias that torment him. Like Adam, Cormier suffered from migraines. Also like Adam, he was afraid of dogs and claustrophobic about elevators. But the daily events of his life were peaceful. For forty years he lived in the same two-story shingled house in a pleasant wooded suburb of Leominster, three miles away from the house where he was born. Here he and his wife, Connie, raised four children. His modest brown Volvo sedan stood in the driveway. The living room had big soft chairs, a snug window seat, and a baby grand piano that was given years before to Connie's mother by her father. Several shelves held tokens and mementos from fans, in the shape of ceramic beehives or plastic school buses or homemade miniature bicycles.

Until the Cormiers added on a room for his study, he worked for many years in a small alcove at one end of the dining room. Amid the clutter of books and papers was a stereo console where he played the Beatles and the Eagles and Bruce Springsteen and old jazz, and near the desk was his battered standard reporter's L C Smith manual typewriter. Cormier was superstitious about abandoning the old machine on which he had written so many successful novels. Though in 1997 he and Connie did reluctantly buy a computer for final drafts and e-mail, he continued to compose on the typewriter. Here in this office without a door Cormier often wrote late at night. He once said, "My daughter Bobbie recently told friends that, for as far back as she can remember, she could hear the tap, tap, tap of typewriter keys as she went off to sleep. She said it was a comforting sound."[3] His insomnia was a factor in the extraordinary closeness he had with his children as they were growing through their teen years. "I'd be awake when my kids came home at night. They knew I wasn't spying on them and we'd just talk. There are a lot of things a kid will tell you at one in the morning that he won't at one in the afternoon. I found their lives exciting and tragic. A kid could go through a whole lifetime in an afternoon on the beach."[4] The four Cormier teenagers, Bobbie, Peter, Christine, and Renee, are grown up now and have children of their own, and all show their creative inheritance in various ways. All are frequent and welcome visitors at the house where they grew up.

Cormier's rapport with his own and other young adults made him extremely open and available to his readers. In *The Catcher in the Rye* Holden Caulfield says, after finishing Isak Dinesen's *Out of Africa,* "What really knocks me out is a book that, when you're all done reading it, you wish the author that wrote it was a terrific friend of yours and you could call him up on the phone whenever you felt like it."[5] Cormier was that kind of author. Teenagers *could* just call him up anytime. It is a well-known secret that Amy Hertz's phone number in *I Am the Cheese* was Cormier's own. His readers did call, often. Sometimes, if they were especially sharp, they would ask for Amy. "Sorry, she's not home, but this is her father," Cormier would say, or if Renee was visiting and answered the phone she would respond, "Speaking." Some callers were so shocked by this collision of reality and fantasy that they hung up, but those who persisted found Cormier willing to discuss their questions about the books with seriousness and respect. The only time his patience wore thin was when young callers forgot time-zone differences and rang the Cormier phone very late at night. "Do you know what *time* it is?" he would growl, like everybody's father.

Letters poured in, too, from readers who wanted to find out why a certain character did what, or the meaning of a puzzling turn in the plot. The intricate last chapter of *I Am the Cheese* drew so many questions that a class at Fitchburg State College taught by Dr. Marilyn McCaffrey once prepared an answer sheet for Cormier to mail out, revealing the enlightening nuggets of plot facts that can be ferreted out of earlier chapters. But usually he felt that a thoughtful question deserved a personal answer, sometimes as long as two closely written sheets. He valued the discipline of answering this feedback from his audience highly. "They keep me sharp. They ask some very tough questions about things I haven't really thought through."

Cormier's willingness to think things through, to face up to the absolute truth without cynicism or bitterness—these qualities give his work strength and integrity. Some of that courage may have come from the solidity of a childhood in the secure, self-enclosed community of French Hill, and from the safety of a good marriage and a lifetime in the same town. "I love it here," he said. "I like being able to go downtown and run into some guy I was in the first grade with."[6]

Although Leominster was founded in 1740, the French Hill section was built between 1900 and 1915 to house the labor being recruited from Canada for the new comb factories. The French were not the only immigrants—Italians and Irish also poured into the town during this period—but members of each ethnic group kept to their own sections. Robert Cormier's grandfather brought his young family there so that he could seek his fortune, and he was soon a man of substance with a three-story tenement house and a horse and wagon of his own. His son Lucien Joseph Cormier married an Irish girl, Irma Collins,[7] and brought her back home to live on the third floor of the tenement his father owned in French Hill.

The first of their eight children, Norman, arrived soon, and two years later, on January 17, 1925, Robert Edmund Cormier was born.[8] With grandparents downstairs and aunts and uncles as neighbors, he was surrounded with love and attention as a small child, although his earliest memory was a sad one. When Robert was five his three-year-old brother, Leo, died. "My mother said that he was a blond, beautiful child," he remembered. "I was sort of his protector because we were close in age." The family mourned the loss, and the tragedy became a landmark in Cormier's adult emotional landscape. But other siblings soon filled the house: Gloria, John, Ann, and later, when Robert was fourteen, the twins, Constance and Charles.

Life in French Hill was good for young Bob, and he evoked this time and place lovingly in *Fade* and *Frenchtown Summer.* "There was a great sense of family. I always felt as if my father would take care of us." Bob played in the yard of St. Cecilia's Parochial Grammar School with his brothers and sisters and cousins, or watched the men pitch horseshoes after work. The games of the factory baseball clubs were major social occasions. Everyone would come to cheer for fathers or uncles, and afterward the men and older boys would go off to celebrate the victory with a few beers.

Local businesses catered to the needs of the French Hill population: Sauve's Market, Nimee's Department Store, Aubuchon Hardware, Vallee's Dairy. . . . Nobody had a telephone, because there was no need. Best friends lived next door or across the street. It was easier just to open the window and shout. Nor did anybody need a car, because all the working adults walked the few blocks to the comb factories, which by then had diversified to other plastic objects, baby carriages, and even, for a time, Arrow shirts.

Because Bob's mother was Irish, the Cormiers spoke English at home. The nuns at St. Cecilia's taught in both languages: English in the morning and French in the afternoon.

At school life was not so easy anymore. "I wasn't athletic. I was a lousy ballplayer who would rather be off reading a book someplace," he recalled. "On the streets I was alone."[9] And he was humiliated by his wire-rimmed glasses. "I would sort of lose them and have to fake my way in the classroom, until finally I realized that I had to wear them. They were really a burden."[10] But there was always the secure retreat of home. It wasn't all bad. "I had a horrible time in parochial school and I also had a great time," he admitted.[11] But in another context he spoke revealingly of "the hell I went through with nuns."

St. Cecilia's school is part of the church that the rest of Leominster calls the French cathedral. The tall spire is the central landmark of French Hill. St. Cecilia's size and beauty are amazing achievements for such a tiny community. Built in the early thirties in the midst of the Depression, it was considered an act of faith by the factory workers, who scraped together their pennies to erect an extravagant house of God. Its soaring white interior is full of light and is almost Calvinistic in its restraint and lack of superfluous decoration. One truly fine piece of sculpture—a graceful reclining statue of the martyred Saint Cecilia—adorns the chancel. The congregation ran out of money before they could buy proper stained glass, so in Bob's childhood the light streamed in through rippled orange-gold windows. It was like being inside the sun, he often thought with awe.

But some of his experiences in the church were more awful than awesome. On the first Friday of the month the nuns brought each class in turn to the front of the church where the confessionals were to make confession in preparation for Sunday Mass. The confessionals were simple curtained alcoves at both sides of the nave. The class was seated conveniently nearby, in a long row in a pew, and one by one they went into the confessional to kneel and confess. But the priest inside was deaf. "Louder! Louder!" he'd demand. The nuns had told them that if they held anything back they'd be unclean for Communion, and then they'd go straight to hell when they died. So, stiff with agonized embarrassment, Bob would shout out all his small shameful secrets to the avid eavesdroppers behind him.

Other nuns were more sensitive to the budding talent of young Bob. One especially, Sister Catherine, he remembered with affection as a "big boy's nun." One day, when he was in seventh grade, he sat under the playground stairs and wrote a poem for her. When he handed it to her with trepidation, she read it carefully and said, "Why, Bob! You are a writer!" A casual kindness, but a remark that deeply influenced his self-definition. "Are," not "will be"! From that moment on, he thought of himself as a writer.

His aspirations were refined and shaped by a momentous gift on his twelfth birthday. His godmother, Aunt Victorine, presented him with *The Adventures of Tom Sawyer*—the first real book he had ever owned. He laughed and cried with Tom, dreamed and schemed with him. "More than that," Cormier wrote in an essay on his childhood reading, "this novel pointed out the drama possible in the life of an ordinary boy and thus the potential drama in my own life. I looked at French Hill as if for the first time and saw its mysteries and its beauties and the drama that can be found in ordinariness."[12]

Although he had always been in love with words, in earlier years young Bob had not been a devotee of the children's room of the Leominster Public Library. "I never found what I was looking for in that children's section because, I see now, I didn't know what I was looking for . . . I searched in vain for books that would satisfy a yearning in me that I could not identify."[13]

But in 1991, in a moving speech he delivered to an august assemblage of librarians on the occasion of his winning the American Library Association's Margaret A. Edwards

Award, he traced the beginnings of his discovery of literature and his lifelong love affair with libraries:

My dream as a boy was to be admitted to the adult section of the library, to leave the limited precincts of the children's room, and enter the limitless bounds of that mysterious and marvelous place called the stacks. . . . On occasion, I sneaked past the women at the circulation desk . . . and made my way into the stacks. I would run my hands across the spines of books, reading the names of the authors. This was excruciating because I was not allowed to borrow them. So I'd draw one from the shelf and sit on the glass floor, knees jackknifed, my back to the wall, and read. Miss Wheeler found me there one afternoon and we talked of books and authors. She issued my first adult card—one of the great moments of my life, possessing my passport to a world that I still explore with wonder and delight. The library from that moment on was my second home—my home of the spirit. . . .[14]

And then, just before his graduation from eighth grade, something else happened to mark the end of his accepting childhood and the beginning of his rebellious and questioning adolescence. On the morning of June 10, 1939, he looked up from his school desk and glanced out the window. There, across the street and beyond a vacant lot, his house was one solid sheet of flame. His mother and baby sister were home, he knew. He leaped to his feet in horror to run, but the teacher cried, "Wait! Bob, sit down! We're going to have some prayers before you run out!" And then, while the flames crackled, she forced him to take out his rosary and say a decade—an Our Father, ten Hail Marys, and a Glory Be to the Father. When he finally was allowed to leave, he found to his relief that his mother and sister were safe, but the anger from the incident was a force in his life for many years.

Although his precious graduation suit had been ruined by the fire, the neighbors rallied and brought clothes for the Cormiers, and he was able to leave St. Cecilia's in dignity. Attending the Leominster public junior high school was another matter. For the first time in his life, he was thrown in with people from a variety of ethnic and religious backgrounds. The French and Italian Catholics entered junior high with a distinct disadvantage: not only were they an exotic minority by religion and national origin, but since their parochial school went on through eighth grade and public junior high began with seventh grade, they entered an already established social order as outsiders. It was tough. There were bullies in the halls and in the yard after school, and snarling dogs on his paper route. But there was always comfort at home. "Once I got in the house I was safe."

Then, too, there were compensations in his intellectual life. He discovered William Saroyan, who had written so movingly of his childhood in an Armenian community in California not unlike French Hill. He admired the clear simplicity of Hemingway's language. And in ninth grade at the library he found Thomas Wolfe, a writer who was to influence him all his life. "His prose thundered like mountain torrents. I simply plunged into his work, somewhere in the middle, reveling in the marvelous tumult of language, getting to know the characters, working back and forth through the chapters."[15]

He adored the movies, too, and went faithfully to the Saturday-afternoon matinees at the Plymouth and Met theaters. Because his mother had given up motion pictures as part of a religious vow, Bob would often hurry home and tell her the week's movie scene by scene—an exercise that he later wrote taught him "vital lessons in plotting and story structure, narration and pacing, and dialogue."[16] He continued writing poetry, too, and some of it was good enough to be published in the *Leominster Daily Enterprise,* much to the pride of French Hill.

In high school his world widened further. For the first time he met a Jew, a girl. In a series of long, intense conversations they told each other everything they knew about their respective religions. More teachers recognized his writing as something special. Several encouraged him. He especially remembered Lillian Ricker, who worked with him, edited his writing, and induced him to start acting. Much to his surprise, he found he was good at it. When the school put on a production of *The Devil and Daniel Webster,* he played the second title role with flamboyance and style, and won a "best acting award" for his performance.[17] A youth group sponsored by the WPA (like the Rec Center in *Heroes*) was "a very big part of my life," he told me. The group put on shows, and he won table tennis tournaments. "Ping-Pong was the only sport I was ever good at," he commented. His shy friendliness even got him elected president of the senior class. In spite of his triumphs, he seemed to himself to be a social disaster, particularly with girls. He remembered adolescence as "a lacerating experience."

World War II was raging when he graduated in 1942. Most of his male classmates were snapped up by the army, but Bob was rejected because of his nearsightedness.[18] He went to work at the factory, as all French Hill sons were expected to do, but he took a night shift so he could go to classes during the day at Fitchburg State College.[19] One of his instructors, Florence Conlon, noticed his skill with words and asked to see something he had written. He showed her a short story, "The Little Things That Count." A few weeks later on a summer Saturday afternoon she drove up to the Cormier house, got out of the car, and ran up the walk waving a check. She had had the story typed and had sent it to *Sign,* a Catholic family magazine. They had accepted it immediately and sent a check for seventy-five dollars, the first money Cormier had ever earned for his writing.

Encouraged in his ambition to earn his living at the typewriter and eager to get on with it, he left Fitchburg State and took a job writing commercials for radio station WTAG. It was excellent discipline for a new writer. Everything had to be packed into a hundred words, and sponsors were severe critics.[20]

Young bachelors were scarce and consequently popular in French Hill. Every Saturday night there were community dances, and Bob loved to dance. The first dance would always go to his sister Gloria, and then he would dance with each of her girlfriends in turn, spreading himself around out of courtesy. One Saturday night Gloria arrived with her friend Constance Senay. Connie had been only a sophomore when Bob was a senior at Leominster High. He had been aware of her, though he had never paid much attention to the pretty French Hill girl whose mother ran the pharmacy. But politely he invited her to dance, and they stepped onto the floor together. Forty-two years later he still got starry-eyed when he described the next moment. "She was fantastic! We just floated away." They danced the next dance, and the next, and then there were a succession of Saturday nights, and then they were going together.

Soon he was offered his first real newspaper job. He joined the night staff of the Leominster bureau of the

Worcester Telegram,[21] the paper that owned radio station WTAG. On the strength of the new salary he and Connie were married in 1948 at St. Cecilia's. The marriage was solid from the very beginning. Connie provided the safe home that gave Cormier a firm foundation for his writing, and her quick intelligence was a match for his. "The great thing about my wife, Connie, is she has been able to create an atmosphere in which I could work," he was to say many years later.[22] In a short story titled "Another of Mike's Girls" he put a tribute to Connie into the mouth of one of his characters. "We have been married twenty-one years and she still has the ability to turn my knees liquid when she holds her head a certain way and looks at me."[23]

In 1955, with two babies at home, he transferred to the competition, the *Fitchburg Sentinel.* He was to work there for the next twenty-three years, first as a reporter and then as a wire editor, from 1959 to 1966, and finally as an associate editor and columnist until he left to write fiction full-time in 1978.[24] From the beginning Cormier was in love with his typewriter. He wrote night and day. In the evenings, after a full stint at the newspaper, he wrote publicity releases for two Fitchburg paper companies to help feed his growing family. On the weekends he dove into fiction. "That was my dessert. I wrote stories the way other guys play golf."[25] *Sign* printed more of his work, and later he became a regular contributor to *Redbook, Woman's Day, McCall's,* the *Saturday Evening Post,* and other popular magazines. He wrote about the small happinesses and disappointments of human relationships, often drawing on his French Hill childhood and adolescence for characters and settings.

This family history soon grew into a novel, a story of French Canadian emigrant life told from the point of view of his grandfather. Although he was not satisfied with the book, he titled it "Act of Contrition" and sent if off as an experiment to Houghton Mifflin. They rejected it, not to his surprise, but editor Ann Barrett was impressed enough to recommend that he find himself an agent. She referred him to the Curtis Brown Agency, where he was taken on by a capable young newcomer from the Midwest, Marilyn Marlow. She encouraged him to continue to explore the novel form in the scarce moments of free time left after his journalist's workday.

Cormier had become a very good newspaperman, especially when the assignment had an element of human interest. He won three major journalism awards for his work. In 1959 a piece about a child burned in a car accident earned him the Associated Press in New England award for the best human interest story of the year. In 1973 he was awarded the same prize for an article about a workshop staffed by mentally retarded people, which was written from their perspective. And in 1974 his human interest column was judged the best column in the Thomson Newspapers chain, the syndicate that owned the *Daily Sentinel and Leominster Enterprise.*[26]

Life was good, pleasant, ordinary. And then suddenly the world, like an elevator with a broken cable, dropped from beneath his feet. His father, the strong refuge of his childhood and the closest friend of his adult years, developed lung cancer. Cormier's memories of the progress of his illness were etched deep with the acid of pain. "I remember the most terrible day of my life. My father had been coughing and losing weight. He went to the doctor to find what the trouble was. As soon as he left the office the doctor called my mother and said, 'The X-ray has revealed a growth, quite large.' So my mother called me and I came down. My father's car pulled up, and through the front window we saw him get out. This endearing typical way he had of tucking up his chest and buttoning his coat with one hand whenever he left the house or got out of a car—he did that, and I thought, *'He does not know.* We know and he doesn't know, and his life is going to change.' He looked so innocent, and it broke my heart. The doctor told him he had to have an operation or he would be dead in six months. He had the operation, but he was dead in six months anyway."

Cormier recalled the prevailing emotion of that time as anger more than sadness. He began to write about it. At first it was only therapy, an attempt to rid himself of the anger and shock. But gradually a structure began to emerge. One day his agent, Marilyn Marlow, called to find out why she hadn't gotten any stories from him lately. "Well. I haven't done much writing," he said, "because I've been putting down my thoughts about my father's death."

"I'd like to read it," she said. "I think everything a writer writes is important." He sent her the haphazard heap of paper. She read it through and called him back. "You know, Bob," she pondered aloud, "with a very little form and work I think this would make a novel that would really affect people."

By that time he had worked off the raw edge of his grief, and had begun to gain insight into his father's death and into the nature of death itself. He saw that Marlow was right. Starting again, he rewrote with an objectivity that had been missing before.

The result was, and was not, autobiographical. Alph LeBlanc in *Now and at the Hour* is not Lucien Cormier. The story, as Robert Cormier later summarized it, tells "how an ordinary man learns of his approaching death, gathers himself to meet it, learns to endure, reaches for shreds of comfort and finally achieves a kind of triumph, lonely though it may be."[27] In the darkness of his grief Cormier had found the theme that was to move through all his novels: the nonhero who struggles to hang on to humanness even under siege from an all-powerful Them—or It.

The book was published almost immediately—a first for both Marlow and Cormier—and critics, including those at the *Atlantic*[28] and *Time* magazine[29], were stunned by its power and honesty and praised it lavishly. The *New York*

Times gave it a place on their list of best books of the year. Sales were small—fewer than five thousand copies—but the word was out that Cormier was a first novelist to watch.

Soon a publisher who had heard of his small-town background approached him with a proposition: a big French Hill epic. But it was not a congenial task, and eventually Cormier gave it up in disgust. "It was just hack work with no emotion involved," he said later. To Marlow he confided, "I work best with a microscope, not a telescope."[30] Cormier needed to build a novel from a deeply felt emotion, not just a marketable idea. In a few months that emotion came along. He was sent on assignment to do a story about a woman whose young daughter had been murdered. The assignment included the difficult task of asking the mother for a photograph of the dead child. He sat in the woman's living room and talked with her, established rapport, and got his picture. Later he found that his compassion drew him back for another interview and a human interest story about the woman's tragedy.[31] But he couldn't stop thinking about it. What if, he wondered, this woman were widowed by her husband's reaction to the tragedy? And what if she reached out for just a little comfort—and got pregnant? The "what if" led to a second novel—*A Little Raw on Monday Morning*—published in 1963.

Two years later he wrote another novel that had its genesis in a newspaper assignment. This one came from a visit to an old people's home on the edge of Leominster. Some of the inhabitants impressed him with their spunk. What if a feisty old man ran away from the home? The comic novel *Take Me Where the Good Times Are* was the answer. The reviews of both books were favorable, but Cormier was beginning to be misunderstood and typecast as a writer who glorified "faceless little people." *Now and at the Hour* cast a giant shadow, and although they were fine in their own way, neither of the next two books measured up to its dark promise.

In 1966, with the pressures of an expanding family, Cormier left newspaper work for a year to experiment with freelancing. He took nonfiction assignments from the magazines that had learned to respect his writing through his short stories. But the hustle of the freelancer's life left him no energy for fiction. Back at the newspaper, he threw himself into short-story writing at night. Magazines like *Redbook* were paying as much as fifteen hundred dollars for a story, and he could turn one out in two weeks. He continued to write novels and to learn and grow from their creation, though no book he wrote in this period reached publication.

For the next year and a half he was immersed in a book that was his favorite of any he had written up to that time. "In the Midst of Winter" was important to him, both in terms of his personal and spiritual development and in terms of his development as a writer. The title is from the French Existentialist Albert Camus: "In the midst of winter, I found that there was in me an invincible summer." It is the story of a worldly young girl, Lily, who is suddenly called to become a nun. Her father is baffled and troubled by her choice, and only years later, after her death, is he inexorably brought to his knees before God.

Vatican II, a world council of Catholic authorities in 1962, had brought sweeping changes and modernization to the Catholic church, and faith, too, was undergoing a revitalization. The book was a vehicle for him to explore the meaning of this spiritual renewal. The character of Lily, too, is significant because she is an early version of the troublesome figure of Cassie, who in first drafts was the protagonist of *The Bumblebee Flies Anyway*. "In the Midst of Winter" was a failure in that it was too intensely Catholic for general publication, but for its author it was a success because of the pleasure and growth he experienced in the writing of it.

These were his children's teen years. He has described that time vividly in *Eight Plus One:* "The house sang those days with the vibrant songs of youth—tender, hectic, tragic, and ecstatic. Hearts were broken on Sunday afternoon and repaired by the following Thursday evening, but how desperate it all was in the interim. The telephone never stopped ringing, the shower seemed to be constantly running, the Beatles became a presence in our lives."[32]

One day Peter came home from Notre Dame Preparatory with two big shopping bags of chocolates to sell to raise money for the school. At the dinner table that night the family kidded him a bit; then his father came up with three alternatives. Cormier reconstructed the conversation: "I told him, 'Look, Peter, let's just look at the options. First of all, let's have you sell the chocolates. I sold them when I was a kid, and it didn't hurt. You can bother the neighbors and the relatives, and that's all right. Then the second thing would be that we could buy the chocolates.' (Twenty-five boxes, a dollar apiece—I was hoping he wouldn't say yes.) Then the third thing I said was 'You know, you don't have to sell the chocolates. It's a free society. It's not going to appear on your report card: CHOCOLATE SALE—FAILURE.' And Peter being who he was, said, 'That sounds fine, Dad. I don't want to sell the chocolates.' So I wrote him a note, and the next day I drove him to school, and as I watched him go up the walk, I thought, 'My God, what am I letting him in for?' "[33] It was September, Peter was a freshman in a very jock-oriented school—but nothing happened. He gave the headmaster the letter and the chocolates and that was that.

But something had happened to Cormier. His "what if" had started again. What if the headmaster had been unscrupulous? What if there had been peer pressure? The characters started to come alive, and he began to write the book that would become *The Chocolate War.* When Marilyn Marlow saw the first chapters she said, "Bob, I think what you have here is a young adult novel." Cormier was alarmed. Would he have to go back and simplify and take things out and clean up the language? Marlow reassured him, "Don't worry about it. Just go on writing what you think is true to what you want to do, and let us determine the market."[34]

But some publishers were not as convinced as she that the book was suitable for young people. They found it too downbeat and pressured Cormier to change the ending. He resisted firmly, and eventually, after seven rejections, editor Fabio Coen at Pantheon recognized its quality and put it into print in April 1974. It was an instant sensation. Reviewers roared—some in pleasure, some in rage. Controversy developed, but the book's reputation only increased from the tangles with would-be censors. Cormier had found his theme, his tone, his audience.

Another dark novel of dazzling complexity followed in 1977: *I Am the Cheese.* With his first two young adult novels Cormier achieved critical and financial success. When the idea for *After the First Death* began to consume his thoughts, he asked for six months' leave from the newspaper. They offered eight weeks. He went home and discussed it with Connie. "She said those magic words," he told a British interviewer. "She said, 'Why don't you quit?' I'm a child of the Depression, you know! You don't cut off the umbilical cord to the weekly paycheck. It kind of took my breath away, really."[35] But he realized that she was right—he needed to give all his energies to his writing. Connie had a secretarial job with New England Telephone as a safety net, so in 1978 Robert Cormier became a full-time writer. *After the First Death* followed; then came an intermission in 1980 in the shape of the short-story collection *Eight Plus One,* and in 1983 the strange puzzle of *The Bumblebee Flies Anyway.* In 1985 this first period of his work came full circle with *Beyond the Chocolate War.*

By this time there was no question that Cormier had become the country's leading young adult author—and some critics believed that that was too narrow a definition of his genius. Honors and awards were heaped on each of his books, and also on Cormier himself for his body of work: the American Library Association's Margaret A. Edwards Award, the ALAN Award from the Assembly on Literature for Adolescents of the National Council of Teachers of English, an International Reading Association Commendation, and an honorary doctorate from his alma mater, Fitchburg State College. When that college established a Cormier archive in 1981 he was pleased but a little puzzled that anybody would want all his old papers. "It's nice, though, to have all those boxes out of the house," he said. "The closets were getting pretty full, and Connie was starting to complain."

With *Fade* in 1988, Cormier moved into his mature powers. In the next ten years he wrote six more novels, each very different but each at the same time completely faithful to his themes and style. These were productive years for Cormier, but his daily life was quiet. Although he and Connie enjoyed traveling all over the world to speak and to attend conferences, he always liked coming home best of all. "Superficially my life probably sounds very prosaic," he told an interviewer. "I write every morning and in the afternoon I visit my libraries and the bookstores and see friends. I run into a lot of them at the libraries. And then some time at night I take out the work and look it over. And that's pretty much it."[36]

Cormier regarded libraries as his spiritual home, and so it should come as no surprise that he visited at least one, and sometimes as many as five, of the local public libraries almost every day. He often delighted the teen book discussion groups at the Leominster Public Library by dropping in unannounced, and for fifteen years he was a trustee of that library. If he had an appointment for an interview, or a call from a teacher passing through town, the meeting place was often in the room at the library that was held open for him.[37]

In 1989 the Cormiers had fulfilled a dream by buying a summer home on a little lake in Hubbardston. There was an upstairs study where Bob could write and look out over the water. The Cormiers took great joy in their "getaway house," although it was only nineteen miles from Leominster—close enough for Bob to make frequent trips into town to pick up the mail and drop in on his beloved libraries.

Then, on the first day of summer in 1997, Cormier climbed to an upstairs loft to get the American flag and un-furl it on the deck—always their first action on arriving for the season. Losing his balance, he stepped backward into empty space and fell heavily to the floor below, breaking his back. The injury was debilitating and kept him from sitting at the typewriter for many months. But lying in bed, he continued to work on polishing *Heroes,* dictating his changes to Connie, who sat nearby at the computer. A photo taken several weeks after the accident, on the challenging occasion of his speaking about *Tenderness* at a boys' prison facility, shows him looking gaunt and wan. Nevertheless, he continued to speak at local schools, and the next year saw the publication of *Heroes,* followed by *Frenchtown Summer,* which went on to win the prestigious Los Angeles Times Book Prize for Best Young Adult Fiction in 1999.

Although his health was failing and he was often in pain, he had a calendar full of appearances and engagements. Only days after a speaking trip to Chicago, he had a stroke that interfered with his power of speech for twelve hours. Then the doctors discovered a circulation blockage in his legs that had begun to turn his foot gangrenous. Rushed to Massachusetts General Hospital in Boston, he was the un-willing subject of multiple tests that disclosed two inoperable cancerous masses in his body. Connie bravely made arrangements for him to be moved to a hospice, but time had run out, and he died early on the morning of November 2, 2000, with his family around him.

Robert Cormier ended his life still writing, putting a final polish on *The Rag and Bone Shop* as he lay in the hospital. And so we come back to the paradox: Robert Cormier, this author of dark novels full of complex ambiguity, lived a simple, happy life, content with his family and friends, his town, and most of all, his writing. Sustained by his faith until the end, he reassured a friend a few days before his death that he was not afraid to die. He himself said it best, with characteristic humility: "My dream was to be known as a writer and to be able to produce at least one book that would be read by people. That dream came true with the publication of my first novel—and all the rest has been a sweet bonus."[38]

Notes

1. Lingeman, Richard R., "Boy in a Trap," *The New York Times Book Review,* May 22, 1977, 51.

2. "From the Inside Out—the Author Speaks," in "Robert Cormier" [pamphlet], New York, n.d.

3. Courtemanche, Dolores, "Overnight Success—After *30* Years," *Worcester Sunday Telegram,* July 16, 1982, 11.

4. Schwartz, Tony, "Teen-agers' Laureate," *Newsweek,* July 16, 1979, 87.

5. Salinger, J. D., *The Catcher in the Rye,* Boston, Little Brown, 1951.

6. Davis, William A., "Tough Tales for Teen-agers," *Boston Globe Magazine,* November 16, 1980, 22.

7. Commire, Anne, ed., *Something about the Author,* Vol. 10, Detroit, Gale, 1976, 28.

8. Ibid.

9. Davis, 12.

10. "Robert Cormier," www.achuka.co.uk/special/cormier01.htm, July 11, 2000.

11. De Luca, Geraldine, and Roni Natov, "Taking True Risks: Controversial Issues in New Young Adult Novels," *The Lion and the Unicorn,* Winter 1979–80, 125.

12. Cormier, Robert, "Books Remembered," *The Calendar,* Children's Book Council, June/December 1986, unpaged.

13. Ibid.

14. Cormier, Robert, "A Fragile Triumph," *School Library Journal,* September 1991, 184.

15. "From the Inside Out," 2.

16. Courtemanche, Dolores, "Robert Cormier—in the Movies," *Worcester Sunday Telegram,* July 18, 1982, 9.

17. Courtemanche, "Robert Cormier—in the Movies."

18. Davis, 24

19. Ibid, 26.

20. Ibid.

21. Ibid.

22. McLaughlin, Frank, *Cheese, Chocolates, and Kids: A Day with Robert Cormier,* videotape prepared for PBS, n.d., (Robert E. Cormier Collection, Fitchburg State College, Fitchburg, Massachusetts).

23. Cormier, Robert, *Eight Plus One,* New York, Pantheon, 1980, 45.

24. Commire, 28.

25. Davis, 30.

26. Ibid.

27. Serebnick, Judith, "Triumph in Tragedy," *Library Journal,* June 1960, 2203.

28. Adams, Phoebe-Lou, review of *Now and at the Hour, The Atlantic,* September 1960, 118.

29. Review of *Now and at the Hour, Time,* August 1, 1960, 68.

30. Davis, 32.

31. De Luca and Natov, 112.

32. Cormier, *Eight Plus One,* vii.

33. Cormier, Robert, audiotape of speech at Young Adult Services Division luncheon, American Library Association Conference, Dallas, 1979.

34. De Luca and Natov, 111.

35. "Robert Cormier," www.achuka.co.uk/special/cormier01.htm, July 11, 2000.

36. Ibid.

37. Ibid.

38. Campbell, Patty, "Conversing with Robert Cormier," www.amazon.com/exec/obidos/tg/feature/-/5191.

Chapter Three

At the Typewriter

When Robert Cormier sat down each morning at his old L C Smith and faced a blank sheet of paper, what happened? Where did the words come from, how were they shaped into great novels? What was his writing process, and what might have been the unconscious origins of his characters, his symbols, and his themes? Who was he speaking to, and how have they responded to his work? And underneath it all, what was Robert Cormier *really* saying?

The writer himself was generous in interviews and speeches with the details of his working day, because, as he often said, he wanted to keep young people from the delusion that books were produced without human struggle, by some sort of "writing machine." And because his "writing machine" was a typewriter, not a computer with a Delete key, he has left the Cormier archive at Fitchburg State College a treasure trove for scholars and student researchers, in the form of first drafts, letters to and from editors, personal notes, and outlines relating to his work. Janice Flint-Ferguson, in an article on using an early manuscript of *We All Fall Down* in the classroom, describes its revelation of Cormier's compositional methods.

"Originally typed using an old manual typewriter and onionskin paper, it carries none of the earmarks of high technology. Words are crossed out, written in, and crossed out again. Entire passages are struck with swirls and x's. Notes appear in the midst of text, and outlines list events that never happen in the published novel. They are close readings just waiting to happen. They are also the evidence of the writing process. The process is not neat; it is not linear; it happens over and over again before it is even given up to a reader for feedback."[1]

Cormier once said, "I write until I lose perspective. I come back and the problem is solved; the perspective is restored. You get so close to a thing, and then you have to draw away from it."[2] The late night, when the house was quiet, was his time to look over what he had done that day, to cut and hone and refine. This was the part of writing he loved best: tinkering and polishing, looking for exactly the right word and the strong verbs that would leap and dance. "When I want to capture a certain scene or a character, I just . . . write it to the fullest and then go back and pare it down and cut and look for that perfect word or phrase. To me, that is the joy of writing."[3] "And then I go to bed with the writing on my mind, and the next morning I get up and there's a very lovely kind of momentum that goes on."[4] He took great pleasure in this whole process, calling it "an act of love and an act of joy and fun." Even on the occasional days when he felt that the "words [weren't] coming, and they [were] flat and stale," he still wrote.[5] Every book for Cormier was an unfolding adventure. "I don't sign contracts with publishing houses," he declared emphatically. "I don't tell them when a novel will be done. I don't know myself."[6]

In the morning, he often said, he went to his typewriter

to see what his characters were going to do that day. They were very real to him, and acted out their own lives in his head even while he was walking or driving or waiting in line at the grocery store. "I think characters are the most important element in a novel," he declared. "You can have a clever plot and fine writing but if the reader doesn't believe in the characters, doesn't love them or hate them or doesn't identify with them, then the story won't work. . . . Until I 'hear' the voice of a character I can't proceed. . . . And what happens eventually to that character, as well as others, affects me greatly. I was very upset when I saw the way doom was descending on Kate Forrester in *After the First Death* and felt helpless to avoid it. I'm often reluctant to finish a novel because that means letting the characters go. I often write about them for my own purposes after a novel is published."[7]

And yet he was aware of the paradox that these people who were so real to him were created by his own mind. With amused satisfaction, he told a story that illustrated this point:

When *The Chocolate War* was first accepted for publication, I went down to an editing meeting in New York and met a young editor who looked at me and said, "If I ever met Archie Costello I think I'd thrash him." (I thought that word was so terrific; I always remembered it.) Well, I thought to myself, you're looking at him. Because I thought up all those terrible things that Archie Costello did. When I was writing at the typewriter, I was Archie. I devised all the assignments, I spoke

through his voice and saw the
world through his eyes.[8]

And Emile Janza? Artkin? Eric Poole? Creations, yes,
but not out of thin air. Yet who would suspect that such crea-
tures could emerge from the dark corners of a heart as loving
and kind as that of Robert Cormier?

The trigger that set the characters in motion, that started
them moving purposefully into a story, was always an emotion. Sometimes a seemingly trivial incident, a news story, a
family anecdote, could bring up strong feelings that res-
onated in Cormier's subconscious and initiated his need to
try to find just the right words to create that same state in his
readers. "Something happens that affects me emotionally—
disturbs me, upsets me, angers me—and sends me to the
typewriter. . . ."[9] Capturing that emotion in words, so that the
reader could feel it, was his driving force. And then would
come the question he called the "what if." Given this emotion, this character, this situation, what would inevitably
happen next? And so the story was on its way.

Character and emotion are important in the creation of a
novel, but telling a good story was always Cormier's over-
riding goal, the whole point of the endeavor. "Sometimes we
forget that the story is the thing," he said, when questioned
about his ideas. "You can have all the great plots and themes,
but if it doesn't work first as a story, the reader will never get
to the themes."[10]

When asked by interviewers how many pages he wrote a
day, Cormier would always protest (after politely answering
"Four or five") that he didn't think of the writing as pages or
chapters, but as scenes—an approach he credited to his lifelong love of movies. Indeed, his writing has often been described as "cinematic" in its tautness and economy of
dialogue. The multiple points of view in his books can be
compared to the cross-cutting techniques used in film to

increase dramatic tension.[11] There are many subtle, perhaps unconscious, references to films throughout his work, especially the black-and-white film noir of the thirties and forties, the movies of his childhood.

But Cormier's style owes more to his years as a newspaperman than to his devotion to the movies. He learned his craft in the newsroom, under the discipline of deadlines and the need to get it right the first time, and his style reflects the rules of good journalistic writing—though it is not journalism. A reporter must use simple words, no fancy language for its own sake. He must use as few words as possible and the right words to convey the situation clearly and vividly. He must strive for short, punchy sentences; brief, tightly focused paragraphs. And he must start his story with a lead that grabs the reader. Cormier excelled in all of these requirements, especially the last, as illustrated by the startling opening sentences of his novels: "They murdered him." "Me, I get fixated on something and I can't help myself." "My name is Francis Joseph Cassavant and I have no face."

The one journalistic rule he ignores is the familiar stipulation to tell who, what, where, when, and why in the first paragraph. Cormier stretches out the five w's—the exposition—far into the book (almost to the end in the case of *I Am the Cheese*), giving out hints, raising questions and puzzles, giving readers only tidbits of information to keep them eagerly following his lead. And many of these clues, and even a whole second level, are buried beneath the narrative surface. "I always am conscious of layering," he revealed. "And if people don't find it, fine, but I like to think it is there just in case somebody cares to look for it."[12]

It is one of the many paradoxes surrounding Cormier and his work that his books can be read simply as good stories—they move quickly and easily along to an epiphany and a satisfying (or challenging) ending. And yet a more sophisticated reader will find on a second reading hidden links and allusions and subtleties that clarify what the story is *really* about. And it gets even better on a third reading. As librarian Linnea Hendrickson wrote: "One of the amazing things about Cormier's work is that . . . when you read the book the first time, it is one story, but when you read it a second time (now knowing the ending) you are reading a very different book. In fact I have found that upon rereading I see clues I've overlooked because they portended an ending that I didn't want to happen."[13]

This *interactivity* is one of the most striking characteristics of Cormier's work. His books can be a partnership with the reader. Although they can be read on the surface as just exciting stories, these hints and clues are invitations he offers the reader to enter the story and interact with it, to dig for rewards, to solve puzzles. Or to recoil with horror or resistance. Cormier's love of ambiguity embeds many questions in the narrative to which we must respond, taking sides, before the story can continue satisfactorily. The reader's participation completes the literary creation, rounds it out, and Cormier has deliberately left room for this action— eliciting the heartfelt cry of "No! This isn't the way it should be!" as we close the pages of *The Chocolate War,* for example. Or forcing upon us the necessary decision beyond the end of *The Rag and Bone Shop* as to what Jason will or won't do with that butcher knife. Or allowing us to make up our minds in *After the First Death* as to whether Artkin was really Miro's father.

Many critics, scholars, students, and reviewers have realized that this ambiguity and interactivity, as well as the depth and subtlety of Cormier's work, give them a wealth of material to examine. Countless articles, dissertations, and scholarly papers have been devoted to analyzing one aspect or another of his novels. Sometimes these focus on peripheral issues: the use and meaning of color in his work, for example,[14] or the significance of names[15] or landscape.[16]

Others deal with more central subjects like Cormier's heroines[17] or protagonists[18], or the psychology of adolescence as it appears in his work[19]. And lately still others have attempted to deconstruct his writing in the light of radical feminism[20] or other theories of twenty-first-century literary criticism. Of these, the most successful has been the attempt to position Cormier as a postmodernist, first in an exploratory essay by Patricia Head, and then in a brilliantly conceived master's thesis by Robert LeBlanc from, appropriately, Fitchburg State College.[21]

But Cormier was always uncomfortable with this sort of close analysis. Though he was happy to talk about his characters and stories, whenever critics and reviewers would shift their focus from his actors to sweep aside the curtain and reveal the puppeteer at work, he would grow self-conscious and uneasy. His modesty had something to do with this, but also there was an almost superstitious feeling that looking too closely at the magic gift of inspiration might make it disappear. "For a long time," he said, "I was reluctant to analyze my writing and grew uncomfortable when I encountered articles arguing certain aspects of it. . . . I felt like one of those characters in a cartoon who flies through the air until he becomes conscious of what he's doing and looks down in horror, loses the ability to fly, and plummets to the earth. Too much theorizing worries me. . . . It makes me feel as though I am looking into a mirror as I write."[22]

Because Cormier was unwilling—or perhaps unable— to articulate his central vision, many critics, speakers, and essayists have had a try at analyzing it. Some have settled for generalities. His themes, they say, are betrayal, vulnerability, guilt, paranoia, fear, or psychosis. Others have groped for a nucleus in these ideas. "His novels deal with the struggles of the individual against often malicious, sometimes unidentified, external forces and stress the importance of self-reliance."[23] Or "the most common description of his world-view . . . is 'the plight of the individual versus the system.' "[24]

All of this is too easy, too superficial. In earlier versions of this book, I, too, struggled to find a center in Cormier's dark vision. Who is the enemy? I asked. Isolating the central fixed point, the immovable factor, the solid wall against which the action crashes, is the key to understanding the fiction of Robert Cormier, I argued. It was tempting but not quite accurate to think of this force as "the enemy." Looking back at the initial formation of Cormier's themes in his adult novels, I found that the immovable force as it appeared in these books was pregnancy or old age or death. And most revealingly, I felt, in the unpublished novel "In the Midst of Winter," the force was God Himself, the Holy Spirit who pursues the agnostic with implacable love until he finally surrenders.

The "enemy," then, I wrote, is not necessarily evil. The unifying characteristic in all these manifestations of the concept can be neatly pinned down with the word *implacable*. Unalterable, inflexible, inexorable—that which cannot be appealed to. Incidental but concrete symbols of this quality appear often in his work in the form of cold-eyed bullies, snarling dogs. What fascinated Cormier, I theorized, the eternal question that drew him back again and again, is, How can we confront the utterly Implacable and still remain human? His emotion centered on the individual made powerless, cut off from all recourse. Thus Cormier's plots often turn on the symbolic regaining of humanity through one supremely irrational but self-determined gesture. When I wrote this I was thinking of the flight of the Bumblebee, Adam's circular bike ride, and Jerry's triumphant nonresistance in *Beyond the Chocolate War* (rather than his doomed passive refusal to sell the chocolates in the earlier book).

Revealingly, Cormier recalled an incident from his childhood that was a metaphor, or perhaps one of the sources, for the rage he felt about helplessness at the hands of the Implacable, an incident that gave him a sense of fragility and mortality and perhaps was responsible for his lifelong claustrophobia. "They" had decided that he was to have his tonsils out, in spite of all his pleading and protests. So when the day came, he was wheeled into the operating room, trying to make the best of the situation. A nurse, evidently having heard that he was in the church choir, said to him, "I understand that you sing—would you do us a song?" Pleased and flattered, he opened his mouth to let out the first notes, and instantly the anesthetic mask was clamped down over his face. Betrayed! He still feels angry when he remembers the moment. "They tricked me! I thought they loved me because I sang, and they tricked me. I'll never forget it. Authority sucks you in, and then—!" No matter how lovable or deserving or pitiful you are, there is no appeal. The Implacable has its own purposes.

But then Cormier himself read my analysis and perhaps was made self-conscious by it. No matter what the reason, starting with *Fade* my little theory about the Implacable no longer applied so neatly as it had to the first five YA novels. Instead of focusing on that one redemptive irrational gesture, Cormier took side trips into other themes like guilt and forgiveness, the corruption of innocence, hidden and revealed identity. But behind it all was still a determining Force that more and more showed its face as Ultimate Evil. It had other names, like the Fade, and sometimes it had the face of a person who had surrendered to it, like Harry Flowers or Lulu or Mr. Hairston. But the question was still how to remain human, how to stand on your feet and face It—or him or her—down.

But where was God in this unequal battle? In an interview with Roger Sutton published in *School Library Journal*, Cormier made a supremely revealing remark. Asked "Do you think that God is present in the world that you portray?" he answered, "Probably a silent watchful God who

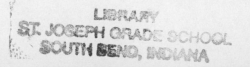
43

doesn't interfere, who probably hopes that people do the right thing. But we have free will to do what we want, even though God knows what the next step will be."[25]

And so it turns out that the key to understanding what Cormier is really saying is theology, specifically the beliefs he absorbed in his Catholic upbringing, but also the theology that grew out of his mature understanding of faith. These ideas in his work are often mistakenly understood to be dualistic—that is, a belief in the struggle between the two equal and opposing powers of good and evil—a construct that is known historically as the Manichaean heresy. The more enlightened and contemporary view, and one that Cormier was undoubtedly taught, is that God the Creator is supreme, and the devil, as part of the created order, is allowed to exist by God but subject to Him. God trusts us with freedom, as Cormier implied in his remarks to Sutton, and evil is inherently one of the choices in free will. In his stories it gets its power to act in the world not from its own malicious force but through the agency of human weakness and error—from Trent's ambition and pride, Buddy's cowardice, Lulu's desire for revenge, Larry LaSalle's lust, the idolatrous love of country shared by Artkin and the general. In *Other Bells for Us to Ring,* Darcy is told by the wise and saintly Sister Angela, a character who can be understood as voicing Cormier's mature beliefs, "Let the days come, the darkness and the light, and don't concern yourself."[26] In other words, whatever happens is in God's hands, if we let it be, and is therefore ultimately good. But on the other hand (and with Cormier there is always an "on the other hand"), he has also said, "Happy endings are not our birthright. You have to do something to make them happen."

Many of the later novels are lit not with the brief spark of irrational gestures, but with real gleams of hope. Characters who embody goodness begin to appear, and there is even an occasional happy ending. In *Fade* Susan finds a life purpose. Darcy, in *Other Bells,* reaches understanding through Sister Angela's counsel. While Buddy is lost in *We All Fall Down,* Jane rises to a new life. In *Tunes for Bears to Dance To,* Henry destroys the victory of the evil Mr. Hairston by refusing to accept the bribe. In the sunlit pages of *Frenchtown Summer,* evil appears only in Eugene's vague suspicions about his Uncle Med, and the Implacable is finally defeated when the bully is killed in an accident.

But Mark Oppenheimer, in a review of *The Rag and Bone Shop,* takes issue with this interpretation by maintaining that Cormier does project a fictional world in which evil and good are equal powers at war with each other. "Even when the good wins, as he often allows, it's a Pyrrhic victory, for so much evil remains. So many more dragons to slay, and all just inside the schoolhouse door. Cormier's victory was not to give youngsters a solution, but to name the problem."[27] Once, just to see Cormier's reaction, I quoted Roberto Rossellini to him: "To perceive evil where it exists is, in my opinion, a form of optimism."[28] His face lit up. "Oh, yes!" he cried.

His last editor, Karen Wojtyla, had some relevant words on this subject:

```
Cormier's books have enormous emo-
tional honesty, I think, but most
of them are dramas in which he
creates a crucible where individ-
ual moral choices shape the lives
of the characters, for better or
worse. . . . He often places his
characters at crossroads, explor-
ing what happens depending upon
which choice they make. In that
sense his novels are about free-
dom, and the consequences of our
```

> freedom to choose good or evil,
> defiance or conformity, truth or
> complicity in lies. . . . Of course
> Cormier was an enormously tal-
> ented deviser of twisty plots,
> master of suspenseful pacing and a
> stylist of uncommon economy and
> grace, but it is the rich moral
> dimension of his stories that I
> think makes the novels so end-
> lessly fascinating.[29]

Cormier was a deeply moral man, in the finest sense. He cared profoundly about the world's pain and was scrupulous about ensuring that his own daily actions helped to erase rather than increase that suffering. This beauty of character probably came naturally from the loving integrity of his personality, but he also was very much in touch with his Catholic conscience. He often spoke, with some resentment, of the guilt instilled in him by the nuns. "I was made aware of evil," he admitted, "and I'm aware of it now. I mean, we constantly try to be good, and most of us are because of the lack of the opportunity to be evil. . . . But I'm aware all the time of trying to do the right thing, the good thing, and of often not doing it. As I've said, it's the sins of omission that hound me."[30]

That moral sensibility was drawn, clearly, from his Catholicism. He was diligent in his religious practice, attending Mass every week, even when he was away from home. His agent, Marilyn Marlow, remembered many Sundays when she and the Cormiers would drive around in unfamiliar cities at conferences looking for a Catholic church. He had come to terms with his religion since the era of Pope John XXIII in the 1950s opened the windows, and in later life he felt much more relaxed with his faith. "A theology of love," he called it, contrasted with the "theology of fear" of his childhood.[31] He was even secure enough with his religion to make fun of naïve interpretations of those practices in *Other Bells for Us to Ring*.

Nevertheless, the darkness of Cormier's work must be acknowledged, no matter what the theological interpretation. Over the years he was asked about its origins so many times that finally, in the 1999 Frances Clarke Sayers speech at UCLA, he made a determined effort to trace the roots of this darkness in the events of his life. He began with a day when he was five years old, playing in a nearby field, and was suddenly seized with an overwhelming conviction that his mother, "my refuge and the center of my life,"[32] was dead. He ran home to find her lying on the bed, but just resting, not dead. In the next months those daytime naps became a torment to him, as each day he was sure that *this time* she would never get up. Later that year his beautiful, blond younger brother, Leo, died suddenly, and Cormier remembers "that heartbreakingly small white coffin in the front room" during the three days of the wake.[33] Other deaths shadowed his childhood—his cousin Jacqueline, and the boy who was the prototype for all the implacable bullies in his books.

"Those years, those deaths; do they account for darknesses in my unconscious life, the things that guide my imagination as I write?" he asked. "And yet— don't all lives, all childhoods, hold tragedies? And darkness?"[34] Typically, his conclusion was a question: "These tragedies, these traumatic events obviously went inside of me into the deep cellars of my own heart and remained there all those years. Is all of this a clue to why I am impelled to write those books that seem to be so opposite to the person I appear to be?"[35] A later childhood anecdote recalled by Cormier in other writings may be a clue to an alternate explanation of his darkness. As a boy, he would often write little stories and read them to his mother. "That's very nice, Bobbie," she would say. "But why are your stories always so sad?" It is my guess that Cormier's terror of his mother's death, his fearful reaction to his tonsillectomy and the deaths of his brother, cousin, and schoolmate were more symptoms than causes. The music of some minds is naturally in a minor key. Cormier shows us the light by focusing on the shadow that is its consequence.

The ultimate Cormier paradox is to ask whether this most important of all young adult writers may *not* have been writing young adult novels at that old L C Smith. His books break the "rules" and defy the assumptions of the form, even though those are the very qualities that have made him a leader in this literature's development. Are his novels, with their darkness, complexity, universal themes, and moral depth, over the heads of young readers? Or even harmful to them—an idea that has fueled many a censorship attack on his work? Conversely, is it a waste of his talent to be classed with "kiddie lit," as the adult literary establishment regards young adult literature? Does the label cut him off from the readers and respect he deserves?

Remember, it was the publisher, not the author, who made the decision to market *The Chocolate War,* and consequently all Cormier's other novels, to teens. In 1988 Delacorte Press made an attempt to break out of this mold by marketing *Fade* from the adult side of the publishing house as well as from the juvenile division. Several journals, including the *San Francisco Chronicle,* the *Washington Post Book World,* and the influential *New York Times Book Review,* chose to judge it as a work for adults. Nevertheless, the effort failed because Cormier by this time had been typecast as a juvenile author, at least in the United States. In other parts of the world Cormier's work has long had a readership among adults as well as teens.

Certainly he himself resisted the label but at the same time embraced that audience. "I don't regard myself as a 'young adult' author," he often said. "I always have in my

48

mind an intelligent reader who likes me and will forgive me my trespasses and errors and go along with me. And thank goodness, that intelligent reader often turns out to be fourteen years old." He was grateful for the discipline that audience imposed on him: "The fact that . . . my . . . novels found their way to classrooms made me a better writer. Spurred on by hundreds of letters from young readers, teachers, and librarians, ignited by the knowledge that my work would be studied, dissected, and probed in classrooms—these facts demanded that I seek the best within myself. One cannot write casually or carelessly for that kind of readership. The beauty of it all, I discovered, is that I could use all the craft at my command, could be sly and subtle, complex and confounding, and still have a young audience turning the pages of my books."[36]

Notes

1. Flint-Ferguson, Janis D., "Being and Becoming a Real Writer Through Reading the Manuscripts of Robert Cormier," *Ohio Journal of the English Language Arts,* Winter/Spring 1999, 14.

2. McLaughlin, Frank, *Cheese, Chocolates, and Kids: A Day with Robert Cormier,* videotape prepared for PBS, n.d. (Robert E. Cormier Collection, Fitchburg State College, Fitchburg, Massachusetts).

3. Hoffman, Laura B., "Beyond the Shadows of Robert Cormier." Writes of Passage, 1996, www.writes.org/conversations/conver_4, accessed May 14, 2004.

4. Zitlow, Connie S., and Tobie R. Sanders, "Conversations with Robert Cormier and Sue Ellen Bridgers: Their Life and Work as Writers," *Ohio Journal of the English Language Arts,* Winter/Spring 1999, 35.

5. Ibid.

6. McLaughlin.

7. "Robert Cormier," Teenreads.com, April 21, 2000, http://teenreads.com/authors/au-cormier-robert.asp.

8. Hoffman, 3.

9. Teenreads.com.

10. Zitlow, 36.

11. Myszor, Frank, "The See-Saw and the Bridge in Robert Cormier's *After the First Death,*" in *Children's Literature,* vol. 16, 1988, 77, as quoted in Tarr, C. Anita, "The Absence of Moral Agency in Robert Cormier's *The Chocolate War,*" in *Children's Literature,* vol. 30, edited by Elizabeth Lennox Keyser and Julie Pfeiffer, New Haven, CT, Yale University Press, 2002, 96.

12. Zitlow, 37.

13. Hendrickson, Linnea, CCBC-Net, August 10, 2001.

14. Kobayashi, unpublished paper. Robert E. Cormier Collection, Fitchburg State College, Fitchburg, Massachusetts.

15. Nilsen, Alleen Pace, "The Poetry of Naming in Young Adult Books," *ALAN Review,* Spring 1980, 3.

16. Lundin, Anne, "A Stranger in a World Unmade: Landscape in Robert Cormier's Chocolate War Novels," in *The Phoenix Award of the Children's Literature Association, 1995–1999,* edited by Alethea Helbig and Agnes Perkins, Lanham, MD, Scarecrow Press, 2001, 127.

17. Monseau, Virginia R., "Cormier's Heroines," *ALAN Review,* Fall 1991, 40.

18. ———, "Studying Cormier's Protagonists," *ALAN Review,* Fall 1994, 31.

19. Stringer, Sharon, "The Psychological Changes of Adolescence," *ALAN Review,* Fall 1994, 27.

20. Tarr, C. Anita, "The Absence of Moral Agency in Robert Cormier's *The Chocolate War,*" In *Children's Literature,* vol. 30, edited by Elizabeth Lennox Keyser and Julie Pfeiffer, New Haven, CT, Yale University Press, 2002.

21. Head, Patricia, "Robert Cormier and the Postmodernist Possibilities of Young Adult Fiction," *Children's Literature Association Quarterly,* Spring 1996, 28, and LeBlanc, Robert, "Postmodernist Elements in the Work of Robert Cormier," M.A. thesis, Fitchburg State College, Fitchburg, Massachusetts, 2005.

22. Cormier, Robert, "Forever Pedaling on the Road to Realism," in *Celebrating Children's Books: Essays on Children's Literature in Honor of Zena Sutherland,* edited by Betsy Hearne and Marilyn Kaye, Lothrop, Lee & Shepard, 1981.

23. *Contemporary Literary Criticism,* edited by Sharon Gunton, Farmington Hills, MI, Thomson Gale, 1973, 133.

24. Davis, William A., "Tough Tales for Teenagers," *Boston Globe Magazine,* November 16, 1980, 35.

25. Sutton, Roger, "Kind of a Funny Dichotomy," *School Library Journal,* June 1991, 28.

26. Cormier, Robert, *Other Bells for Us to Ring,* Delacorte Press, 1990.

27. Oppenheimer, Mark, "Murder in Frenchtown," *The New York Times Book Review,* November 18, 2001, 54.

28. Rossellini, Roberto, interview in *Cahiers du Cinema,* 1954.

29. Wojtyla, Karen, e-mail to the author, August 24, 2001.

30. De Luca, Geraldine, and Roni Natov, "An Interview with Robert Cormier," *The Lion and the Unicorn,* Fall 1978, 131.

31. Christian, George, "Conversations: Novelist Robert Cormier and Reporter Nora Ephron," *Houston Chronicle,* May 14, 1978, 12.

32. Cormier, Robert, "Probing the Dark Cellars of a Young Adult Writer's Heart," Frances Clark Sayers Lecture, University of California, Los Angeles, 1999, 15.

33. Ibid, 14.

34. Ibid, 21.

35. Ibid, 22.

36. Cormier, Robert, "The Gradual Education of a YA Novelist," introduction to *Twentieth-Century Young Adult Writers,* edited by Laura Standley Berger, Farmington Hills, MI, St. James Press, 1994.

Chapter Four

The Chocolate War

"They murdered him." The opening line of *The Chocolate War.* Three words that describe the whole movement of the plot. The process of "murdering" Jerry Renault is the subject; it remains only to tell who and why and how they felt about it. And what it meant, in this book that is generally acknowledged to be the most important work in young adult literature.

On the surface the story is straightforward enough, moving along quickly in brief, intense scenes. We first see Jerry slamming through a football practice. He is a freshman at Trinity High School in Monument and making the team is important to him, a small compensation for the recent death of his mother and the gray drabness of his life with his defeated father. The camera shifts to the stands, where we meet Archie, the villainous brains of the secret society called the Vigils. With his henchman, Obie, he is plotting "assignments," cruel practical jokes to be carried out by selected victims. On the way home, Jerry is confronted at the bus stop by a hippie vagrant who challenges his passive conformity.

Meanwhile, the malevolent Brother Leon, acting headmaster of Trinity, has called Archie into his office to break the traditional conspiracy of silence about the Vigils by asking for their help in the school chocolate sale. As Archie later discovers, Leon, in a bid for power while the headmaster is in the hospital, has overextended the school's funds to take advantage of a bargain on twenty thousand boxes of chocolates. Archie is delighted to have the vicious brother capitulate to him.

Now we see Archie in action, as an inoffensive kid called The Goober is assigned to loosen every screw in a classroom so that it falls into debris the next morning at the first touch. But no assignment is complete until Archie has drawn from a box containing six marbles—five white and one black. If the black turns up—it never has yet—Archie himself must carry out the assignment. But again the marble is white.

In a scene that underscores the theme of the book, we see Leon in action, tormenting a shy student with false accusations of cheating while the class watches tensely, then turning on the group to accuse them of condoning the cruelty by their silence. An even more vicious character is the bestial Emile Janza, who is in bondage to Archie over a photo that he believes Archie snapped over a restroom stall door while Emile sat masturbating, his pants around his ankles. Now the cast is complete and the action begins.

To show Leon where the power lies, Archie secretly assigns Jerry to refuse to sell the chocolates for ten days. Brother Leon is enraged but impotent as every day at the roll call of sales figures Jerry continues to answer "No." Suspecting a plot, Leon calls honor student David Caroni into his office and threatens to spoil the boy's perfect academic record with an undeserved F unless he reveals the secret. Terrified, Caroni tells him about the assignment. Finally the ten days are up, but Jerry, for reasons he only dimly understands, continues stubbornly to refuse to sell the chocolates. Surreptitious approval for Jerry's stand grows among the other students, and for the first time he begins to understand the question on a poster he has taped in his locker: "Do I dare disturb the universe?" Sales begin to drop off. Leon, panicked, pressures Archie; Archie pressures Jerry before the Vigils, but Jerry clings to his resolve. Soon it becomes apparent that the power of both Leon and the Vigils will be destroyed by the failure of the chocolate sale.

When Carter, the jock president of the Vigils, in frustration resorts to his fists to subdue a contemptuous assignee at a Vigils' meeting, Archie realizes that Jerry's resistance must be utterly squelched. The Vigils take charge of the chocolates, and under their secret management sales mount dramatically. With this turn of the tide, the school is caught up in the enthusiasm. Jerry is ostracized and tormented, first secretly by the Vigils and then openly by the whole student body. Finally Archie prods Emile Janza to taunt Jerry into a fistfight, but characteristically Emile hires some children to do the actual beating. Jerry's friend The Goober, in a belated show of support, decides to stop selling, but his gesture is futile. Soon the sale is over, and only Jerry's fifty boxes of chocolates remain.

Archie conceives a diabolical scheme for final vengeance. Under cover of a supposed night football rally, he stages a "raffle" for the last boxes of chocolates. He offers Jerry "a clean fight" with Emile Janza, and Jerry, wanting desperately to hit back at everything, accepts. Only when he and Emile are already in the boxing ring are the rules explained. The raffle tickets are instructions for blows, and the designated recipient is forbidden to defend himself. But now Carter and Obie come forward with the black box. Archie's luck holds; the marble he draws is white. The fight begins as planned, but Emile's animal rage is quickly out of control, and the mob goes wild as he beats Jerry savagely. The carnage is stopped when one of the brothers arrives and turns out the lights, but it is too late for Jerry. Terribly injured and lying in The Goober's arms, Jerry begs him not to disturb the universe, but to conform, to give in. An ambulance takes him away, and Archie, who has seen Brother Leon watching with approval in the shadows, is left triumphant.

The novel works superbly as a tragic yet exciting piece of storytelling. Many young adults, especially younger readers, will want simply to enjoy it at this level, and Cormier himself would have been the first to say that there is nothing wrong with that. A work of literature should be above all a good story. But a work of literature also has a broader intent than resolving the fate of its characters. For the reader who wants to dig beneath the surface, there is a wealth of hidden meaning and emotion in *The Chocolate War*.

A look at Cormier's style in this book will show first of all his driving, staccato rhythms. His sentences are short and punchy, and the chapters are often no more than two pages. He uses dialogue to move the action quickly forward and to establish character and situation in brief, broad strokes. His technique is essentially cinematic; if he wants to make a psychological or philosophical point he does so through action or dialogue, with a symbolic event or an interchange between characters, rather than reflecting in a narrative aside. Tension is built by an escalating chain of events, each a little drama of its own. "Rather than waiting for one big climax, I try to create a lot of little conflicts," Cormier explained. "A series of explosions as I go along."[1]

The point of view snaps from boy to boy in succeeding chapters. First we see Archie through Obie's eyes; then we are inside Jerry's head; then we watch Leon and The Goober squirm under Archie's gaze; then we are looking up at Archie from Emile's dwarfish mind; then we watch Brother Leon's classroom performance through Jerry's quiet presence; and so on. The variety of perspectives develops our understanding of the characters and reveals the complex interweaving of motivations and dependencies. The shift is unobtrusive but can be easily detected by a close look at the text. Less subtly, there are occasional tags that clue the reader to a change in voice: Brian Cochran and Obie, for instance, are inclined to think, "For crying out loud!" while Archie is addicted to the ironic use of the word *beautiful.* Cormier is too fine a writer, of course, to descend to using imitation slang to indicate that this is a teenager speaking. Nothing dates a book more quickly than trendiness, and his understanding of the quality of adolescence goes far deeper than picking up the latest expression.

Much has been made of Cormier's imagery, and many essays and articles have been written on his metaphors and similes, his allusions and personifications. Sometimes it seems that Cormier is merely exercising his virtuosity for the reader: "His voice curled into a question mark," or "He poured himself liquid through the sunrise streets." But most of the time his images are precisely calculated to carry the weight of the emotion he is projecting. Carter, about to tackle Jerry, looks "like some monstrous reptile in his helmet." Leon, thwarted, has "a smile like the kind an undertaker fixes on the face of a corpse." Jerry, happy, scuffles through "crazy cornflake leaves" but, sad, sees autumn leaves flutter down "like doomed and crippled birds." Sometimes the imagery is vividly unpleasant, as some critics have complained, but it is always appropriate to the intensity of what Cormier is trying to say. There is a whole bouquet of bad smells and ugly imagery in *The Chocolate War,* starting with Brother Leon's rancid bacon breath. The evening comes on as "the sun bleeding low in the sky and spurting its veins." Sweat moves like "small moist bugs" on Jerry's forehead. The vanquished Rollo's vomiting sounds like a toilet flushing.

Literary and biblical allusions, too, enrich the alert reader's experience of the novel. Shakespeare and T. S. Eliot are the most obvious sources. "Cut me, do I not bleed?" thinks

Emile, like Shylock. And the quotation on the poster in Jerry's locker is from Eliot's "The Love Song of J. Alfred Prufrock." One critic has gone so far as to write an essay drawing parallels between Jerry and Hamlet, Archie and Iago.[2]

Many of these allusions are not isolated flourishes, but fit together into larger structures of meaning. As one example, the Christian symbolism in *The Chocolate War* is an indication of the importance of the book's theme to Cormier. Before tracing that imagery, however, it is essential to clarify that the school itself is not part of this symbolism. It is a gross misunderstanding of the theme of the book to interpret it as an attack on parochial schools or the Catholic Church. The fact that Trinity is a Catholic school is as irrelevant to the meaning of the story as that fact is irrelevant to the characters. But Cormier does use Christian symbolism to show the cosmic implications of the events he is relating. When Jerry refuses to sell the chocolates, the language suggests the book of Revelations: "Cities fell. Earth opened. Planets tilted. Stars plummeted."[3] In the second chapter, the goalposts remind Obie of empty crosses, and in the last chapter, after Jerry's martyrdom, they again remind him of—what? In his graceless state, he can't remember. When Jerry is challenged to action by the hippie, the man looks at him across a Volkswagen so that Jerry sees only the disembodied head. The image is of John the Baptist, who was beheaded by Herod after he cried in the wilderness to announce the coming of Christ. Archie's name has myriad meanings from its root of "arch": "principal or chief," "cleverly sly and alert," "most fully embodying the qualities of its kind." But most significantly, the reference is to the Archangel, who fell from Heaven to be the Fallen Angel, or Lucifer himself. The Vigils, although Cormier admitted only to a connotation of "vigilantes," resonate with religious meaning. A vigil is a watch on the night preceding a religious holiday, and the candles placed before the altar in supplication are vigil candles. The members of the gang stand before Archie, who basks in their admiration like a religious statue before a bank of candles.[4] But most important, the understanding of the ultimate opposing forces of good and evil in *The Chocolate War* is a deeply Christian, or perhaps even a deeply Catholic, vision.

How does the theme of this book fit into Cormier's fascination with the nature of human confrontation with the Implacable? All of the three villains are vulnerable, and if they cannot quite be placated, they can at least be manipulated. They are quick to see each other's weaknesses and quick to take advantage of them for more secure positions of power. Leon's overreaching ambition has put him in a shaky place, and Archie sees him "riddled with cracks and crevices—running scared—open to invasion." Archie fears Leon's power over him as his teacher, and his domination of the Vigils is dependent on thinking up ever more imaginative assignments. And then there is the black box—a nemesis over which he has no control. Emile's vulnerable point is his stupidity; he is easily conned by Archie into believing in the imaginary photograph. So none of the three is an implacable, unconquerable force; all are subject to fears and weaknesses.

Why, then, does Jerry's lone refusal seem so doomed from the beginning? Why does the contest seem so unequal? Why does the action move so inevitably toward tragedy? The answer lies in the nature of what it is he is saying "no" to. What he is opposing is not Brother Leon, not Archie, not Emile, but the monstrous force that moves them, of which they are but imperfect human agents. The Goober echoes Hamlet when he gives it a name: " 'There's something rotten in that school. More than rotten.' He groped for the word and found it but didn't want to use it. The word didn't fit the surroundings, the sun and the bright October afternoon. It was a midnight word, a howling wind word." The word is *evil*.

The unholy trinity of Trinity are studies in the human forms of evil. Brother Leon, who as a priest is supposedly an agent of the Divine, has sold his soul for power, even down to his exultation in the small nasty tyrannies of the classroom. Cormier said that he chose the name Leon, a bland, soft name, to match the brother's superficial blandness. "And so is evil bland in its many disguises," he added.[5] Leon's appearance is deceptive: "On the surface, he was one of those pale, ingratiating kind of men who tiptoed through life on small, quick feet." "In the classroom Leon was another person altogether. Smirking, sarcastic. His thin, high voice venomous. He could hold your attention like a cobra. Instead of fangs, he used his teacher's pointer, flicking out here, there, everywhere." Leon's skin is pale, damp, and his moist eyes are like boiled onions or specimens in laboratory test tubes. When he blackmails Caroni into revealing Jerry's motivation, his fingers holding the chalk are like "the legs of pale spiders with a victim in their clutch." After he has demolished the boy, the chalk lies broken, "abandoned on the desk, like white bones, dead men's bones." The image that gradually accumulates around Leon is that of a hideous, colorless insect, a poisonous insect, crawling damp from its hiding place under a rock. Or perhaps he has emerged from even deeper underground, as Jerry suspects when he sees "a glimpse into the hell that was burning inside the teacher."

Archie is far subtler and will ultimately, when he is an adult, be more dangerous, because he is not in bondage to ambition. True, he revels in the captive audience of the Vigils, but he is not really part of that or any political structure. "I am Archie," he gloats, Archie alone. For him, the pleasure is in building intricate evil structures for their own sake. "Beautiful!" he cries as Brother Eugene falls apart like the furniture in his room, as Leon squirms under the pressure of Jerry's refusal, as Jerry struggles ever deeper into the exitless trap Archie has made for him. Yet, Archie, too, is in hell, the hell of understanding only the dark side of human nature. "People are two things," he tells Carter. "Greedy and cruel."

From this knowledge comes his strength, his ability to make anybody do anything. But for him reality is bottomless emptiness. "Life is shit," he says without emotion.

Emile is the purest embodiment of evil. In him we see the horror of evil's essential quality: silliness. Emile loves to "reach" people. He giggles when he leaves a mess in the public toilet, when he secretly gives an already-tackled football player an extra jab, when he loudly accuses a shy kid of farting on a crowded bus. Essentially evil is pointless. Purpose and structure belong to goodness; evil can only turn back on itself in chaos. Archie and Leon have clothed their evil with intelligence and worldly power, but Emile's surrender to darkness is revealed in all its terrible nakedness. The others recognize his nonhumanity quite clearly. "An animal," they call him.

Archie is amused by Emile's simplicity but also chilled by the recognition of a kinship he is not willing to acknowledge. Emile, however, in his perverse innocence, easily sees that he and Archie are "birds of a feather," and that their differences are only a matter of intelligence. An even more terrible innocence is that of the children whom Emile recruits to ambush Jerry. "Animals," he calls them in turn, and they emerge crouching from the bushes to do his bidding like twittering hordes of little devils.

All three villains are completely devoid of any sense of guilt. Indeed, Archie often congratulates himself on his compassion. Brother Leon is all surface; his soul is hollow, and he is the one main character whose interior monologue we never hear. Repentance is totally foreign to him. Emile is even a bit defensive at being defined as a bad guy. "All right, so he liked to screw around a little, get under people's skin. That was human nature, wasn't it? A guy had to protect himself at all times. Get them before they get you. Keep people guessing—and afraid."

Cormier deliberately gives us no hint of the origins of

their devotion to darkness. "People can't say Archie did this because he was a deprived child or he was a victim of child abuse. I wanted him judged solely on his actions."[6] To understand is to forgive, and to forgive real evil is to make an alliance with it. To render these characters psychologically understandable would be to humanize them, to undermine their stature as instruments of darkness, and therefore to erase the theme of opposition to the Implacable.

For those who would turn their eyes away from the ultimate and prefer a smaller and more comfortable theme, Cormier has thoughtfully provided an alternative. It is possible to view the book as an examination of tyranny. The themes' patterns overlap but are not identical. Seen this way, the trinity has a different cast. There are three structures of misused power: the school, as headed by Brother Leon; the athletic department, as headed by the coach; and the mob, as headed by Archie. Each has a passive assistant to tyranny, characters who have decent impulses but are ineffectual because they lack the courage to act. Obie is Archie's reluctant stooge; Carter agrees with the coach's approval of violence, and Brother Jacques despises Leon but condones his actions by not opposing them.

The question ultimately turns back, no matter whether tyranny or absolute evil is the enemy, to "How can we resist?" If evil had inherent power, there would be no answer. But Leon, Archie, and Emile all find their power source in their victims' weaknesses. Leon even plays contemptuously with them in the classroom, when he tells the boys that they have become Nazi Germany by their fearful silence. Emile has very early discovered that most people want peace at any price and will accept almost any embarrassment or harassment rather than take a stand or make a fuss. "Nobody wanted trouble, nobody wanted to make trouble, nobody wanted a showdown." Archie, too, has realized that "the world was made up of two kinds of people—those who were victims and those who victimized." But the moment Jerry, of his own volition, refuses to sell the chocolates, he steps outside this cynical characterization. In that defiance is the source of hope.

Jerry at first has no idea why he has said no. "He'd wanted to end the ordeal—and then that terrible *No* had issued out of his mouth." But Jerry's life has been "like a yawning cavity in his chest" since his mother's death. His father is sleepwalking through his days, a man for whom everything and nothing is "Fine!," a pharmacist who once wanted to be a doctor and now denies that such an ambition ever existed. Like Prufrock, he is too numb to live and too afraid to act. When Jerry looks into the mirror he is appalled to see his father's face reflected in his own features. The hippie and the poster dare him to disturb the universe, and when he finally says no on his own, he is taking a stand against far more than a chocolate sale. And it is Brother Leon himself who has taught Jerry that not to resist is to assist.

Jerry is the only one who learns that lesson, and this is what makes his destruction inevitable. Evil is implacable and merciless to a Lone Hero, in spite of the folk myth that he always wins. *The Chocolate War* betrays that expectation, and the reader cries, "No! This is all wrong!" In that cry is Cormier's very intention. The reader's outrage is the interactivity that Cormier has built into the ending, and in it lies the meaning of the story.

But could it have turned out differently? What if the marble had been black and Archie had had to step into the ring to confront Jerry directly? This is the ending imagined by screenwriter Keith Gordon for the 1988 film of *The Chocolate War,* which is otherwise faithful to the book. In Gordon's version of the story, Jerry batters Archie unmercifully, and then realizes that he, Jerry, has become one of the enemy. In a final scene, we see Archie defeated and humiliated, an ending that has the probably unintended effect of making him a tragic hero and the central figure of the story.

Returning to Cormier's vision, the key to the real triumph of good, ironically, comes again from Brother Leon's lesson about group responsibility. If others had joined Jerry . . . There are a number of places in the story where this might have happened. The Goober, of course, is often on the verge of acting on his friendship for Jerry, but in the end, like Hamlet, he only thinks, and doesn't act until too late. For a moment he even hopes that it will all end in a stalemate. The Goober speaks for all the others in wanting to avoid confrontation at any cost. Obie might have acted on his disgust for Archie: "I owe you one for that!" he thinks when pushed too far. In the end he settles only for hoping that fate will punish Archie with a black marble. Carter, too, might have used his simple strength to end Archie's regime.

Any of these isolated actions might have started the group movement that would have saved Jerry and defeated Leon and the Vigils. Even without such a spur the school comes close to following Jerry's example at the midpoint in the sale. But their motivation is negative—they are tired of selling and selfishly individual—"let each one do his own thing." Without a conscious joining together for the good of all, they can easily be maneuvered separately back into doing the Vigils' will.

So here at last is Cormier's meaning. As one critic has written, "Jerry's defeat is unimportant. What is important is that he made the choice and that he stood firm for his convictions."[7] Only by making that irrational gesture can we hold on to our humanity, even when defeat is inevitable. But there is more—when the agents of evil are other human beings, perhaps good can win if enough people have the courage to take a stand together. Evil alliances are built on self-interest with uneasy mutual distrust, but goodness can join humans with the self-transcending strength of sympathy and love.

1. De Luca, Geraldine, and Roni Natov, "Taking True Risks: Controversial Issues in New Young Adult Novels," *The Lion and the Unicorn,* Winter 1979–80, 125.

2. Clements, Bruce, "A Second Look: *The Chocolate War,*" *The Horn Book Magazine,* April 1979, 217.

3. Carter, Betty, and Karen Harris, "Realism in Adolescent Fiction: In Defense of *The Chocolate War,*" *Top of the News,* Spring 1980, 283.

4. Donelson, Kenneth L., and Alleen Pace Nilsen, *Literature for Today's Young Adults,* Scott, Foresman, 1980, 186.

5. Nilsen, Alleen Pace, "The Poetry of Naming in Young Adult Books," *ALAN Review,* Spring 1980, 3.

6. De Luca and Natov, 122.

7. Hoxie, Renee, letter, *Wilson Library Bulletin,* January 1982, 327.

Chapter Five

The Dark Chocolate Controversy

A border of funereal black enclosed the review of *The Chocolate War* that appeared in the American Library Association's *Booklist* on July 1, 1974, just a few months after the book's release in April. The reviewer, Betsy Hearne, the magazine's children's book editor and a highly respected critic, wrung her hands over what she perceived as "the trend of didactic negativity" in books for young people. While acknowledging Cormier's power, she deplored the vision he portrayed with that power, calling *The Chocolate War* "a book that looks with adult bitterness at the inherent evil of human nature and the way young people can be dehumanized into power-hungry and blood-thirsty adults." Her words were the opening salvo in a battle that still rages over Cormier's writings in particular and young adult literature in general, a passionate confrontation between the advocates of the therapeutic value of honesty and those who would protect young people from knowledge of dark realities.[1]

Hearne was not alone in her distress. Although most of the critics were enthusiastic about Cormier's skill, only some of them were brave enough to praise his dark vision. Mary K. Chelton, a leading teacher and mentor of young adult librarians, was one of these. In *School Library Journal* she called the book "unique in its uncompromising portrait of human cruelty and conformity."[2] Richard Peck, himself a highly regarded young adult author, was equally impressed with the theme. Writing in *American Libraries,* he said:

> Too many young adult novels only promise an outspoken revelation of the relevant. *The Chocolate War* delivers the goods. . . . Surely the most uncompromising novel ever directed to the "12 and up reader"—and very likely the most necessary. . . . And anyone looking for a pat triumph of the individual had better avert his eyes. . . . The young will understand the outcome. They won't like it, but they'll understand.[3]

Theodore Weesner of the *New York Times* was specific in his praise: "Masterfully structured and rich in theme, the action is well crafted, well timed, suspenseful; complex ideas develop and unfold with clarity. . . . Written for teenagers but a strong read for adults," he declared, and "an ideal study for the high school classroom."[4]

But there are still critics, teachers, librarians, and parents who are uncomfortable with this lumpy package that Robert Cormier hands them. In a number of ways *The Chocolate War* jarred expectations. Superficially, it looked to some older readers like a standard school story, the kind of tale about boyish pranks right under the headmaster's nose that began with *Tom Brown's Schooldays* and continues today with the Harry Potter series. To other, more sophisticated readers it evoked the deeply ingrained American myth of the lone heroic stand—the showdown at high noon. Except that this showdown wasn't triumphant for the hero. And for those who were already familiar with patterns in young adult literature, Cormier's preoccupation with the universal rather than the personal was disorienting, and the lack of helpful adults and a happy ending violated a sacred tradition. As Donald Gallo said later, "Somebody had challenged the status quo. Not just Jerry Renault, but Robert Cormier. *Robert Cormier had disturbed the universe of young adult books!*"[5]

It is important to remember that, as far as the critics were concerned, Cormier had come out of nowhere; he was a complete unknown to the world of juvenile fiction. It had been almost ten years since he had published a novel of any kind, and fifteen years since the flurry of critical excitement over *Now and at the Hour.* His three adult novels were out of print and virtually forgotten. So it is no wonder that, when confronted by *The Chocolate War,* many critics saw only bleak hopelessness where Cormier intended an uncompromising but therapeutic honesty. "I was kind of surprised by the initial controversy about *The Chocolate War,*" he remembered much later, "because to me there was the implicit lesson. . . . I thought I was portraying what happens when good people don't come to the rescue. Which didn't mean that was the way life is all the time, just in that particular situation."[6]

But some critics remained unconvinced, and lively exchanges continued to appear in the pages of literary and professional journals and even popular magazines. These early debates laid the battle lines for many that were to follow. Seventeen years later the issues were still drawing blood. In May 1998, on the occasion of Cormier's delivery of UCLA's annual Frances Clarke Sayers lecture, the *Los Angeles Times* published an article that praised his work and characterized its darkness.[7] A week of stormy letters to the editor followed, from readers who took one or the other side of the by now familiar controversy. The unconscious presumption beneath these and other exchanges is clarified by an insightful sentence from a review in *Signal* magazine: "It seems to me that too many children's book 'professionals' . . . still work on the assumption that literature makes people better only so long as the books themselves show a life, however unreal, which is the 'better' they want children and young people to be."[8] Again Cormier's words are illuminating. In a letter to the students of the Cohen Hillel Academy, he explained: "To write a book in which the evil is victorious is not to condone it."[9]

Before the book was published, Cormier stood by the inevitability of Jerry's bleak defeat, even when three editors rejected the book because of the ending. "I knew that in my mind the curve of the story was to build and then go down. And I had this crazy image in my mind of trying to fix up the ending to make it go up—'zip'—which seemed untrue, but it was tempting."[10] But when the chips were down, he stuck by his convictions. "A happy ending attached to a novel whose flow and tone and development is downbeat fatally flaws the work," he maintained.[11]

Another kind of Cormier critique, an objective analysis of a particular aspect of his writing, appears more and more often in scholarly and professional journals. As college students discover the rich critical possibilities in his work, it is one measure of his literary importance that many papers and even masters' and doctoral theses have been devoted to Cormier deconstruction. In recent years these have sometimes been from a postmodern or feminist perspective.

For instance, a critique of *The Chocolate War* from this perspective was written in 2002 by C. Anita Tarr in Yale University Press's *Children's Literature.*[12] In her essay, titled

"The Absence of Moral Agency in Robert Cormier's *The Chocolate War*," Tarr faults the novel for a lack of female characters and deplores the book's depiction of the very real but very politically incorrect tendency of young men to regard all girls as interesting collections of body parts. However, Tarr does make a convincing case for Cormier as a postmodern novelist, with his emphases on angst and interactivity with the reader. Jerry, she insists, is not to be seen as rebel hero, but as "the prototype of a popular kind of protagonist in young adult literature, one who is paralyzed by postmodern society's anxieties." She maintains that current textbooks reveal that teachers are perceiving the plot as an example of moral decision making and using it mistakenly to impart the value of nonconformity. Jerry, Tarr demonstrates, is deeply conformist, and it is Archie who is the real nonconformist. Responding to Cormier's mandate for collective good, Tarr points out provocatively that all the collective agencies in the book, all the examples of people working together (the school, the Vigils, the football team, the campaign to sell the chocolates) have evil—not good—results.

The controversy surrounding *The Chocolate War* reaches beyond literary criticism, however. The novel is one of the books most challenged by censors in our times. From 1981 to 2001 it was reported by the *Newsletter on Intellectual Freedom* as the target of thirty-one censorship attempts—and the American Library Association estimates that for all books there are twenty-five unreported challenges to every one that makes it into print.[13] However, it should be noted that many of these challenges were what the *Newsletter* calls "success stories"—in the end the book was returned to the classroom or library shelves.

One of the earliest challenges took place in Cormier's home state of Massachusetts. In the summer of 1976, just a year and a half after the book had been published, teacher Connie Manter assigned *The Chocolate War* to the freshmen who would soon be entering her ninth-grade humanities and communication class in Groton. "The book is structurally sound," she said later, in defending her choice. "It is a good example for plot sequence and it shows character development. And after we selected the book, we learned that the author lived nearby, and we thought that if he could address the class then it would be a human experience that we could not duplicate."[14]

One or two mothers in the town disagreed. After glancing through the book their teenagers were reading for school, they went straight to the telephone and complained to school committeeman Andrew Zale. By the time school opened in mid-September feelings had grown so intense that it was necessary to call a town meeting to air the matter. Nearly 150 people came to see the fireworks. Zale presented his case. *The Chocolate War,* he argued, "is on the whole a depressing text which casts school authority in a completely adverse position to the students of the school and contains a wearisome abundance of violence and disruption coupled with veiled references to less than wholesome sexual activities. Also included is the figure of a member of a Christian denomination in a totally evil light." He proposed that the community establish a curriculum and textbook review committee to act as an authority in keeping such books out of the hands of students.[15]

Connie Manter, as well as the school librarian and even some parents, spoke out in favor of the book, but the most telling piece of testimony was a letter written by two students from Manter's class and signed by thirty-eight others. "A high school student does not have to open a book to read far worse things than *The Chocolate War.* Any trip to a public restroom will expose him to far more obscene written material. The book has a good story to tell. The supposed immoral statements are there to tell part of the story. You cannot protect us from hearing such things unless you lock us up." The audience and the school board, except Zale, gave overwhelming support to keeping the book in the classroom.[16]

The challenges continued in other parts of the country, and not all of them ended so happily. As teachers discovered the literary excellence of *The Chocolate War* and its ability to spark passionate discussion, it became a standard study in high school classrooms. And a standard target for would-be censors, who hurled accusations that it is "pornography,"[17] "filth," "garbage,"[18] "a continued assault on Christian principles,"[19] and even that it contains "an explicit rape scene."[20] One parent claimed to have found 171 "swear words" in the novel.[21] But eleven-year-old John McGrath in New Milford, Connecticut, put this issue in perspective: "I think it's a very reflective book. The language? Some of it's obscene, but if you could look on the [school] bus, this would be a Little Bo Peep story."[22]

As Cormier continued to write more fine novels, the censors' ire occasionally spread to those books, too. So when *I Am the Cheese* was singled out for removal from Mowat Middle School classrooms in Bay County, Florida, in April 1986, it was not unusual that school superintendent Leonard Hall justified his order with unfounded claims that the book contained "profanity and sexually explicit passages,"[23] as well as "depressing themes" and "filthy language."[24] Hall was responding to a directive from the school board, who in turn were responding to pressure from Charles E. Collins, a wealthy and influential developer who felt that his granddaughter's teacher had assigned "a trite little book with terrible sentence structure." Never mind that Mowat's English department had been named a Center of Excellence by the National Council of Teachers of English. Award or not, the teachers were overruled, and *Cheese* had to go.[25]

The Bay County school board decided that every book to be used in the classrooms of the county's twenty-five schools should be approved by the superintendent. Hall, who by his own description is "not an English type of guy,"[26] set up a breathtakingly simplistic method for making these decisions.

According to reporter Barbara Stewart, who later wrote a vivid history of the whole affair for *The Orlando Sentinel*, "Hall ordered teachers to count up the dirty words in books and list the pages on which they appeared. The worst offenders, including books that had racy plots as well as those with dirty words, were designated Category III, the blacklist. (Category I books were those fully approved, like *The Hobbit;* Category II books could be taught, but they weren't pristine, like *The Hound of the Baskervilles.*) There were sixty-four Category III books, including books taught in Bay County for generations: *Wuthering Heights, Twelfth Night, Macbeth, The Great Gatsby, Great Expectations,*"[27] *Lord of the Flies, To Kill a Mockingbird, The Chocolate War,* and fifty-three others.[28] All were banned from Bay County classrooms. The media got wind of the packed, steamy school board meetings and descended like flies. Hall was hounded by *60 Minutes, World News Tonight,* the *Washington Post,* and the *Atlanta Constitution.*

Cormier himself flew to Florida in the thick of the battle, "to show them," he said, "that I was a human being and not some monster from New England trying to corrupt their children."[29] ReLeah Lent, one of the teachers under siege, remembers the scene:

I couldn't wait to introduce Cormier to these Bay Countians, many of whom had signed petitions against his books, to show them his gentle spirit, his wise and tempered words reflecting an introspective life. I was nervous, but it was an excited anxiety, as if I were about to introduce Ghandi. I trusted him to calm the masses, to face narrow-minded fear with honest openness. And, indeed, as the auditorium filled beyond capacity, as people stood in the aisles looking at this man who had "started this whole mess," they seemed a bit pacified. Then, like Moses coming down from the mountain, he spoke and they listened. He spoke about how writing a book is both terrible and wonderful, about how he went to a boys' school and wrote what he knew, about how life isn't always bright and glorious; the darkness exists even as we "dare to disturb the universe." His words seemed to diffuse the hostility and I could see many of those who had prejudged him drinking in his tonic of reason. They had confronted the monster and he turned out to be a gentle, kind man with appropriately large owl glasses, speaking about emotions: fear, love, insecurity. As he spoke, it was clear that he was perplexed as to how his words had ignited such a burning controversy. Robert Cormier sparked a connection with the audience just as he had connected with millions of readers.[30]

At last businessmen in Panama City, the county seat, began to worry that all the publicity was giving the town a bad name and scaring away new industry. Public sentiment grew against Hall and Collins, and the school board voted to reinstate most of the banned books—all but Farley Mowat's nature classic, *Never Cry Wolf,* and Cormier's *I Am the Cheese.* It took a courageous lawsuit by teachers Gloria Pipkin and Alyne Farrell and forty-two other teachers and parents and teenagers to reverse the decision on these last two banned books.[31]

It is important to remember that while such censorship attempts make dramatic reading, they are isolated incidents. And in many of these cases, the teachers had been using *The Chocolate War* for years without any problems. Most of the hundreds of teachers who use the book in classes find that parents and school authorities recognize the excellence of their choice and that students enjoy the book and benefit from discussing Cormier's provocative themes. But these peaceful successes don't make newspaper headlines or get reported in the *Newsletter for Intellectual Freedom.*

However, a legitimate source of parental complaint, and the root of many challenges, is the mistake of presenting Cormier novels to readers who are too young for them—not because of sexual content or language, but because young teens are not mature enough to comprehend the subtleties of his ideas and style. For instance, a challenge in Evergreen, Colorado, in 1994 resulted from the inclusion of *I Am the Cheese* in a media center for fifth and sixth graders,[32] who at that age could only be bewildered by the novel's complex structure and its buried secrets. (Significantly, no censorship attacks have been leveled at Cormier's novels for younger readers, *Tunes for Bears to Dance To* and *Other Bells for Us to Ring.*) Popular computerized reading programs like Accelerated Reader bear some of the blame here, because age levels are measured not by a determination of the psychological and emotional—or even sexual—sophistication of the book, but by vocabulary, sentence length, and other quantitative markers recognized by the computer. Cormier's short, tight sentences and simple, direct words often result in his books' being classed by these programs at a much lower grade level than is appropriate.

  Cormier, with his wisdom and compassion, understood the motivation of would-be censors and wrote eloquently of it in Donald Gallo's *Authors' Insights:*

Censorship is . . . the act of sincere, sometimes desperate people who are frightened by the world they live in and in which they are bringing up their children. . . . Instead of preparing them to meet that world, they want them to avert their eyes and remain in impossible exclusion. Beyond that, they insist that this same kind of sheltering be extended to the people next door or down the street or in the next town. Every writer I know whose books are challenged enters that battle, flies across the country, makes the speeches, debates opponents, offers encouragement to educators who find themselves targets of the bookbanners. . . . I believe, however, that the greatest thing writers can do is simply to keep writing. Writing honestly with all the craft that can be summoned. Writing to illuminate as well as entertain. Writing to challenge the intellect and engage the heart. . . . This is what I try to do each day when I sit at the typewriter. This is my best answer to those who would ban my books.[33]

But the war is never over. In June 2000, just months before Cormier's death, the old controversy over *The Chocolate War* erupted in Lancaster, Massachusetts, a town just a few miles from his own Leominster. Some of the challengers were even personally acquainted with him.[34] As he always did, he gave an interview to the press, not in defense of himself or the book, but of the teacher who had assigned it. And publicly he told Diane Williamson of the Worcester *Telegram & Gazette,* "I'm weary of the battle. But a tired fighter can still be a fighter."[35]

Notes

1. Hearne, Betsy, "Whammo, You Lose," *Booklist,* July 1, 1974, 1199.

2. Chelton, Mary K., *School Library Journal,* May 1974, 62.

3. Peck, Richard, "Delivering the Goods," *American Libraries,* October 1974, 492.

4. Weesner, Theodore, *The New York Times,* May 5, 1974, Section VII, 15.

5. Gallo, Donald, "Robert Cormier: The Author and the Man," speech at a reception commemorating the establishment of the Robert E. Cormier Collection, Fitchburg State College Library, Fitchburg, Massachusetts, May 3, 1981, printed in *ALAN Review,* Fall 1981, 34.

6. Sutton, Roger, "Kind of a Funny Dichotomy," *School Library Journal,* June 1991, 28.

7. Smith, Lynn, "Unhappily Ever After," *The Los Angeles Times,* May 26, 1998, E2.

8. Pelorus, *Signal,* September 1975, 146.

9. Cormier, Robert, letter to eighth-grade students at Eli and Bessie Cohen Hillel Academy, Swampscott, Massachusetts, November 13, 1982,

Robert E. Cormier Archive, Fitchburg State College, Fitchburg, Massachusetts.

10. De Luca, Geraldine, and Roni Natov, "An Interview with Robert Cormier," *The Lion and the Unicorn,* Fall 1978, 114.

11. Cormier, Robert, "Forever Pedaling on the Road to Realism," in *Celebrating Children's Books: Essays on Children's Literature in Honor of Zena Sutherland,* edited by Betsy Hearne and Marilyn Kaye; New York, Lothrop, Lee & Shepard, 1981.

12. Tarr, C. Anita, "The Absence of Moral Agency in Robert Cormier's *The Chocolate War,*" in *Children's Literature,* Vol. 30, edited by Elizabeth Lennox Keyser and Julie Pfeiffer, New Haven, CT, Yale University Press, 2002, 96.

13. Kister, Ken, "Censorship in the Sunshine State: Florida Libraries Respond," *Wilson Library Bulletin,* November 1989, 29.

14. ". . . in Groton Social Studies Dept.," *Public Spirit* (Groton, Massachusetts), September 16, 1976, 1.

15. Ibid.

16. Ibid.

17. *Newsletter on Intellectual Freedom,* March 2001, 57.

18. *NIF,* May 2000, 78.

19. *NIF,* March 1985, 45.

20. *NIF,* January 1991, 12.

21. *NIF,* September 2000, 145.

22. *NIF,* May 1992, 96.

23. *NIF,* November 1986, 209.

24. Kister, 29.

25. Ibid.

26. Stewart, Barbara, "Dangerous Books, Dangerous Deeds," *The Orlando Sentinel, Florida Magazine,* July 12, 1987, 10.

27. Stewart, 9.

28. Kister, 31.

29. Williamson, Dianne, "Censorship an Endless Challenge," *Telegram & Gazette* (Worcester, Massachusetts), June 13, 2000, A1, 3.

30. Lent, ReLeah, and Gloria Pipkin, "We Keep Pedaling," *ALAN Review,* Winter 2001, 10.

31. Stewart, 13.

32. *NIF,* May 1994, 97.

33. Cormier, Robert, "A Book Is Not a House: The Human Side of Censorship," in *Authors' Insights: Turning Teenagers into Readers and Writers,* Donald Gallo, ed., Boynton/Cook-Heinemann, 1992, 74.

34. Nugent, Karen, "Forum to Examine Eighth-Grade Book," *Telegram & Gazette,* (Worcester, Massachusetts), June 12, 2000, 1.

35. Williamson, A1, 3.

Chapter Six

Beyond the Chocolate War

"And then what happened?" The question that is put to rest at the end of a good story. But a question that, after a while, revives and tugs enticingly at readers when an author has created characters that live their own lives beyond that particular set of events. "What happened to Jerry? And Archie?" young readers of *The Chocolate War* asked Cormier continually. "And how about Tubs Caspar? Did he buy the bracelet for Rita?" Privately Cormier himself also wondered, especially about Obie. How had the dark days of the chocolate war changed him and the others at Trinity? And then what happened?

So, eleven years later, Cormier began to play around at the typewriter to find out. He conjured up the characters again and let them show themselves in new scenes. He pared and refined and distilled. The result is a work that upon close analysis reveals itself as complex and dense, but on first reading has the spare and compelling clarity of great storytelling. The plot is an intricate delight of glittering illusions, magic tricks, and surprises, yet paradoxically it moves with the utter simplicity and inevitability of absolute truth. The reader has no trouble at all keeping track of the more than a dozen major characters. Unanswered questions and unresolved tensions layer from scene to scene as the characters collide in a rich choreography of shifting expectations, allegiances, and perceptions. Cormier revealed to the *Horn Book Magazine* how he achieved this tension: "You have a rubber band that you keep pulling and pulling and pulling, and just at the moment of snapping you release it and start another chapter and start pulling again."[1]

It is the paradox of surprise and inevitability that is the chief pleasure of the book. In spite of all the unexpected jolts around each corner of the plot, the overwhelming experience for the reader is a sense of rightness. We know these characters, and this is just what they *would* do, just what *would* happen. We knew it all the time—except we didn't, until Cormier told us. As Tubs Caspar says to Obie, when Obie asks what happened when Rita didn't get her bracelet: "You know what happened." And when Tubs, as we were always sure he would, comes to Archie's attention as a natural victim, the assignment—to gain twenty pounds—is a perfect fit. The surprise is our sudden recognition of the inevitability of that fit.

The question that immediately comes to mind about any sequel is whether it can stand alone. Must the reader have experienced the chocolate war to be able to follow the action of *Beyond the Chocolate War*? In a limited sense, no. Cormier has dutifully written in all the events that went before, so that a newcomer can pick up the thread of the narrative. But the real heart of the story lies in the emotions and the characters, and these it is hard to grasp fully from a synopsis. The deeply satisfying inevitability of the action is rooted in our prior understanding of the actors. Indeed, so closely are the books linked as cause and result that perhaps the real question is whether they are two halves that should be published between the same covers.

For the new reader Cormier needed a new character, someone who also needed to be told what went on last term. His name begins the first sentence of the book: "Ray Bannister started to build the guillotine the day Jerry Renault returned to Monument." A lapel grabber of an opening, and one that sets up appropriately sinister expectations. A guillotine means an execution. Whose? Having gotten our attention, Cormier immediately denies everything with the second sentence: "There was no connection between the two events." But we know there's going to be. Cormier explained in another context, "I think Chekhov said it—if you have a rifle on the mantel in the first act, it must be fired by the last act."

The important thing to remember about *this* guillotine is that it is an illusion. It cuts, and it doesn't cut. Cormier plays with our uncertainty about its nature and thus sets us up for the whole bag of magic tricks that he will perform in *Beyond the Chocolate War.* "Are you sure it's fool-proof?" asks Obie.

"Is anything really sure in this world?" Ray counters.

The guillotine casts a tall, dark shadow. While the story is unfolding in the halls of Trinity, we are aware of Ray at home building the instrument of execution. Cormier has even given us in this first chapter a capsule preview of what the guillotine's final role will be, as Ray imagines himself performing for the student body: " 'May I have a volunteer from the audience?'—and hearing the guys gasp with astonishment as the blade fell, seeming to penetrate the volunteer's neck."

Ray is basically a simple soul, a carpenter. Although the deviousness of the magician would seem to be a foreign role to someone so straightforward, he finds its secrecy congenial because he is a private person, a natural loner. In the first chapter we see Monument through Ray's eyes, and the simile is drawn from his loneliness and boredom: the town is "like a movie set from one of those old late-night films about the Depression." Trinity seems to him in his innocence to be "not wicked but only unfriendly and suffocatingly small." For us, who have come to know it as a whole dark world, his perception is ironic. His simplicity makes him immune to the evil at Trinity—"that Vigils stuff" only puzzles him. His name—meaning "a limited beam of light"—is a significant symbol. Cormier's first title for the book was "In the Darkness," a phrase that ends *The Chocolate War* and describes the condition of the world afterward. Ray's sunny wholesomeness is a bit of light in that darkness, and even when he is maneuvered into becoming the executioner, his simple good sense, in the form of the safety catch, deflects the ultimate moment of evil.

This first chapter is written in a rather flat narrative (as contrasted with the vivid scene on the football field that opens *The Chocolate War*). The effect is like a prologue, a statement before the real action begins, establishing the unanswered question of the guillotine. That done, Cormier the conjurer sweeps aside the curtain, and here we are back at Trinity, plunged with a shock of glad recognition into the familiar scene of a Vigils meeting. It is fall term, and at first glance everything looks the same—Carter with his gavel, Archie plotting an assignment. But things have begun to change. Obie and Carter are restless and distracted. There are some new people in the darkened room—the sophomore Bunting and his henchmen, Cornacchio and Harley.

The memory of the chocolate war hangs over the whole student body like a bad dream. It has made differences in the lives of the people we know from last term. Not surprisingly, Brother Leon has been appointed headmaster after the retirement of the former head. After all, this is what the chocolate sale was all about. Not a surprise, either, is the fact that Leon has had the decent Brother Jacques transferred. Brother Eugene, we learn later, has died from the mental and physical disruption that began with the collapse of his beloved Room Nineteen. Jerry Renault has been in Canada recovering but is now back home, although not at school. Emile Janza is the same, or maybe even worse—a little heavier, a little more menacing, a little more of a brute. He and Archie seem untouched by the events of last term. But Obie and Carter, Jerry and his friend The Goober, David Caroni—the passage of evil has left them struggling in its wake.

It is Obie whom Cormier sees as the protagonist of *Beyond the Chocolate War.* "A tragic figure" he has called him, and the instrument of revenge.[2] Obie has lost everything because of his devotion to Archie: his high school years, his own potential, his self-respect. Before the story is over, he has even lost the salvation of his love for Laurie Gundarson, because she is repelled by his connection with the Vigils. Pathetically, he tries to define himself to her, when she asks about the secret society, as "one of the good guys," but the name he gives himself as Ray's partner in the magic act is closer to the truth: "Obie the Obedient." When Archie forces him to face his identity as "a selector of victims" and perhaps even a murderer, he sees with horror that he has misplaced the blame all along. The face of evil is not Archie's but his own. "You could have said *no* anytime, anytime at all. But you didn't . . ." Here again is the theme of *The Chocolate War,* made even more explicit. Evil must be resisted collectively, but collective resistance begins with one *no.* Cormier spelled it out for the *Horn Book Magazine:* "The power of the leader comes from those who allow themselves to be led."[3]

Each of the other characters provides variations on this theme. Carter makes a gesture of resistance, but it is misdirected, too late, and too weak; he ends up being destroyed by it. The aftermath of the chocolates has left him unmoored, unanchored, and he blames Archie. "The tragedy of Carter's senior year was the ban on boxing imposed by

Brother Leon. Carter had been captain of both the boxing team and the football squad. With the boxing team disbanded and the football season a distant memory, he was now captain of exactly nothing. His simple claim to distinction these days was his presidency of the Vigils. And as president he had to respond to Archie, play his games, shadowbox with words." He has to do something to re-establish his manhood. The big, beefy varsity guard is more decent and sensitive than anyone suspected. When Archie plans a caper that will humiliate the bishop, Carter is appalled at the attack on the representative of goodness. He turns his outrage into action—but the wrong action. Instead of confronting Archie, he writes an anonymous letter to Brother Leon, thus becoming a traitor. Archie makes him pay dearly by demolishing the two pillars of his self-respect: honor and pride.

The trophies Carter is so proud of winning for Trinity are stolen from the hall case and replaced with a little ceramic toilet. His pride is further ravaged when he must make a groveling confession to Archie, and when he almost betrays Obie's guillotine scheme as a bargaining point, he realizes that he has lost his honor by nearly becoming a traitor a second time. A halfhearted gesture of resistance that does not directly confront the source of evil can backfire.

David Caroni, too, has misdirected his resistance. "Kill yourself and you also kill the world," he thinks as he draws the hot bath and lays out the razor blade. Ben (in *After the First Death*) and Barney (in *The Bumblebee Flies Anyway*) would have agreed. But at the last minute Caroni finds it is not enough; he must take Brother Leon with him into death more directly. David's opposition to evil becomes obsession and madness, out of proportion to the offense. Because Brother Leon has given him an F, he puts a knife to the headmaster's throat. Even we, who know the extent of all Leon's evil doings, don't want a revenge like this. There is no justice in it; it is too much. As Brian Cochran thinks, "He wouldn't wish for Leon to be killed or wounded, but a good scare would be terrific." Caroni fails, and says *no* by ending his own life.

Leon does eventually get his just deserts, in a way that is completely appropriate. In this book he appears primarily as an antagonist for Archie, rather than as an agent of his own evil doings. But Leon is still loathsome enough. In his new role as headmaster he has affected a repulsively mod seventies style, with sideburns down to his earlobes. "He wore a silver chain, from which dangled a cross so fancy that you had to squint to make certain it was a cross." A diabolical symbol: the man of God who is not a man of God wears a cross that is not a cross. Again, as in *The Chocolate War,* he is the one character whose interior monologue we never hear—pure unexplained evil. It would have been pleasant if he had not been quite so brave under Caroni's knife, if he had blubbered a bit more. But when he stands pompously before the students of Trinity and tries to transfer the guilt for Caroni's suicide to them, the flung tomato that explodes against his cheek in juicy fury is the perfect rejection of his hypocrisy. It is not a comic moment. The tomato is more satisfying than the knife—an appropriate nay-saying perfectly aimed and perfectly timed. No wonder the thrower, Henry Malloran, is elected president of the senior class the next day.

Jerry Renault is the character from the first book who is the most problematic. Some readers even believed that he died from the terrible beating at the end of *The Chocolate War.* In any case, we have worried about him, and of all the characters from the first book we want most of all to know what happened to Jerry. His inclusion in the sequel posed great difficulties for Cormier, as he explained to *Horn Book Magazine:* "I suppose the natural thing would have been to bring Jerry back to Trinity and have him confront Archie again. But I didn't want to do that. It would be like rewriting *The Chocolate War.* I wanted to keep him away from Trinity and yet have him involved with a Trinity character. . . . To me he was stubborn and refused to come to life; I worked so hard on him."[4]

The basic problem is that Jerry is inherently passive. His natural instincts are to do nothing. This is why the poster that challenges him to disturb the universe is so fascinating to him. His refusal to sell the chocolates only *seemed* like a heroic action because of the circumstances that led up to it. Actually, once the refusal is set in motion, Jerry's natural inertia keeps it in place. The only uncharacteristic thing he does is to strike out at Emile in the boxing ring, and as soon as he does it he knows it is wrong. That single blow guarantees that he will lose.

It is hard for a novelist to work with such a character. How can passivity be made interesting, or even—as it needed to be in this case—heroic? Cormier experimented in early versions of *Beyond the Chocolate War* with sinking Jerry even deeper into inertia. "I had him mute for a good time. In that version because of the language problem in Canada, he wasn't speaking, and suddenly he realized that he couldn't talk anymore. So when he came back to the States, he wasn't able to communicate at all during The Goober's first visit. In fact, because he wasn't able to talk, he let out a terrible scream of frustration that sent The Goober out of his home in horror. I wrote several scenes in which he was trying to talk and was talking haltingly. It just wasn't working for me; it just didn't ring true."[5] Glimpses of this version remain in Jerry's attraction to The Talking Church.

It is necessary for dramatic reasons that Jerry balance Archie's evil and transcend his own previous defeat. But how to achieve this without doing violence to the character's basic nature? The triumphant solution comes when Jerry discovers the power to defuse evil with an active commitment to passive resistance. With The Goober trailing along, he tracks down and confronts Emile, knowing that he will be beaten again. But this time Jerry wins. "Arms at his sides, looking defenseless but knowing where his strength *was,* where it had to be, he advanced toward Janza." Emile hits and hits, and Jerry absorbs the blows without ever lifting a fist, until Janza retreats, confused and disappointed. It is the beginning of victory for Jerry.

"He'll probably go back to Trinity and go through a Purgatory but be triumphant in the end even though he looks as if he's defeated," speculated Cormier. "I was very tentative about writing those scenes, and I really had to work hard on them. I didn't want a fourteen-year-old kid to sound like a Christ figure. He still had to sound like a kid. That's why I made him groping, not quite sure what he wanted to do. But he still has a quest, a mission. . . . He may become a contemplative; in a way I tried to hint at that in the first scenes when he was praying in Canada, repairing his mind and body and soul."[6]

So here again is the theme that has given Cormier so much trouble: the young person who is irresistibly drawn to leave the world for religious seclusion. This is the theme that he struggled unsuccessfully to bring to life in the unpublished "In the Midst of Winter," the theme that flaws *Bumblebee* in the shape of Cassie's unmotivated and unexplained attraction to the Hacienda. But here in *Beyond the Chocolate War* it works at last. Jerry is a natural-born contemplative, and it does make sense that he should eventually find solace as "a good and kind brother like Brother Eugene . . . someone to fight the Archie Costellos and even the Brother Leons."

The truly tragic figure, it now becomes apparent, is not Jerry, but The Goober. He has admirable instincts for good—but always too late. "I should have refused," he thinks about his part in causing the collapse of Room Nineteen and Brother Eugene. But he didn't. He should have fought by Jerry's side that terrible night, but he stayed away until the moment was past. He tries to find forgiveness by confessing his guilt to Jerry and by trying to help fight

Emile. But again fate makes him a traitor. When Jerry tries to make him understand how "you can get beat up and still not lose," The Goober doesn't get it. All he knows is that he is dogged by guilt and that he will have to give up his friendship with Jerry rather than continue to betray him. Jerry, too, is planning to spare The Goober by letting the friendship fade away, rather than let him tag along and be hurt by a mission he doesn't understand. But they are each acting out of concern for the other, and after all, they have all summer to talk. Can we hope that Jerry will manage to share some of his salvation with the poor old Goob?

Archie, of course, is the most interesting character in the book. The more we know about him, the more fascinating he becomes. Although Cormier has shown Archie in scenes that reveal his essence in new ways, he has not yielded to the temptation to humanize him, perhaps by allowing him a weakness or two or an occasional endearing quality. He remains completely evil, utterly cold, aloof, and alone. "I am Archie!" he exults. Other people exist only to be used by him.

In metaphor, Archie is the Pope of Darkness. At the Vigils meeting, when Obie and Carter ceremoniously elevate the box of marbles like a demonic chalice, Archie lifts his hands, "palms downward, almost as if he were about to bless the Congregation." Later, he thinks of "the gospel of Trinity as written by Archie Costello." When he offers false sympathy to Obie, he takes his loss "upon himself like a cross." Leon, in his arrogance as headmaster, is king to Archie's pope: "He treated the students as if they were underlings, mere subjects in the kingdom of his royal highness, Leon the First." But Archie is no follower to anyone, not even the Prince of Darkness. "Archie recognized no eternity, neither heaven nor hell." The external world is for him a hellish projection of his own internal chaos. As he waits in the twilight for an encounter with Brother Leon, he imagines that the dark is providing places for people to hide. "Archie always envisioned lurkers, predators, watchers in the shadow or around corners, peeking out of windows, waiting behind closed doors. . . . It was a rotten world, full of treachery and evil. . . ."

Archie is above the messiness of human relationships. "I don't hate anybody or anything," he says, truthfully. Only one thing arouses his fury and scorn: goodness. Obie's new-found happiness in his love for Laurie disgusts Archie, and he lashes out venomously at Carter's "honor and pride." Although he is brilliantly, subtly intelligent, real thinking is as repellent to him as emotion. "People thought too much, anyway," he observes. Because evil, as we have said before, is essentially pointless; think it through, and it loses its meaning and power. Archie cannot afford to think.

Neither can he afford to feel. In this book Cormier has finally allowed us to see the sexual dimension of Archie's nature. The passage in which Archie has sex with Jill Morton in his car is passionless. He fears the goodness of the body, allowing himself "measures of enjoyment . . . but always holding a part of himself aloof, never letting go completely." Archie cares nothing about Jill, so he can talk to her. "He told her everything. And nothing." Although we know that Miss Jerome's is a girls' school, Cormier evokes a whore-house and a loveless encounter between professional and customer. "Archie usually came to Morton, his favorite of all the girls at Miss Jerome's," because of "her willingness to please and her knowing ways." "You haven't been around for a while," she says coyly, like a floozie in an old movie.

Although the coupling of Archie and Jill is cold, it is fairly explicit. Other scenes in *Beyond the Chocolate War* are also sexual. The passionate explorations of Obie and Laurie, for example, and the "rape." Up to this point in Cormier's career, his young adult novels had had almost no overt sexual action, so it is interesting that he chose to write such scenes in the eighties, a period that he admitted was "a very conservative time." When he sent the completed manuscript to his publisher he worried that someone might ask for cuts; he was pleased when he got full support for the book just as he had written it.[7]

In *Beyond the Chocolate War* Cormier comes into his full strength as a storyteller, and there is no need for that play with metaphors and allusions for the sheer joy of virtuosity that characterized the style of *The Chocolate War*. Still, there are many arresting phrases that strike home a meaning like Carter's gavel, "a hammer driving a nail through wood into flesh." Jerry and his father occupy their apartment "the way mannequins inhabit rooms of furniture in a department store." Archie's laugh is "a sound as dry as rolling dice"; his words are "as cold as ice cubes rattling in a tray." When Obie reminds him, with a look, of the chocolates, "something flickered in Archie's eyes, as if an invisible branch had snapped across his face." Ray thinks wistfully of "the sea lapping the shore like the tongue of an old and friendly dog." There are brief references from the Cormier symbology: a menacing dog, a whiff of lilac, a forbidding nun.

Cormier, who often entertained his family with amateur legerdemain, always entertained his readers with secrets and games, illusions and surprises. In *Beyond the Chocolate War* his bag of magic tricks yields one astonishment after another. Ray Bannister calls misdirection "the magician's most powerful tool," and, as he explains it, "a magician guided the audience to see what the magician wanted them to see, made them think they were seeing one thing while another surprise awaited them." Cormier is a master of this technique. Caroni's oblique references to "the Letter" misdirect us to think of it as a missive like Carter's note to Leon, until it is revealed as a test grade. The realistic tone of the scene in which Leon opens a package lulls us, so that we are astounded when it blows his head off, and jarred again when at the end of the paragraph we realize that it is Caroni's fantasy and we have been fooled. Other illusions of death abound: Leon shot by a sniper, Obie's dream of the guillotine, Ray as a killer in the false newspaper clipping, the near-miss of Caroni's first try at suicide, Leon pricked by his knife—and Obie's murder attempt.

But the illusion of the black marble is Cormier's most amazing and complex effect. Archie has always drawn the white marble, which releases him from responsibility, and we never wondered why. But at the first Vigils meeting his draw is a bit too quick and glib. Remembering Ray's sleight-of-hand practice, we begin to wonder if perhaps Archie's good luck has had some help. Later, Obie is struck with the same insight when he sees Ray make a red ball, "no larger than a marble," vanish and reappear. He remembers that Archie had been presented with the box by surprise only once (at the disastrous boxing match), and on that occasion "sweat had danced on his forehead—Archie, who never perspired—and he had looked apprehensive." We are sure that his discomfiture was because he was not prepared with a sleight. Our suspicions are confirmed when we learn (through the incident of the fake clipping) that he is no stranger to the magic store in Worcester. So we are as startled as Archie is when he draws the black marble from the box that Obie has so carefully rigged to expose his sleight of hand. Cormier has misdirected us, and much later we are surprised yet again, when Archie tells Obie that he deliberately took the black marble to find out what would happen, how far Obie would go. But why then was he startled? Mysteries remain even after the trick is completed.

All through both books we have longed for Archie to get the black marble. But when he finally does, Cormier plays one last masterpiece of a trick. He cheats us of the sweetness of retribution by manipulating our sympathies. The delicious first sight of Archie as the Fool is not as delicious as we thought it was going to be. As he is led (the great

Archie—led!) across the parking lot, head held high in spite of the "Kick Me" sign on his back, suddenly we very much do *not* want to see him humiliated. When he sits quietly on the platform of the Water Game, "neat and spotless in his chino pants and white jersey," he has dignity, grace, even nobility. The crowd is silent and hangs back. When Obie tries to bribe a boy to throw the ball at the target that will drop Archie, splashing and struggling, into the pool, he protests, "I'm not dunking any Archie Costello." Neither are we. When the hawker dismisses him ("I'd go broke with you there all day long . . .") and he leaps gracefully to the ground, we feel like cheering. It is no surprise when nobody is willing to *kick* any Archie Costello, either.

But what about the guillotine? It must fall, but if we didn't want Archie dunked, we certainly don't want him beheaded. As he kneels so coolly to be "executed," he becomes a heroic figure, and it is Obie who is despicable. The tension at this point is almost unbearable. Cormier has built it to the shrieking point with one emotional scene quickly following another. The audience is in the palm of his hand. The blade descends—but before it reaches its target we are plunged into the midst of Caroni's suicide. Only when his body hits the ground with the "hollow, thudding sound" we expected from the guillotine, only then is the tension released.

The illusion is ended. In the next line Archie marvels, "You wanted to kill me, Obie," and we know we have been misdirected again. Archie, of course, did not know that he was about to lose his head. What seemed to be dignity and bravery was only casual acceptance of a silly magic show. The trappings of an execution made us believe in Archie as the heroic condemned criminal. Now suddenly he is the old Archie and our loathing is firmly back in place as he demolishes Obie by praising him for attempting murder.

And then he shows Obie where the guilt really lies for all the evil at Trinity. But can it be that this is one final piece of misdirection? Obie knows that he could have, should have, refused to follow Archie. But isn't it true that things would have been different if Archie Costello had never registered at Trinity? Obie cries out in anguish, "This could have been a beautiful place to be, Archie. A beautiful time for all of us." If he had said no—or if Archie had not been there to require a no.

Archie has had it all his way for four years, and now, as he leaves Trinity, he sets one last scheme in motion that will bring the school down around Brother Leon's ears for good. Cormier said, "It bothered me that I'd created Bunting to be the Assigner, because he is so unlike Archie. Then it occurred to me that Archie has a motive for picking a kid like Bunting. Archie doesn't want someone there who would outdo him. He really isn't going to tell Bunting his secrets about how to manipulate people."[8] Subtlety goes right over Bunting's head. He is a thug, and an incompetent one at that. Archie is pleased when he botches the rape—"he was delighted because he saw that Bunting was perfect for what he had planned for the future." The plan is diabolical in its simplicity: he saddles Bunting with Emile Janza as right-hand man, and then he offers Emile a number of suggestions about how things might be run next year. Bunting bites the bait gladly—violence is something he understands.

So the book ends as it started—in deepening darkness. Or does it? There *is* hope for next year if you know where to look for it. Henry Malloran, with his knack for well-timed action, is president; levelheaded Ray Bannister will still be around; Jerry and The Goober may be back with new strength. And doesn't Brother Leon know very well how to squelch the kind of disturbance Bunting and Janza have in mind? Things may work out for Trinity with Archie gone.

Ah yes, but it might be wise to remember that Archie has now been let loose on the *world*.

When the critics were let loose on *Beyond the Chocolate*

War at the time of its publication, they generally agreed that it was a worthy sequel. Gayle Keresey in *Voice of Youth Advocates* even hailed it as "the best of Cormier's highly acclaimed novels."[9] Roger Sutton, however, writing for *School Library Journal,* felt that "individually, many scenes are vividly horrific, but as a whole this is less compelling as fiction than it is as a commentary on *The Chocolate War*— Cormier here intensifies and explicates what was powerfully implicit in the first book."[10] Hazel Rochman made a similar comment in the *New York Times Book Review:* "With its complexity, *Beyond the Chocolate War* is not as starkly dramatic as its predecessor. It relies too much on Mr. Cormier's explication, and there is less action and more emphasis on the internal lives of many characters."[11]

Despite all its shimmering brilliance, this novel has never become a favorite with readers. Like all sequels, it suffers by comparison with its antecedent, lacking the depth and compelling ambiguity of *The Chocolate War.* Cormier's carefully considered and psychologically valid explanation for Jerry's behavior has been generally disregarded, as readers new to *The Chocolate War* continue to be distressed by the ambiguous ending, presumably unaware that the answer lies in the sequel.

Notes

1. Silvey, Anita, "An Interview with Robert Cormier," Part 1, *The Horn Book Magazine,* March/April 1985, 145.
2. Ibid.
3. Ibid.
4. Ibid.
5. Ibid.
6. Ibid.
7. Silvey, Anita, "An Interview with Robert

Cormier," Part 2, *The Horn Book Magazine,* May/June 1985, 289.

8. Silvey, Part 1, 145.

9. Keresey, Gayle, review of *Beyond the Chocolate War, Voice of Youth Advocates,* June 1985, 128.

10. Sutton, Roger, review of *Beyond the Chocolate War, School Library Journal,* April 1985, 96.

11. Rochman, Hazel, review of *Beyond the Chocolate War, The New York Times Book Review,* May 5, 1985, 37.

Chapter Seven

I Am the Cheese

TAPE YAK001 0213 date deleted
P-R
P: Stop.
R: You mean stop reading?
P: Yes. You, the reader. Right
here. First, before you go on,
you must answer one question.
R: What do you want to know?
P: Have you read *I Am the Cheese*
yet?
R: No. I thought I'd read this
chapter first.
P: That would be a great pity. It
would spoil things for you—the
suspense, the intriguing perplexities, the myriad shocks of discovery, the false leads—in a word, the
fun. I would emphatically advise

```
that you make the journey with Adam
before you cover the same ground a
second time with me.
R: All right.
P: Excellent. We shall continue
afterwards. Let us suspend now.
END TAPE YAKO01
```

Having finished *I Am the Cheese,* the reader is irresistibly compelled to turn back to the beginning and, like Adam, begin all over again. The story circles back on itself, revolving like the wheels of a bicycle, like children in a ring playing "The Farmer in the Dell." But for the reader, unlike Adam, each time the experience is different. The first time through, we know only what Adam knows. Our blank spaces are his, and the truth comes to us—and to him—in a series of disorienting jolts.

But this is far too simple a description. Perry Nodelman, in his incisive article "Robert Cormier Does a Number," has attempted to analyze the complex and unsettling experience of a first reading of *I Am the Cheese*. A reader's first impulse, Nodelman observes, is to approach the story as a logical, detached detective. The key, it seems, is in understanding the events of the mysterious past. But this leads to anxiety, disorientation, and confusion—"that uncertainty we call suspense"—because the events of the present are not clear. "Cormier cleverly makes us accept and enjoy our confusion by providing *one* genuine past . . . and what appear to be *two* different presents that that past led to. . . ."[1]

The possibility that never occurs to us, continues Nodelman, is that both presents are happening at once, that Adam is at the same time on a journey to Rutterburg and being interrogated by Brint. "Cormier cannot allow us to consider it, for it depends on our knowledge that the bike trip is a fantasy, knowledge that is the key to the entire mystery. He deflects our attention from the literal truth of the novel, the impeccably chronological ordering of events that seem to have no chronology, by making them seem to have no chronology. How Cormier manipulates readers into believing the wrong things and ignoring the right ones is fascinating to explore."[2]

A close look at the two opening chapters, first as a novice and then as an experienced reader of *I Am the Cheese,* will illustrate this process. In the beginning we know only that someone is riding a bicycle from Monument to Rutterburg. Who? Why? A young person, evidently, who has been close enough to his father to still want to use an old bike like his, even though it makes him pedal "furiously"—a strangely intense word. The rhythm of the paragraph suggests the steady pumping of his legs. Then the first tiny hint of something sinister: "the wind like a snake slithering up my sleeves."

In the second paragraph we learn that the sight of a hospital reminds the rider of his father in Rutterburg. Is he ill there? Is the journey to visit him? Whatever it is, it must be urgent because the cyclist accelerates his pedaling at the thought. Then another hint of chill—the rotten October. The love of Thomas Wolfe that the cyclist has shared with his father confirms our guess about their relationship, and the elderly phrase used to describe a teacher—he "regarded me with suspicion"—tells us that the person is a student, young but bookish and probably solitary. And he is kind—he waves when he passes a child who looks lonesome. But why does he think someone might be following him? Now he tells us he didn't wave good-bye to anybody when he left on this trip. Why not? Where were they? This is not the kind of person who skips school and goes away without at least telling someone. It doesn't fit. We begin to feel puzzled.

Immediately, Cormier gives us what seems to be an explanation of sorts: the irrational fears, and later, the pills, tell us that the bike rider has emotional problems. But why? Other questions come fast now. What is the gift package? Why are his father's clothes in the cellar? If he has money, why doesn't he take the bus? His reasons ring a bit hollow. Why is it so important that he make the trip on his own power? And why must he do it this way "for his father"? The intensity of his determination seems inappropriate—but perhaps it is a sign of his unbalanced state.

Then another character is introduced: Amy Hertz. She, we know immediately, is a very different kind of person. "What the hell, as Amy says, philosophically." A tough, cocky, self-assured sort of person. The fact that such a girl is the object of the bike rider's love tells us more about his needs (and also confirms that he is a young *man*). But his reasons for not phoning her before he leaves seem logical. When he dumps his pills into the garbage disposal he seems "reckless and courageous" to us as well as to himself, and when a car howls its horn at him "for straying too far into the roadway," we think it is a result of that recklessness. It becomes apparent that the journey is going to be long and grueling, and as the boy struggles through, breaks free, and is off on his way, we are too busy exulting with him to notice that we have been left with a double handful of unanswered questions.

The second chapter clarifies nothing; indeed, it adds a second layer of perplexities. The preceding chapter was in the present tense, and so is this one, at first. Has the boy been in some sort of an accident that has put him here in the hands of a doctor? Or is this even the same boy? Is one of the chapters a flashback to the other? Which? The form is even more puzzling. It seems to be some sort of official record of a tape recording, but for what possible reason can the date have been deleted? Why is the questioner labeled "T" when his name is Brint? Does it stand for "tape"? Or "therapist," perhaps? (Cormier himself said that he used "T" because it is the *last* letter of Brint's name[3]—but, then, can that statement be part of the Number?) Even for a psychiatrist his speech is strangely stilted and formal: "We shall," "I have been advised," and that ominous phrase from the torture chamber, "the better it will be for you." But when the questioning turns to the boy's earliest memories we are on familiar ground again. Isn't that how people always begin with a therapist? The sense of menaced flight that pervades the boy's story could be explained by his mental illness, as could his perception of Brint as threatening. When the boy dissolves in panic, almost, but not quite, we believe in Brint's benevolence when he says, "Everything's going to be all right." But there have been no answers to some basic questions, nor will there be any until many, many pages later. As Perry Nodelman says, "Novelists usually make us ask such questions at the beginnings of novels, in order to arouse our interest. But they usually quickly answer them, and then focus our attention on new developments. . . . In keeping us in the dark . . . Cormier extends throughout most of *I Am the Cheese* the disorientation we usually stop feeling a short way into other novels.

"A second reading . . . is a different experience. Now the novel seems filled with clues, with obvious evidence of what seemed incomprehensible before, and with huge ironies."[4] All of Adam's forgotten past is still available to us, and we can see his buried knowledge at work on the fabric of his fantasy. As he goes about his preparations for the journey to Rutterburg, we at the same time see him preparing for the ride around the hospital grounds, and we know that the road he will travel in his imagination is the same route he and his parents took on the fatal "vacation" trip, in a different Thomas Wolfe October. This time we know why he doesn't wave good-bye to anyone and why he talks himself out of calling Amy. It is his own loneliness that stands on the sidewalk in the form of a child and his own fear of Them that follows invisibly. His fear needs a face, so he tells himself that he is afraid of elevators, exposed open spaces, rooms without windows, dogs—all animals, in fact, plus snakes and spiders ("They are not rational," he explains cryptically). He knows there is good reason for terror, but he dare not give it its true name.

Even though he has money, he must talk himself into pedaling the bike because where he is going there are no buses, and he "travels light" because he needs no "provisions or extra clothing" for that trip inside the fence. His father's jacket and cap are, to him, in the basement because that is where he last saw them in his past, even though Dr. Dupont has brought them to him here in the hospital. And Pokey the Pig, who represents the safe comfort of childhood and will be gift-wrapped, is in "the cabinet in the den" where Adam searched for and found the first terrible evidence of his own nonexistence. He dresses in his father's clothes and looks in the mirror as if to bring him back to life. But he must justify his actions to his conscious mind by remarking how good the cap is for the cold. It is the hospital that has provided him with the mind-clouding green and black capsules that he pours into the sink. And it is the memory of the car that killed his mother that blares past as he leaves the driveway. Only his thoughts of Amy are fresh and clear and not overlaid with anything else.

Now when Adam tells Brint the story of his parents' escape we know why "their voices scratched at the night," why Adam's father never smoked again, why there were purple half-moons under his mother's eyes. The slightly inappropriate word "clues" has, of course, been implanted in his mind by Brint during earlier investigations. When Adam says, "It's as if I was born that night," we appreciate the irony, and when he wants to tell Pokey how brave and clever he has been, we recall with poignance that in the end—and now—there is no one *but* Pokey to listen sympathetically to such confidences. Even the number of the tape—OZK001—

is significant. It reminds us of *The Wizard of Oz* and Dorothy's return to Kansas, where she, like Adam, is reunited with the real people who appear as fantasy characters in her dream.[5] But Cormier is still not through playing games with us. Adam associates the lilac perfume with his mother—but in the last chapter of the book he has noticed that fragrance in the hallway of the hospital. And we still don't really know why Brint is recorded as "T."

The triple strands that are braided together to make the story, the three alternating levels on which the narrative progresses, are an intricate but internally consistent device. The bike ride is told in first-person present tense. The tapes, as dialogue, have neither person nor tense (but we assume they are happening in the present), and the revelation of Adam's past that grows out of the tapes proceeds chronologically and is in third-person past tense. A slightly confusing factor is that in the early phases of the bike ride Adam enjoys some memories of the warm, safe times of his childhood—and these fit into the chronology of the memories he is sharing with Brint. This is all perfectly clear the second time around, but a first-time reader feels that the events of the story have been scrambled intriguingly.

Of all the sinister characters Cormier has created to embody his ideas about evil, Brint is perhaps the most chilling. Indeed, it is tempting at first to jump to the conclusion, because of Brint's stiffly formal speech, that he is a machine, perhaps some kind of interrogation computer. Tempting, because the worst thing about Brint, the most appalling realization, is that he *is* (or *was*) a human being, but he has been so corrupted by his immersion in evil that he can sit year after year across from Adam, calmly herding him through lacerating self-discoveries and feeling not one flicker of pity or mercy. Only twice does he seem human, but in both cases it is immediately clear that the pose is a trick. At one point he exclaims about the beauty of the weather—but only to jolly

Adam out of a deep withdrawal. Later, when Adam is remembering his father's distrust of Grey, he suddenly sees something in Brint's expression that makes him suspect that he is "one of those men who had been his father's enemy." Brint, realizing that he has almost given himself away, covers quickly. "I am sorry that you were disturbed by the expression on my face. I, too, am human. I have headaches, upset stomach at times. I slept badly last night. Perhaps that's what you saw reflected on my face." But Adam is not entirely convinced. "It's good to find out you're human," he grants uncertainly. "Sometimes I doubt it."

Much of the content of the dialogue portion of the tapes is the progress of Adam's reluctant realization that Brint is his enemy. He wants so much to believe in him as a benevolent father figure that sometimes he even tries to prompt Brint into this role. He wonders aloud why Brint never asks him about his mother; another time he is a bit hurt when Brint interrupts his reminiscences, and he says plaintively, "You sound impatient. I'm sorry. Am I going into too much detail? I thought you wanted me to discover everything about myself." Later he finally cannot avoid noticing that only certain kinds of information interest his interrogator, though Brint repeatedly protests that he has only Adam's welfare at heart. But Adam really does know the truth about Brint, and he cannot entirely hide it from himself, even at the beginning. In the second tape he says, "He had a kindly face although sometimes his eyes were strange. The eyes stared at him occasionally as if the doctor—if that's what he was—were looking down the barrel of a gun, taking aim at him. He felt like a target." Adam is completely in Brint's power, both physically and mentally. The windows of the interrogation room are barred; the shots and the pills control his feelings and his thoughts. To recognize his captor as the enemy is unbearable, and so he pushes away the knowledge as long as he can and tries to find goodness in Brint. And so does the reader. It is this blurring of the distinction between good and evil that gives the tapes their peculiar horror, and that point to the larger theme of the book.

Cormier has had some revealing things to say about Brint. He chose the name, he says, to suggest someone bloodless and cold, to rhyme with *flint* and *glint*.[6] At first he was not sure whether the character was a psychiatrist or not. "But I thought this would be the way it would sound if a character were using a slight knowledge of psychology to take advantage of a situation."[7] Brint's knowledge may be "slight," but he has certainly learned the superficial tricks of the trade, as when he turns Adam's suspicions back on himself by accusing him of attacking his therapist to create a diversion whenever certain buried information is approached. In the Brint-Adam interchange there is a hint of a theme that Cormier was to explore more thoroughly in *After the First Death* and *The Rag and Bone Shop*: "Adam comes to him completely innocent in his amnesia, and Brint corrupts that. That's what evil is, the destruction of innocence." Although Cormier emphasizes Brint's machinelike quality by never giving us any description or background, he claims he has a home life in mind for him. "I picture Brint in a two-car garage, a family, belongs to the Elks. . . . He has this job in an agency where he's got to keep questioning all these people, but at night he leaves the area and goes home and has a regular life. . . ." Somehow the idea of Brint presiding over a suburban household seems like part of the Number. Has Cormier forgotten that Brint is instantly available to Adam in the night? Obviously he sleeps nearby in the hospital, probably in a spartan room where he hangs his impeccable suit neatly in the closet. Then he lies rigidly on a narrow cot all night without rumpling the covers, stretched out on his back with folded arms. He does not allow himself to dream.

At a crucial point in the narrative, Brint lays out some priorities. "Permit me to summarize. The first landmark was that day in the woods with the dog. The second landmark was that call from Amy." The Dog and fearful encounters with it, as both symbol and event, recur often in Adam's narrative. In the first chapter, the very thought of "all the dogs that would attack me on the way to Rutterburg, Vermont," almost keeps him from setting out on the journey. He keeps an eye out for dogs when he does get on the road, and sure enough, soon he is threatened by one. As soon as we know that the bike trip is unreal, it is clear that this is a dream dog. It is a German shepherd, a breed associated with official power, police, Nazis. He is black, and, like Brint, he looks at Adam silently, "with eyes like marbles." And, contrary to the normal behavior of dogs, he is guarding an empty house where there is no owner to defend. As in a nightmare, the direct attack is deflected to the tires. The beast tries "to topple the bike, send it askew and have me crashing to the roadway, his victim," just as Brint with his persistent questions tries to topple the delicate structure of defense that allows Adam to delude himself with the imaginary escape of the trip to Rutterburg. Even when Adam has eluded the animal, he has a prophetic feeling that "the dog will pursue me forever."

And finally, it is a dog that brings the whole complex narrative structure into focus. As Adam returns sadly and quietly from his long trip, he wheels through the grounds of "the hospital" and is met by a kindly doctor. Has he at last broken free and come to a safe place? But as soon as he meets the dog Silver in the hall, the momentary hope is blasted. We have seen Silver before, through the window of Brint's office, and we know now without a doubt that Adam has never left the place of interrogation.

Brint's second landmark is the call from Amy. The reader, like Brint, suspects that there was more to this incident than met Adam's ear. "Was Amy part of the conspiracy?" was a frequent question in Cormier's mail. The letter writers wondered shrewdly if she was prompted by the enemy to probe Adam's past, or if perhaps the name Hertz is meant to suggest that she "hurts" him. This Cormier denied emphatically. Amy is innocent and, as Adam wished, quite separate from the structure of intrigue, and the reason she is no longer there after three years is not that the enemy got her, but simply that her family moved away. In fact, Amy is helpful to Adam. She, as he says, "brought brightness and gaiety to his life." Cormier introduced her out of compassion for his protagonist: "I was conscious that Adam was leading a very drab life—his father a shadow, his mother withdrawn, and he was introverted—and I thought, this is getting pretty dull. So I introduced her to liven up the book, to give him a little love and affection, and, of course, instantly I fell in love with her."

Amy, with her quick imagination, her antic sense of humor, her tender toughness, and her nonchalance, is truly a charming creation. But what lies behind that toughness? Does her mother's preoccupation with committee work have something to do with it? We see her only through Adam's adoring eyes, but actually all is not well with Amy's soul. Amy, like Adam, is an outsider, a loner. Her Numbers have more than a little anger in them; they are not funny to the victims. Sometimes they have a strained quality, like the caper in the church parking lot, or depend for their effect on an enigmatic quirk of thought, like the cartful of baby-food jars left in front of the Kotex display in the supermarket. She really needs Adam to laugh with her. There is nobody else in the audience.

To Adam, the Numbers are "heady and hilarious but somehow terrible." Defying authority is foreign to his nature. But through his participation in the Numbers he gains the courage to investigate the mysteries about his past. "I, too, am capable of mischief," he thinks as he eavesdrops on his father and Mr. Grey. Thoughts of Amy give him courage on the bike ride, too. "What the hell, as Amy would say," he tells himself. Her last words to Adam are a casual "Call me," and throughout his eternal bike rides he tries. Or thinks he tries. He makes excuses, or he calls at the wrong time, or he hangs up because the wise guys are approaching. He really knows that after three years Amy Hertz has disappeared from his life, and there is no comfort to be found at 537–3331. When he does finally make the connection with that number, the Number is over, and it is the beginning of the end of this illusion.

Adam is to some extent based on Cormier himself as a boy. Not only Adam's fears and phobias and migraines, but also his personality and ambitions recall Cormier at fourteen. He is shy and book loving, and home is a warm, safe retreat from a hostile world where wise guys lie in wait at every corner. Like Jerry in *The Chocolate War,* he knows only too well the outcome of the scenario that begins, "You lookin' for trouble?" Cormier's betrayal in the operating room is vividly evoked when Adam says, "I don't like to be confined or held down. My instinct, then, is to get up on my feet, flailing my arms at anything that might try to hold me down, confine me." When Adam explains the writer inherent in his attitude toward life, it is also the young Cormier speaking:

```
Anyway, his terrible shyness, his
inability to feel at ease with
people, had nothing to do with his
mother. He felt it was his basic
character; he preferred reading a
book or listening to old jazz
records in his bedroom to going
to dances or hanging around down-
town with the other kids. Even
in the fourth or fifth grade, he
had stayed on the outskirts of
the schoolyard watching the other
```

kids playing the games—Kick the Can was a big thing in the fourth grade—anyway, he had never felt left out: it was his choice. To be a witness, to observe, to let the events be recorded within himself on some personal film in some secret compartment no one knew about, except him. It was only later, in the eighth grade, when he knew irrevocably that he wanted to be a writer, that he realized he had stored up all his observations, all his emotions, for that purpose.

Between creator and creation there is an ironic contrast in one respect. "I'm not built for subterfuge and deception," says Adam. It is this quality that makes him a too-perfect subject for interrogation. Because he is so guileless, the enemy—who are so complex in evil that they cannot comprehend simple honesty—persist in thinking he must be hiding something. Again and again he willingly turns the pockets of his mind inside out for them, but they still suspect he has something up his sleeve. It occurs to him to hold back, but he always ends by telling all.

His resistance has been channeled in other directions. The fantasy bike ride is Adam's gesture of defiance in the face of the Implacable. This explains the fierce intensity of his determination to make the journey "for my father," and the inevitability he feels in the beginning about his decision to go—"I knew I would go the way you know a stone will drop to the ground if you release it from your hand." Like Jerry's, his gesture is stubborn and half aware, not the grand, controlled action of a hero. "I am a coward, really," he admits, but in the refrain "I keep pedaling" there is persistent courage. Adam must repeatedly overcome obstacles and break through his fears, but each time he does he can soar for a moment and find new hope and strength.

As in dreams real emotions are translated into fantasy people and events, so as the bike ride progresses Adam's hidden awareness of the menace all around him begins to come to the forefront of his mind and take on personification, shape, and form as Whipper and the wise guys, as Fat Arthur and Junior Varney, as snarling dogs and the terrible, ferocious vomit-pink car with the grinning grille. Meanwhile, in the interrogations he is bringing to consciousness memories that bleed their terror into his secret life of the mind so that he is less and less able to sustain the fantasy. As he approaches the final truth, his newly discovered knowledge of the amount of time that has passed intrudes into the dream in a collision of logics. When he gets to the motel where he and his parents spent a safe night "last summer," he finds that it "feels as if it has been neglected for years and years." The effect is eerily disorienting. One last time he tries to call Amy, but the gruff man on the phone and in his own mind tells him she is gone; Adam is no longer able to delude himself with hopes of her comfort or with the defiant illusion of escape. He wants to leave this reality—"I would give anything to be folded into bed, the pills working their magic, soothing me"—and in a moment he does. The dream begins to smear and waver like the woman's face through the wet windshield. Everything slows down; sounds are distorted, like a movie in a disintegrating projector. The darkness gathers him. Yet still—on a first reading—still we believe this is reality.

Like Amy, Cormier always withheld "information about the Numbers until the last possible moment, stretching out the drama." Even here at the end, there is one last, tiny gleam of false hope. We think Adam has arrived in Rutterburg at last. Then he turns the corner and sees the hospital, and as he greets one by one the people from his fantasy, the shattering truth crashes down. For the first time he sings the *last* verse of "The Farmer in the Dell." The cheese stands alone, and he is the cheese.

The final tape, with its cold, bureaucratic verdict, has been the subject of much speculation. With a little study, a key can be puzzled out:

Subject A = Adam

Personnel #2222 = Thompson, or Grey

File Data 865–01 = the record of Adam's father's testimony and subsequent official events related to it

OZK Series = the interrogation tapes between Adam and Brint

Department 1-R = the government agency to which Adam's father testified

Tape Series ORT, UDW = the tapes of Adam's two previous interrogations

Witness #559–6 = Adam's father

Policy 979 = a rule that "does not currently allow termination procedures by Department 1-R."

And Department 1-R, notice, is the agency to whom Adam's father gave his witness, presumably the good guys, but it is they who have imprisoned Adam, and they who are being asked to "obliterate" him. Who, then, are the Adversaries? And Grey? Up to now, it has seemed that Adam saw Grey's legs as he lay on the ground after the crash, but was that just because that person wore gray pants? And Grey, remember, did not "necessarily" wear gray clothes.

Even Cormier's own words from the answer sheet he mailed to questioners do not completely clear up the ambiguity: "Grey was not part of the syndicate. He was not a double agent in the usual sense, although he double-crossed Adam's father, setting him up for the syndicate and the accident. He was present at the scene to clean up afterward, but hadn't counted on Adam's survival—an embarrassment to the agency."[8] So whose side is he on? In terms of Adam's future, it matters not at all. As Anne MacLeod puts it, "The two systems are equally impersonal, and equally dangerous to the human being caught between them. What matters to the organization—*either* organization—is its own survival, not Adam's."[9] In the third chapter the old man at the gas station asks Adam, "Do you know who the bad guys are?" He doesn't, and neither do we. What is so overwhelming here is not just that evil is powerful, but that the good guys and the bad guys turn out to be—probably—indistinguishable. It is not a matter of good against evil, but of the cheese standing alone against everything, the whole world revealed at last as evil. Where now is Cormier's imperative for collective good? There is nobody left to come to Adam's rescue. This is not a metaphor. MacLeod says, "This stark tale comments directly on the real world of government, organized crime, large-scale bureaucracy, the apparatus of control, secrecy, betrayal, and all the other commonplaces of contemporary political life."[10] We could each be the cheese.

"A magnificent accomplishment," said *The Horn Book Magazine*.[11] "Beside it, most books for the young seem as insubstantial as candyfloss," said the *Times Literary Supplement*.[12] "The secret, revealed at the end, explodes like an H-bomb," said *Publishers Weekly*.[13] "A masterpiece," said *West Coast Review of Books*.[14] The *New York Times* and the Young Adult Services Division of the American Library Association both included it on their respective lists of best books of the year for young people. But Newgate Callendar wondered in the *New York Times Book Review* if the novel might turn out to be "above the heads of most teenagers."[15] Cormier, too, was afraid that he was in danger of losing his newfound young adult audience.[16]

The book had begun as a time filler. "Sometimes when there's nothing that's compelling, I do exercises. So I put a boy on a bike and had him take off on a Wednesday morning with a box on his bike. Then right away I wondered, what's he doing out of school on a Wednesday morning, where's he going, what's in the package? . . . I started to give him a lot of my own fears, phobias. . . . And I wrote virtually all of the bike part without knowing where it was going."[17] For a while he searched for a second level among religious themes of pilgrimage, the Stations of the Cross, death and resurrection. Then one day, "across my desk at the newspaper . . . came this thing about the Witness Relocation Program. This was at a time when very little was known about it." He began to wonder about the hardships of giving up a past, and "then it struck me. . . . How much harder for a teen, who doesn't even know who he is yet!" He knew he had found his second level. He went back to the bike ride to make it fit.[18] The creation of *I Am the Cheese* was a very intense experience for him. "During the time I was writing the book, no one saw any part of it. I felt like the mad doctor in a laboratory, because I didn't think it would ever work, yet I felt compelled to write it. It was coming out at breakneck speed."[19] "I still picture Adam riding that bike around the institution grounds, as real now as the day I discovered him."[20]

Notes

1. Nodelman, Perry, "Robert Cormier Does a Number," *Children's Literature in Education,* Summer 1983, 94.

2. Ibid.

3. De Luca, Geraldine, and Roni Natov, "Taking True Risks: Controversial Issues in New Young Adult Novels," *The Lion and the Unicorn,* Winter 1979–80, 12.

4. Nodelman, 96.

5. De Luca and Natov, 129.

6. Nilsen, Alleen Pace, "The Poetry of Naming in Young Adult Novels," *ALAN Review,* Spring 1980, 3.

7. Ibid.

8. Cormier, Robert, answer sheet for readers' questions on *I Am the Cheese,* Robert E. Cormier Collection, Fitchburg State College, Fitchburg, Massachusetts.

9. MacLeod, Anne Scott, "Robert Cormier and the Adolescent Novel," *Children's Literature in Education,* Summer 1981, 74.

10. Ibid., 76.

11. Heins, Paul, review of *I Am the Cheese, The Horn Book Magazine,* August 1977, 427.

12. Salway, Lance, review of *I Am the Cheese,* London *Times Literary Supplement,* December 2, 1977, 1415.

13. Review of *I Am the Cheese, Publishers Weekly,* March 7, 1977, 100.

14. Review of *I Am the Cheese, West Coast Review of Books,* September 1977, 55.

15. Callendar, Newgate, "Boy on the Couch," *The New York Times Book Review,* May 1, 1977, 26.

16. Cormier, Robert, "The Cormier Novels: The Cheerful Side of Controversy," speech given at the Cervantes Convention and Exhibit Center, sponsored by the Children's Libraries Section of the Catholic Library Association, March 29, 1978, printed in *Catholic Library World,* July 1978, 6.

17. De Luca and Natov, 123.

18. McLaughlin, Frank, *Cheese, Chocolates, and Kids: A Day with Robert Cormier,* videotape prepared for PBS, n.d., (Robert E. Cormier Collec-

tion, Fitchburg State College, Fitchburg, Massachusetts).

19. De Luca and Natov, 124.

20. Cormier, Robert, letter to the author, January 25, 1984.

Chapter Eight

After the First Death

In 1979 Robert Cormier wrote a novel that was a piercing examination of the mentality of terrorism. It was read, admired, puzzled over—and then overlooked in favor of novels like *The Chocolate War* and *I Am the Cheese* that seemed less remote from our daily lives. After all, terrorism happened in places like Ireland and Israel, never in New England, where Cormier had visualized it. But twenty-two years later, on September 11, 2001, *After the First Death* suddenly became hideously relevant. What Cormier had to say about how terrorism obliterates compassion and how it has its source in patriotism was not comforting, but it was searingly honest, and as real as the smoldering embers of the World Trade Center. Teens rediscovered the book, and teachers led passionate discussions of the novel, discussions that led to new insights and questions from young people as they pondered, as always, Cormier's hard truths.

"Miro's assignment was to kill the driver. Without hesitation." It is to be his "first death," an eagerly awaited ritual terrorist murder that will mark his transition to manhood and full acceptance into the brotherhood of "freedom fighters." Artkin, the leader of their small band of fanatics, has planned the operation scrupulously. The theater he has chosen for their terrorist act is a school bus full of children, which unexpectedly turns out, much to Miro's consternation, to be driven this morning by blond cheerleader Kate Forrester. The terrorists drug the children and force Kate to drive the bus onto an abandoned bridge, where they announce their intentions to the world and the drama begins.

They demand ten million dollars for their cause, the release of all political prisoners, and the dismantling of Inner Delta, a secret counterterrorist organization at nearby Fort Delta. For every one of their number who is killed, they will kill a child. These events are overlaid and interwoven with what seems to be the journal of young Ben Marchand, whose father, General Marcus Marchand, is the secret high command of Inner Delta. Inside the hot, claustrophobic confines of the bus, the tension-filled waiting goes on. One of the children dies from an overdose of the sedative in the candy they have been given by Artkin. Afraid of the effect on his plans of another such accident, he gives Kate a temporary stay of execution so that she can keep the children quiet.

Miro is disturbed at losing his victim, and at the same time intrigued by the sexual attraction he is feeling for Kate. She tries to forget her own fears by caring for the children, but is aware of Miro's attraction and attempts to use it to her advantage by making conversation with him. As he tells her about his childhood, his terrorist training, the violence he has been part of in the name of a homeland he has never seen, she realizes that he is without human feeling, "a monster," and that her efforts are pointless. Her horror is intensified, when, to convince the watching world that they are serious in their demands, Artkin makes a display of showing the dead child outside on the bridge.

But later Kate finds a gleam of hope. She has a weak bladder under stress, and while changing her damp underwear in the back of the bus she discovers an extra ignition key in her wallet. Also she has noticed that one of the children, bright-eyed and chubby Raymond, has not been eating the candy and so is alert but faking sleep and could be an ally in an escape attempt. Even though this last hope is blasted when Artkin discovers Raymond's ruse and forces him to eat the drugged candy, she still has the key. After careful planning and mental rehearsal she desperately tries to back the bus off the bridge and succeeds until the engine stalls. Artkin blames Miro, and reprimands him severely.

When night comes, the two young people are awake in the dark bus. Miro is puzzled that he is beginning to have emotions: sadness and hate. Kate senses his new vulnerability and tries again to reach him. When she touches his arm he is deeply moved and confused.

Suddenly one of the terrorists is shot by an overanxious sniper, and in retaliation Artkin decides to make Raymond a sacrificial victim, a plan he carries out in spite of Kate's wild offer to take the child's place.

Simultaneously, these events are told a second time from the viewpoint of General Marchand, as his son Ben recalls in his journal the day of the hijacking, when his father summoned him officially to his office. The journal comes to an end, and the general continues. Ben is missing from the room. Where has he gone? The general suspects that he has gone to a nearby bridge to kill himself in remorse. He remembers how he and the terrorists agreed on Ben as a suitably innocent messenger to deliver a stone that would prove to the hijackers that their world leader had been captured. But in the bus Artkin tortured Ben, as his father knew would happen, and Ben revealed what he had learned by accident— the time of a planned attack.

The attack comes, but an hour earlier than the terrorists

expect. Artkin is killed, and Miro escapes with Kate as hostage. As they are squeezed together in a hiding place, she taunts him with the sudden realization that Artkin must have been his father. Miro, convulsed in an agony of self-blame for Artkin's death, pulls the trigger of his gun and kills her inadvertently. In a final dialogue between Ben and his father, it is revealed that the general knew from behavioral tests that his son would break under torture, and so sent him to the bridge with deliberately false information to reveal. Unable to live with the knowledge that his father expected him to be a coward and that the whole world knows it, Ben has killed himself, but now returns to take over the guilt-haunted mind of his father. When last seen, Miro, rejecting everything he has learned from his encounter with Kate, is about to strangle a passing motorist and escape to the world at large.

While the construction of *After the First Death* is not as intricate as the circular triple levels of *I Am the Cheese,* it is still a fairly complex structure with built-in puzzles. There are two main narrative streams: the first-person ruminations, which are presumably the voices of Ben and later the general, and the events on the bus told in the third person from the alternating perspectives of Miro and Kate (and—very briefly—Raymond and one other child).

The first level takes place two weeks before Christmas at (maybe) Castleton Academy, in Pompey, New Hampshire, where Ben has been sent after the summer of the Bus and the Bridge, and (at first reading) seems to last for the space of one afternoon, while Ben types the journal and later his father reads it and waits for him. In the course of these sections the story of the hijacking proceeds in their memory at the same pace that it is being told in the main narrative.

The second level, the Kate-Miro narrative, takes up three times as many pages as the Ben-general sections and is the main device for telling the story. It takes place near Fort Delta and just outside Hallowell, Massachusetts. We know

Monument is somewhere close offstage because the bridge spans Moosock River—a waterway that Adam and Jerry know as Moosock Creek. The action lasts for twenty-four hours—from one morning until the next, with the exception of the introductory scene in which Artkin befuddles a waitress in a café for Miro's benefit. The season is summer, the summer before the time of the Ben-general sections.

In several cases pieces of action are presented twice, once from the point of view of the participants on the bus, and once from the point of view of the opposition command post. This gives the advantage of expanded perspective and lightens what would otherwise be a story stalled in a very static, claustrophobic situation. It also serves to emphasize parallels between the characters, as when Artkin tells Miro of the terrorists' demands and later the general tells Ben the same information.

Perhaps the most difficult element in the book, and one that remains somewhat enigmatic even after close study, is the identity of the voice in the primary narrative, the sections that take place at Castleton Academy. There are two possible interpretations. The first is that Ben sat in his room at the school typing to fill the time before his father was to arrive for a first visit since the hijacking. The general came, was uneasy, and left for a few minutes to recover his composure. Ben typed his feeling about this, then went out to leap off Brimmler's Bridge to his death. His father came back, found the pages, guessed what had happened, and tried to stop Ben but was too late. The shock and guilt unhinged his mind, and in the last section he is in a mental hospital going over and over his need for forgiveness, which compels him to re-create Ben in his own mind and even to give up his identity to him.

A second interpretation, and one that can be substantiated with much internal evidence, is that *all* of these ruminations are the voice of General Marchand, and that we never actually hear Ben. The typing is done by the father in his false identity as the son, and the place is not Castleton Academy but a mental hospital. The general imagines his old school because it is a place where he was happy and where he can easily picture himself as the same age as his son. There are multiple clues to this interpretation. Most obvious is the mother's Freudian slip when she calls "Ben" by his father's name—"Mark." (But this clue loses credence a page later when she calls him back from drifting away mentally: " 'Ben,' she said, her voice like the snapping of a tree branch."—When Ben/Mark quotes a teacher's description of the father, the mother points out, "You realize you were describing yourself, don't you?" Ben/Mark does describe himself, but as "a skeleton rattling my bones, a ghost laughing hollow up the sleeves of my shroud, a scarecrow whose straw is soaked with blood." He refers often to being invisible, or to a feeling that someone is listening, looking over his shoulder. At the typewriter he says, "I am a fake, here," and, "I am trying to deceive myself not anyone else." The son, seeing his father approaching, finds with terror that his face is a blank, and after the visit types, "It's hard to believe he was really here." About his own death and burial, "Ben" says: "Once in the ground, in the military cemetery at Fort Delta. And again inside of you. Buried me deep inside of you." And toward the end he says, "Put yourself in my place. Or put myself in your place."

It is plain that this is the version that Cormier intends us to accept, even though it is far more difficult and far less satisfying. It is clever and yet somehow not convincing; it feels as if the clues have been scattered among the lines like so many crumbs for gullible pigeons and English teachers. And there is even a third possibility: could this be entirely Ben's voice, a Ben deluded by his guilt and shame into believing that he can become his forgiving father? A father who has perhaps ended his own guilt by jumping off Brimmler's

Bridge? In any one of the three interpretations we miss the perfect click of recognition as the piece fits exactly into place—a click we learned to love in *I Am the Cheese.*

Other structural devices enrich the deeper meaning of the novel. As in *Wuthering Heights,* each of the main characters can be seen as a reflection of one of the others, a pairing that brings out similarities and contrasts. Miro recognizes this relationship on his first sight of Ben, "the boy who was almost a mirror to himself." They are two sons, two innocents. Artkin and the general are a pair: both fanatical patriots and both fathers willing to sacrifice their sons. There are even two bridges.

Another kind of pairing is that of the paradoxes that give impact to the themes: murder as virtue, betrayal as service, treachery as patriotism, and above all, innocence as evil. Even the link between Miro and Kate is paradoxical: two young people, sexually attracted to each other and potential lovers but also potential murderer and victim. As *Boston Magazine* said, "Everybody is either killer or target or both."[1]

After the First Death gives Cormier a chance to show off his powers as a stylist. The book is written in two distinct flavors, which are most strikingly contrasted at the point where the reader first encounters the difference, the switch from part one to part two. In part one, Ben has narrated in wavering, limping, truncated paragraphs jumping suddenly from one subject to another. With the introduction of Miro's point of view in part two, the style changes abruptly and becomes strong and taut and purposeful. There are some brilliant set pieces. Artkin's baiting the waitress is a subtle pleasure in a book otherwise devoid of lighter moments. In the long paragraph that ends part eight, in which Kate tries to deny to herself that Raymond has been shot, the words skitter frantically like rats in a maze. Artkin's dance of death as he whirls the body of the murdered child above his head like a priest of evil offering a hideous sacrament is an unforgettable evocation of the Black Mass.

The title itself is also part of Cormier's enigmatic style in this book. The quotation "After the first death, there is no other" is from the Dylan Thomas poem "A Refusal to Mourn the Death by Fire of a Child in London." It applies in one way or another to all the main characters; each has not only a "first death," but also a second. For Miro, of course, his intended "first death" is Kate, his sacrificial victim. But it is Artkin's death that turns out instead to be his first, and Kate's his second. Kate dies a quasi-death from choking long before her actual death at Miro's hand. Ben is "buried" twice, once at Fort Delta after his suicide and once in his father's mind. Both Artkin and the general die morally and emotionally in their commitment to fanaticism and both die again later because of their sons, although the general's "death" is not literal. Cormier said in an interview: "There are so many deaths, you know? Death of innocence, the real deaths, but once there is that first death, it is so devastating that the others pale beside it. It's very intriguing to me, along with the sense that we are dying all the time and killing all the time. Not only with guns."[2]

Cormier traces the genesis of *After the First Death* to several threads of inspiration. One idea that was much in his mind at that time was the parent-child relationship. Renee was an adoring twelve-year-old, and he was very conscious of trying to live up to her exalted concept of her father. But he pondered how terrible it would be if a parent should manipulate a child by using that unquestioning admiration. A second and unrelated thread was a character he had had in mind for years, whom he had dubbed the California Girl. "You find her everywhere—in Massachusetts, New York— she's that lovely, terrific blonde, a cheerleader maybe—that always has a date for the prom. You see her walk down the street and she's lovely to look at, she brightens your day just for that moment." He had always wanted to write about such a young woman and to explore the complications and hidden defects that he suspected lay beneath the bright surface. Then a third thread: "I read about an incident of a bomb being thrown in a post office where innocent children were killed indiscriminately. And I thought, what kind of person could possibly do this? It had to go beyond villainy. . . . An act like that could only be done out of a sense of innocence. A terrible, terrible kind of innocence." Terrorists, he noticed, always went to other places. What reason could they have to come to New England? Then one day, driving by Fort Devens, he got his answer. "In the sky loomed these planes. They were like ugly vultures. From the bowels of the planes came these evil eggs that blossomed into parachutes. It was somehow very ominous to me. And I realized that this army installation fifteen miles away has always been a brooding presence in our lives." What secrets could be hidden there, he asked, secrets valuable to terrorists?

"And then came the characters . . . Artkin and Miro . . . and they began to clash against each other, and I knew that they *had* to snatch that bus, and the first thing they had to do was *kill that bus driver,* that retired man who'd been doing it—but it turned out that it just had to be that driver's day off and here came this lovely girl. And I thought, finally, I'm going to write a love story. This boy Miro is awakening to sexuality, awakening to life, he's a complete innocent (as monstrous as his innocence is), and here's Kate, who feels that she's been untested—she, too, is just opening like a flower, she's questioning herself—and I thought, here's a chance where they'll get together."[3] But it was not to be just that way. Again the inevitability of plot carried the story to a dark ending.

This same irresistible current swept Cormier in painful directions. It dawned on him at some point that at least one child would have to be killed violently by the terrorists. He recoiled, but realized it would have to be. Putting it off as long as he could, he finally wrote Raymond's death, and then went back and developed the character. In retrospect he realized he had done it in this order to spare himself the pain of killing a child he knew.[4] To the reader also Raymond's death is almost unbearable, partly because Cormier has made the character so entrancing. Sketched in two paragraphs and a few lines of dialogue, Raymond comes vividly alive: chubby, intelligent, poignant in his confused sorrow at being a "late child," whispering to Kate in his deep old-man's voice or sneaking a peek at the bad guys with one bright eye.

The third and fourth terrorists are interesting beyond plot necessity, and the name Antibbe, like Miro Shantas, is meant to evoke a generalized Middle Eastern country. Artkin, however, sounds vaguely Slavic. (But of course these are chosen, not given names.) Of the homeland, we know only that it is now controlled by a foreign power and the women are dark and modestly veiled. Cormier has no intention of taking sides in any actual political controversy; he has more important and more eternal matters to consider.

Kate herself, Cormier's California Girl, goes far beyond the stereotype of the pretty blond teenager. Cormier has hit on the perfect device to humanize her—the shameful secret of her weak bladder. Kate's wet underwear makes us forgive her for being otherwise physically perfect, makes us willing to listen sympathetically to her struggle to be brave. Because Kate—uncertain as she is of the fact even to the last—*is* brave. But it is a self-defeating bravery because she doesn't believe in it. She short-circuits all her chances to escape. Artkin looks at her in anger, and she sees "flat, dead eyes, as if they had no life at all except what they reflected. . . ." Those implacable eyes convince her that her gestures of bravery must be futile, and so, futile they are. Artkin is certainly implacable, but, as the reader knows, he is not all-powerful, and Kate has many opportunities. She might throw the ignition key out the window before they reach the bridge, an idea that does occur to her momentarily but one that she rejects. She might dart out the emergency door before Antibbe locks it, or try to escape when Miro allows her to empty the pail outside. Or she might make better use of Raymond's alertness by planning a way for him to help her overpower Miro. Her one real escape attempt need not end when the engine stalls; there is still time to start the bus again, but Kate gives up immediately and even presses the lever that lets the terrorists back on the bus. Instead of actively resisting, she falls back on the one power play her short life has taught her is always effective—she puts all her energy into trying to use her sexuality to manipulate a man. At the end, when she knows better, she still keeps on with her misguided efforts to wheedle her way out of a bad situation, and by going too far, brings on her own death. She is even denied the heroism that might have been hers if Artkin had accepted her flamboyant demand to take Raymond's place—but she knows he won't. Kate is brave, but not very smart about it.

Ben, by contrast, is a victim from the beginning. Nettie, the girl who rejects him, sees this quality as clearly as if he had a "Kick Me" sign hung around his neck, and acts accordingly. His innocence, the general tells him, made him perfect for the role he had to play. He admires his father blindly and does his bidding without question, and when confronted by the Implacable, he gives up immediately, willingly. The only resistance he can offer at last is the angry symbolic gesture of self-destruction. (Cormier was to explore this idea of suicide as the ultimate resistance later in *The Bumblebee Flies Anyway*.) Ben's name conveys sadness to Cormier. He has had "a special feeling for its haunting, evocative powers" ever since he read Thomas Wolfe's lamentation in *Look Homeward, Angel* on the death of his brother Ben, an experience Cormier himself suffered when his brother Leo died.[5]

Four interlocking themes are explored in *After the First Death:* betrayal of trust, identity masked or disguised, innocence as evil, and patriotism as fanaticism.

Betrayal of trust appears, as Millicent Lenz has pointed out, in three central incidents. Each has an ironic dimension. The first is Ben's betrayal under torture of his father's trust by giving away the supposed time of the attack. The irony, of course, is that what his father has actually trusted in is Ben's weakness, and by collapsing under "the fingers" he has fulfilled his father's mission, not betrayed it. The general has set *himself* up for a parallel situation by volunteering to be a public scapegoat if the attack fails. He is willing, as he later explains to Ben, to subject himself to unearned public disgrace just as he has subjected Ben to it. But he fails to notice the crucial difference: he knows he is not a traitor. Ben doesn't. Miro sees "the look of the betrayer" in Ben's eyes. "It was beyond terror or horror or pain. A look of such anguish, such regret. . . . A look that said: What have I done?"

Miro remembers that look when, like Ben, he thinks he has betrayed his father. By grabbing for an escaping Kate rather than shouting a warning to Artkin of the approaching soldiers, Miro feels he has caused Artkin's death. This guilt is intensified unbearably when Kate convinces him that Artkin was his father. The irony is that in all probability he was not. Nevertheless, Kate dies for this dubious insight, and Miro kills in himself all human emotion. "He would keep himself empty, like before." As Lenz concludes, "Miro's 'suicide' is a suicide of his emotional nature; his 'survival' is terrible, in that he lives on as an automaton programmed to kill for the sake of his cause."[6]

Hidden and disclosed identity is a recurring theme with Cormier. He returns again and again to play with the idea—in *I Am the Cheese,* in *Bumblebee,* in *Fade,* in *Heroes,* in *We All Fall Down,* and in *After the First Death.* Here the symbol is the mask—the knitted ski hoods that Artkin and Miro don to hide their faces, but that paradoxically reveal their evil by showing only their cruel eyes and mouths. Kate reads her own fate in the masks because she knows that they will never let her live now that she has seen their real faces: "She knew she was doomed. She had known it the moment she saw them put on the masks." Miro both loves and hates the mask. "Sometimes . . . he felt like a prisoner in the mask, as if he were locked inside, looking out at the world but not part of it." Yet he loves the sense of power and authority it gives him. "Men's faces paled when they confronted him in the mask, men many years older and much bigger and stronger." But he broods about the mask because "he had the feeling that he must be doing something dishonorable if the operations and confrontations had to be carried out with faces hidden. If what we are doing is heroic . . . why must we hide who we are? he once asked Artkin." The older terrorist's answer is that "they had to disguise themselves to remain free under the wrong laws." In disguise Miro then finds meaning, but also another question: "Without the mask, he was Miro Shantas, the boy without even a real name to identify him to the world. With the mask, he was Miro Shantas, freedom fighter. He often wondered which person he really was."

Kate too has disguises. Her public self is the blond, ever-smiling cheerleader, but behind that shiny identity that she presents so carefully to the world she senses other unexplored selves. "All the Kate Forresters. Were other people like that, she wondered, not simply one person but a lot of them mixed together? Did the real person finally emerge? But suppose that real person turned out to be someone terrible? Or someone who never found love?" The risk is too much.

The general also hides his identity, by merging with his dead son. In addition, like Artkin and Miro, he has a false name that represents his patriotic self: General Rufus Briggs. The mystic power of names is suggested in several places. The name of the dead child is unknown at first;

Kate's involvement with the children is intensified as she unwillingly sorts out their names. She is reluctant to know the name of the big man breaking the bus window, and when Artkin chooses to kill the little boy who didn't eat the candy, but is unable to remember his name, Kate tries to protect Raymond by refusing to tell it. Most of all, there is the strange moment when Artkin, to show Miro that he must completely submerge his old identity and the name that went with it, delicately leads the dim-witted waitress to the place where she doubts her own name and, for a second, her own selfhood.

This toying with the idea of hidden identity and names leads to the central theme of *After the First Death*. "The monstrous," says Cormier, "is so often disguised as innocence."[7] Although all the characters are "innocent" in one sense or another, it is Miro who most clearly illustrates the idea of innocence as evil. At first Kate sees him as simple, like an animal—"a dog straining at a leash." Only gradually does she uncover the extent of his corruption. Anne Scott MacLeod says:

> The tentative human relationship created between them when Kate encourages Miro to talk about his past dissolves abruptly when Kate recognizes the depth and the terrible simplicity of Miro's dedication to his political purpose. For the sake of a country he has never seen, and never really expects to see, Miro has made himself into an instrument of guerrilla warfare. Save for his mentor, Artkin, he has no connection with the actual world of

human life, nor does he expect
any. He envisions no future for
himself, takes no interest in
his own qualities except as they
make him an efficient weapon in
a struggle whose political terms
he cannot possibly know. He has
no feeling for the innocent victims, past or potential, of the
undeclared "war" he wages; indeed, he cannot even understand
what it is Kate expects him to
feel for them.[8]

Kate is deeply shocked by this revelation. "And the greatest horror of all was that he did not know he was a monster. He had looked at her with innocent eyes as he told her of killing people. She had always thought of innocence as something good, something to cherish. People mourned the death of innocence. . . . But innocence, she saw now, could also be evil."

To himself Miro seems not guilty but brave and right. As Cormier explained in a discussion of terrorism, "What does he see when he looks in the mirror that night? Not evil. We rationalize our sins, even as we confess them. Who looks into a mirror and says, I'm the bad guy? But the bomber is the bad guy, evil made flesh, and he can live with himself and continue his fatal work only if he is convinced that what he is doing is good. He must be innocent in his own soul. Thus, just as patriotism can reach a point where it becomes evil, so can evil also blossom into innocence."[9]

Artkin and the general are innocent in the sense of "not guilty"—in their own eyes. Both feel that their side is supremely right and the others are always wrong, and anything done in the name of that right is justifiable. In this surrender of moral judgment they have also surrendered their humanity. Once the total commitment to the cause is made, all other choices vanish. The general describes his patriotism as "pure and sweet and unquestioning. We were the good guys. . . . This generation looks at itself in a mirror as it performs its duties and wonders: Who are the good guys? Is it possible we are the bad guys? They should never ask that question, Ben, or even contemplate it."

This fanaticism blinds them to normal human emotions of love and joy and pity. Artkin, in a hideous parody of compassion, "had often said they were not interested in needless cruelty. They had a job to do and the job concerned death. Do not prolong it more than necessary. Deliver it as efficiently as possible with the least mess. We are not animals, after all, he said, but merely a means to an end. Everything is done for a purpose." But Kate sees the truth clearly when she cries out just before her death, "What the hell has purpose got to do with living or dying?"

The general is neither more nor less evil than Artkin; each is capable of anything in the name of patriotism. There are no limits—killing a child, sacrificing a son—they are a pair. The general sees this plainly: "We knew each other across the chasm; we had recognized each other across the ravine, although we had never met." Artkin, too, understands that the general is a fellow fanatic, and even gives grudging admiration to the extent of his madness: "Either you are a great patriot or a great fool." And the general answers, "Perhaps both." In the end remorse overtakes the father for the sacrifice of the son, and in this there is hope.

In a way Artkin is an exaggerated reflection of the general, just as Emile is a caricature of Archie in *The Chocolate War*. Artkin's fanaticism is a warning, the logical result of such a total commitment. The general is for us the more dangerously seductive figure because to some degree we agree with his cause and are in danger of justifying his actions.

He moves, after all, through the landscape of American patriotism—Lexington, Concord—and it is our country he thinks he is defending. Artkin ponders, "Who knows about Americans? Perhaps they cherish their children more than their agencies." But it soon becomes clear that the safety of the children—or of any of us—is not really the central concern. The institution preserves itself—mindlessly, mercilessly—at all costs.

"After the First Death," said *Publishers Weekly,* is "a work of art which like Picasso's 'Guernica' and Goya's 'Disasters of War' stands as a passionate indictment of inhumanity. . . . Cormier bases his flawless tragedy on a plot as ancient as the slingshot, as modern as the H-bomb."[10] Or the destruction of the World Trade Center.

Notes

1. Grove, Lee, "Robert Cormier Comes of Age," *Boston Magazine,* December 1980, 79.

2. De Luca, Geraldine, and Roni Natov, "An Interview with Robert Cormier," *The Lion and the Unicorn,* Fall 1978, 132.

3. Cormier, Robert, audiotape of speech at the Young Adult Services Division luncheon, American Library Association Conference, Dallas, June 1979.

4. De Luca and Natov, 130.

5. Nilsen, Alleen Pace, "The Poetry of Naming in Young Adult Books," *ALAN Review,* Spring 1980, 3.

6. Lenz, Millicent, "A Romantic Ironist's Vision of Evil: Robert Cormier's *After the First Death,*" paper presented at the Eighth Annual Conference of the Children's Literature Association, Minneapolis, March 1981.

7. De Luca and Natov, 132.

8. MacLeod, Anne Scott, "Robert Cormier and

the Adolescent Novel," *Children's Literature in Education,* Summer 1981, 77.

9. Cormier, Robert, "Are You Working on a New Novel? Yes," *ALAN Review,* 1.

10. Review of *After the First Death, Publishers Weekly,* January 29, 1979, 115.

Chapter Nine

The Bumblebee Flies Anyway

It is spring, and there is dying going on. A whole hospital full of dying. Barney Snow—Bernard Jason Snow—whose name, like that of Alph LeBlanc in *Now and at the Hour*, symbolizes his "whiteness," his innocence—and much more. Snow is cold, like death, like a lack of love. "Your heart is as cold as your name," says his friend Billy the Kidney—but he knows it isn't true. Barney's actions are compassionate toward the other inmates of the Complex, an experimental hospital for the terminally ill. He just doesn't want to talk about anybody's past, because—even though he can't admit it to himself—he has no memories of his own to share. His mind is full of "blankness, like snow, suffocating, obliterating snow." The Handyman, as he calls the director of the pediatric unit, has warned Barney to stay in his own emotional "compartment" and to avoid entanglements with the other "guests," because, after all, he is the control, the only one here who is not dying. But Barney Snow is being snowed.

The story begins the day that one of the young patients,

Ronson, "gets the Ice Age"—an experiment with cold in which he is strapped down and hooked up to a lot of "doo-dads" and shot full of chill-producing "merchandise." "Doo-dads" and "merchandise" are Barney's terms for things in the Complex that are too scary to name. The patients at the Complex are all volunteers with terminal illnesses who have offered themselves for scientific experimentation, to give others the hope *they* cannot have. Even the inmates of Section 12, the pediatric unit, are volunteers: pathetic Billy the Kidney, spastic Allie Roon, the doomed Ronson, and rich, handsome, and obnoxious Mazzo. Barney has been here for four or five weeks, time enough for several unpleasant encounters with the merchandise. Although he is not dying, he is to be the subject for some experiments on memory and the brain, the Handyman explains. When they are physically able, the patients are allowed to leave the hospital for short walks. One day Barney, Allie Roon, and Billy the Kidney stroll past a nearby automobile junkyard, and the sight of a red MG among the rusting ruins triggers Barney's recurring nightmare of a wild, rainswept ride in a car that is out of control and about to crash. "Tempo, rhythm," he tells himself, a phrase that he uses to invoke calm and control.

Wealthy Mazzo gets a telephone installed in his room, much to Billy's envy, but refuses to answer it when his anxious mother tries to reach him. Seeing Billy's yearning to use the phone, Barney strikes a bargain with Mazzo. He will stand by in the room when Mazzo's twin sister, Cassie, comes to visit so that she will not be able to persuade Mazzo to see their mother. In return Billy can use the telephone (although he knows no one to call) for an hour a day. Barney takes one look at beautiful Cassie and is instantly in love with her. She, seeing his adoration, manipulates him into becoming a "tender spy" and giving her daily reports on Mazzo's condition. Barney's love for Cassie awakens him to life again, and also to the fear that memories of her will be swept away in the experiments he is undergoing. A terrifying episode with the merchandise temporarily wipes out his knowledge of his identity, but after a few days he is returned to himself, only to learn that the telephone has been a failure for Billy and that Ronson has died. In trying to talk with Mazzo, Barney discovers that the only thing that still interests the dying boy is fast cars. Going back to the junkyard, he finds that the red MG is a balsa-wood fake put together by a woodworking class, and he conceives a plan: he will unscrew the parts of the car and sneak it into the Complex, where he will put it together in the cellar and then take Mazzo for one last wild ride. He shares the plan with Billy and Allie and they are ecstatic at being included in the project.

Meanwhile, several episodes narrated from Cassie's point of view disclose to us (but not to Barney) that her intense interest in her brother's condition is essentially selfish. She has a secret mystic link with him that compels her to suffer in her own body any trauma that happens to him. Now she wonders with dread what will happen to her when he dies.

Barney and the others proceed with the project, but hit a snag when painters arrive to work in the basement. Barney shifts his plan to the attic, where he discovers a skylight opening onto the slanting roof. The plan is transformed: he will give Mazzo a final flight to glory in the car. But as he returns from the attic he idly explores another floor of the Complex and finds a corridor, a room, and a television monitor that he remembers vividly. He turns the TV switch and finds that this room is where his nightmare of the rainy car has been created. The Handyman appears and is forced by Barney's panic to reveal that the nightmare—and the phrase "rhythm, tempo" and his fragmentary memories of his mother—have been experimental screens to shield him from a terrible truth: he, too, is dying of a terminal illness.

Shocked out of remission by the revelation, Barney knows he does not have much longer to live. That afternoon, without really meaning to, he tells Cassie about the car, not revealing who the passenger is to be, and she dubs it the Bumblebee because, contrary to scientific prediction, it will fly anyway.

Seriously ill now, Barney works frantically against time to finish the car. After a farewell visit with Cassie, that night he and Mazzo, followed by Billy, make the agonized journey to the attic, where they struggle to get the Bumblebee up the stairs to the skylight. The effort is too much for Mazzo, and he dies in Barney's arms before they can push off. Barney realizes he doesn't need to ride, either—it will be enough to see the flight of the Bumblebee. They shove it free—and for a glorious moment it flies.

In two final scenes, Cassie suffers through her twin's death and survives by her own will to live, and Barney, dying in the hospital, continues to exult in his vision of the Bumblebee glowing against the night sky.

That one moment of exaltation and hope as the Bumblebee sails out into space was the goal toward which Cormier worked for several years. The novel was troublesome. "The thing is," he said, "I had the concept. I wanted to have that soaring ending. And I was building up to it, and I would get discouraged . . . I had times when my words all seemed cumbersome, dull, when it wouldn't get up and dance, when it didn't sing to me, and I knew it was very downbeat, and I didn't know if I could pull it off. At the end. The soaring moment." There is no doubt he did pull it off. That one chapter is magnificent, unforgettable. But the rest of the novel shows the effects of the not entirely victorious struggle that went into its making.

As with most of Cormier's books, the genesis can be traced to several sources. "It started really one night when I was watching television," he remembered, "and somebody made a brief mention of an experimental hospital in the Midwest where people with no hope came, hoping they could help others." Intrigued, he began to research it. In the process he came across other medical reports of memory experiments, research on the workings of the brain. Always interested in identity, he turned his new knowledge in that direction. Suppose you were dying, he thought, "and if you couldn't wipe away the disease, suppose you could wipe away the memory of it!" But how much of identity would be the cost of that forgetfulness?

Then there was the poster in his study that explained that "according to the laws of aerodynamics, the bumblebee, because of its heavy body and short wing span, isn't supposed to be able to fly. But the bumblebee, not knowing about this theory or law, flies anyway."[1] The idea of doing the impossible like this had haunted him for years. Writing about the impossible turned out to be nearly as difficult. "The problem was, I knew the car had to be on the roof—now how do I get it there? First I went around researching. I went to junkyards, looked at Volkswagens . . . Too heavy, too cumbersome. How could a kid get it up there? Okay, so I made it a sports model like an MG. Still too heavy. Then finally I came up with the idea of the mock-up."

The complex and demanding project almost defeated him. It was five years in the writing. He put it aside in despair for nine or ten months, and then began over again from page one, finally coming to grips with the problems in the manuscript. Basically, the difficulty revolved—and still does—around the character of Cassie. Reviewers complained that there were flaws in the "depiction of Cassie, who we are told is 'vibrant and compelling,' but who remains an abstraction."[2]

"The major weakness in characterization," one said, "is the portrayal of Cassie, who is convincing as Barney's love idol, but less so as her twin's empathetic alter ego."[3] True, it is understandable that Barney would be completely entranced with Cassie, even if she is not really as "vibrant and compelling" as he thinks. After all, except for a few dim memories of spin the bottle at parties, she is the only girl he has ever seen because his past is only five weeks long. But her psychosomatic link with Mazzo is puzzling. Aside from the fact that they are twins, they seem to have neither more nor less closeness than the average friendly brother and sister. There is nothing to explain their almost mystical link, nor does Cormier appear to try. It doesn't seem to work as a metaphor, either—it is just pasted onto the story, and because Cassie is basically unlikable, there is only a mild, abstract suspense in wondering if she will be drawn in to Mazzo's death.

Several false starts added unusable material to Cormier's novel; it had gotten out of hand. It was becoming a whole other book. Whenever the story left the Complex, the tension Cormier had built so carefully evaporated. He was entranced with Cassie, especially her fascination with the convent, but try as he might, he could not make her sympathetic. He even experimented with giving her a saintly aura by having her experience the stigmata—the psychosomatic re-creation of the wounds of Christ. It didn't work, and he took it out, all except a puzzling fragment. But she needed to be there; the Complex without Cassie was unbearably dreary. She released Barney's aspirations to love and revealed his vulnerabilities; she was the motivation for his closeness to Mazzo and the building of the Bumblebee. Finally Cormier acceded to the solution suggested by an editor: Cassie was to be seen only through Barney's eyes except where it was absolutely necessary. As published, the book has only four short sections from Cassie's point of view, in which she shows her half-ashamed manipulation of Barney and her terror of dying with Mazzo. This way she is lovable at least to Barney, although much about her is unexplained in the truncated version.

An additional problem with *Bumblebee* is the *blankness* of the outer and inner setting: the sterile hospital and Barney's amnesiac mind. By the book's very nature there can be none of the sweat, noise, collisions, the *events* of, say, *The Chocolate War.* In the Complex everything is silent, bare, colorless, like the empty, drab gray and dull white corridors. The only sounds are the distant hums of machines; all human noises are hushed. "The passage of feet in the halls of the Complex was quiet, muted, footsteps like whispers as patients and staff ghosted by in rubber-soled shoes or slippers." Barney's memory is equally blank—no allusions, anecdotes, connections from the past to anything he sees or feels. Even his senses of taste and smell are gone, and his emotions are deliberately muted and suppressed. This sterility gives the narrative a peculiar flatness. The story moves along on silent rubber-tired wheels like a gurney carrying a patient to surgery. It feels to the reader as if nothing happens at all until the flight of the Bumblebee—which is one reason for that moment's powerful impact.

Outside on the street it is also silent and sterile. There is no traffic, no people or houses. The grounds are deserted, neglected, the shrubbery cluttered with windblown debris. Behind the fence in the automobile graveyard there is only the dry death of technology—"This terrible place where the only inhabitant was a gray rat lurking in the ruins." In Barney's drug-distorted mind it becomes a surrealistic vision of Armageddon: "He felt as if he were making his way through a battlefield long after the bombs had exploded and the soldiers had fled, taking the dead and wounded with them." A car door banging in the wind is like the sound of doom. It is the end of the world, the dry, dead land without hope of T. S. Eliot's poems "The Hollow Men" and *The Waste Land.* It is the landscape of postnuclear holocaust.

There are other evocations of nuclear terror in the Complex, reminding us that we, like the other patients, may be facing death in a terminally ill society. The Handyman tells Barney, "There are no guarantees about the future even for the man walking down the street this morning in the best of health, the prime of life." Ronson, going into the Ice Age in Isolation, wears "thermonuclear underwear." Barney, awakening in an otherworldly waiting room after his memory has been completely erased, describes the moment of his return to consciousness as if it were the detonation of a neutron bomb: "There had been an explosion of light but no aftermath of smoke and rubble, the way there would be in a real explosion." The automobile graveyard and the Complex are "both filled with busted and broken things." But unfortunately, as Barney reflects, "the junkyard had spare parts and the Complex didn't." Technology can be replaced, but that which is soft and human, once destroyed, is gone forever.

Presiding over this sterile, self-contained place is the enigmatic figure of the Handyman. Who is this Dr. Edward Lakendorp, who has the power of life and death, pain and oblivion over his subjects? Is he evil? The Devil, perhaps, in some existential hell? But hell has no exit, as Sartre made clear, and death is the door here. It is tempting to compare him with Brint from *I Am the Cheese*. Both have mysterious power over the mind with drugs and secrets; both are in hospitals; both speak in euphemisms about painful things. Both are diabolical father confessors to unwilling supplicants, a theme Cormier later carried to its ultimate expression in *The Rag and Bone Shop*. To Barney, the Handyman sometimes looks like a mechanical doll, with hard, cold eyes even when he smiles. But unlike Brint, whose compassion turned out to be a façade, the Handyman is not a monster. After a talk in which he warns Barney not to allow himself to get too close to Cassie, Barney sees a look on his face as if he is sad and lonely. He can be troubled, make mistakes, suffer from a headache. Barney has been delivered to him; the memory experiments did not begin at the Complex. In some ways he is as much a victim as Barney. So, although he is sometimes made insensitive to suffering by his scientific zeal, he is implacable authority but not evil authority. He is not the enemy.

The Handyman never discusses anything except what goes on in the Complex, Barney notices, "as if no other world existed." That is literally true for the orphan children of Section 12, especially for Barney. Five of Cormier's seven previous novels take place in institutions, and in them a steady progression toward equating the Institution with the state of existence itself can be seen. In *Bumblebee* Cormier has taken this idea to the endpoint: the Institution is all. Only Mazzo has a link with the world outside, and he won't answer the phone. This connection, which he might use to reach out for comfort and love, is to him only a way to punish. When Billy tries to find human contact over the phone, he discovers that it is too late. From inside the Complex they are all wrong numbers.

There are hopeful symbols, too, in this book, which at the time of its publication was hailed as Cormier's most affirmative work. On his first excursion to the junkyard, Barney sees a lilac bush growing against the fence, "the purple clusters so heavy they made the branches droop," but it reminds him only that he can no longer smell their fragrance. The blooming bush is the only thing soft and alive in the hard stone and metal of the Complex and the junkyard, growing stubbornly in almost no soil. For American poets— and particularly those from New England—lilacs have always been a potent symbol, blossoming as they do at the end of winter. Cormier has used the symbol of the lilacs in *Bumblebee,* as he did in *Now and at the Hour,* to affirm the renewal of life and the hope of victory over death. Contemplating these ideas, Barney climbs the fence and sees the MG once more. A glimmer grows in his mind: ". . . he let the vision burst full flower. He saw for the first time the flight of the Bumblebee."

Through the symbolism of the lilacs, Barney gropes for

faith in an afterlife that has been erased from his mind. Only fragments of the structure of belief remain—a snatch of a prayer, a brief memory of religious instruction from a nun. "A face flashed before him, pale face enclosed in some kind of starched white collar that concealed ears and hair, and lips moving, saying something about heaven, hell." The dogma is gone, and he is left with only the most banal religious ideas. To comfort Billy after Ronson's death, Barney conjures up a childish vision of heaven: "Maybe Ronson right this minute is boxing away someplace, winning the championship." But he tells himself it is ridiculous, stupid. After he learns that he is dying, the Handyman in pity offers to bring a priest. Barney suddenly remembers that he has been Catholic, but the candles, the wafer, the altar no longer have meaning for him. He finds that he has clothed his faith with the words "tempo, rhythm," the screen that the Handyman has instilled in his mind to disguise Barney's fear of death. But the outer shape doesn't matter—it is still prayer, it is still faith.

"Free choice, the Handyman said, you have free choice here. A laugh, of course," thinks Barney. Yet, outside the terrible, implacable fact of impending death, they do have free choice, and the other characters have used it. Billy the Kidney and Allie Roon have chosen to come to the Complex so that their deaths might help others, and although they are embarrassed to talk about it, the commitment does give each of them some spiritual comfort. Mazzo has made the choice for the wrong reason—to die more quickly—and finds only selfish anger in it. Faith has no reality for him. He sees Cassie's attraction to total spiritual surrender as only a passing fad. Barney, too, has made the choice, but he doesn't know it. The decision to commit himself to the Complex happened in the immediate past, which has been erased from his mind. So Barney must find elsewhere that humanizing gesture against the Implacable that is so central in Cormier's cosmos.

Before he can act he must find out who he is. Or perhaps the other way around, as the existentialists would have it: through action we make our own meaning for our existence. Cassie's first words to Barney are "I know who you are." But *he* doesn't. Just before the terrifying experiment in which his identity is to be entirely obliterated, he writes down what he knows about himself: his name, his age, his weight, his height. That is all. In childhood memory (perhaps a manufactured memory) he recalls losing his mother in a department store. "I started to scream, not only because I had lost my mother but because I didn't know who I was. Without my mother to verify who I was, I was lost." Yet the experiment he is about to undergo is terror beyond that terror because, as the Handyman explains in a misguided attempt at comfort, "You will not remember your name. But consider this: you will also not remember not knowing your name." He is given the drug, and awakes in a room that is a place between worlds: bare, hard chairs lined up against the walls, coffee table with magazines, flat calendar art on the wall—a waiting room for hell. "He was alone, cast adrift, lost, unrelated to anything." A face appears on a television screen and asks him, in the fairy-tale manner, the obligatory three questions. They take the form of word associations. "Snow," "car"—before the third question can be asked, Barney in a panic finds it for himself. *Who am I?* And then *What am I?* He can find no answer. Here, in the existential dilemma, Cormier's preoccupation with identity is laid bare.

Like all of us, Barney thinks he is the only one who is not going to die. Even before, the Handyman tells him, in the other hospital, he had not come to the stage of acceptance as others had. When he is finally confronted with the fact of his mortality, the Bumblebee, which began as an attempt to transform his nightmare of the rainy car, is itself transformed. Now it becomes a defiant affirmation, "a shared vision of freedom and rebirth." When Barney first gazes down from the skylight in the attic he sees only the junkyard, rows of bleak tenements, an old cemetery "with tombstones like small teeth scattered on a rug." But when he stands with Mazzo and Billy on the threshold of the flight, the view, like his soul, is transfigured—"the sweep of sky spinning with stars, the moon radiating silver, turning the sloping roof into a glittering ski slide, the lights of Monument center glowing in the distance, staining the sky with gold." At the last minute he realizes that suicide is irreconcilable with an act of faith. The Bumblebee soars, and in this supremely irrational gesture is ultimate hope.

Notes

1. Graeber, Laurel, "PW Interviews: Robert Cormier," *Publishers Weekly,* October 7, 1983, 98.

2. Rochman, Hazel, review of *The Bumblebee Flies Anyway, School Library Journal,* September 1983, 132.

3. Estes, Sally, review of *The Bumblebee Flies Anyway, Booklist,* September 1, 1983, 37.

Chapter Ten

Fade

What if . . . you could make yourself invisible? What would you do first? How would this ability change your life and your world? What would be its pleasures and dangers? Would it be a gift or a curse?

A suitable subject for science fiction writers. Yet in 1988 Cormier, who had built a firm reputation on realism, on his willingness to look even the grimmest facts straight in the eye, wrote a novel about a boy who could make himself invisible. It is apparent that Cormier delighted in jolting his readers with the unexpected, and he confessed his fear of repeating himself,[1] so it is not really so surprising that after *Beyond the Chocolate War* rounded off the group of four dark young adult novels, he should veer off in a new direction. But while Cormier moved toward science fiction, the story remained firmly rooted in reality, even autobiography. Characteristically, he used the idea of invisibility to explore the intersection of truth and fiction and the natures of belief and guilt, while telling a fast-moving and suspenseful tale dusted with the poignancy of adolescent first love. "Imagine what might happen if Holden Caulfield stepped into H. G. Wells's classic science-fiction novel *The Invisible Man,*" Stephen King said about *Fade.*[2]

Invisibility has always been a part of human folklore. Given the universality of the concept, it is puzzling how seldom it appears in modern literature. Apart from an occasional science fiction short story, *The Invisible Man* stood alone until very recently. (Ralph Ellison's novel, *Invisible Man,* of course, uses the term as a metaphor for the effects of racism.) In Wells's story, an irascible scientist accidentally renders himself invisible during an experiment and is unable to reverse the transformation in spite of his frantic efforts to find an antidote. Raging through the streets of the country village where he has come to find solitude for his experiments, he is eventually undone by his own violence.[3]

The 1933 film based on Wells's novel was certainly a part of *Fade*'s genesis. Few people who have seen this movie will ever forget the scene in which the invisible man slowly unwinds his head bandages to reveal a gaping nothing. *Fade*'s protagonist, Paul, refers to it several times, once, when a child, as "the movie where the man wrapped himself in bandages." And later another character credits it with the genesis of Paul's memoir/novel.

A literary influence that Cormier himself credited was Graham Greene's *The End of the Affair,* in which someone, like Paul's agent, Meredith, who appears in the middle section of *Fade,* "knows the truth but is trying to disprove it all the time." It may or may not be significant that in late 1986 Cormier wrote an admiring review for the *Los Angeles Times* on *The Flight of the Cassowary* by John LeVert, a book in which an ordinary teenager named Paul discovers that he has an unexplained, unexpected supernatural ability that disturbs the course of his life.[4] That this Paul can become an animal and fly, not vanish, makes the coincidence no less intriguing.

And finally there is the question of the effect of the writing of Stephen King on *Fade*. The two writers were friendly acquaintances who enjoyed one another's books. Cormier said, "Stephen King lurked in the background . . . Yet, I wasn't trying to write a Stephen King novel."[5] Certain details—a single eye that stares out of an old man's smashed head, the violence of a knife fight—evoke King's bloody excesses. And the breathless rhythm of the last section as two voices alternate more and more quickly, escalating to a knife fight, is reminiscent of King at his best. Yet in context these passages are pure Cormier, the violence justified by necessities of character and plot. King himself praised the novel extravagantly: "I was absolutely riveted. . . . an exciting, fast-paced read . . . moving and enthralling. Cormier has always been a fine novelist, but *Fade* is easily his best work."[6]

Yet this novel that ends with such drama begins quietly, as if it were going to describe the nostalgic adventures of a French Canadian–American Tom Sawyer. The year is 1938, and Paul Moreaux is thirteen. He lives in the Frenchtown section of Monument with his parents and his older brother, Armand; his younger brother, Bernard; and his twin sisters, Yvonne and Yvette. His best friend, Pete Lagniard, is just downstairs, and nearby are the houses of his grandparents and his many aunts and uncles. The life of this close French Canadian community revolves around St. Jude's Church and the comb factory where most of the adults go to work each day.

Paul is a shy, secretive boy who yearns to be a writer. Although he is happy growing up in this warm family environment, he longs for adventure in the distant places of the globe. This longing is personified for him by his uncle Adelard, a wanderer who returns only occasionally and who is the subject of a mysterious anecdote. Long ago a photograph was taken of the whole family, but when the picture was developed, in the place where Adelard had been standing was only a blank space. Paul is obsessed by this story, and questions his father about it whenever he gets a chance. In the meantime, however, another wanderer returns, Paul's voluptuous aunt Rosanna. Paul falls instantly in love, and she teases him with affectionate flirtatiousness.

As the summer wears on, he secretly follows and eavesdrops on his aunt, and one day surprises her alone in her room. Getting up his courage, he gives her a love poem he has written, but then is inflamed by her beauty to a secret sexual climax, and runs off in mortification. His troubles increase when he is chased by the bully Omer LaBatt but mysteriously escapes his pursuer's notice. He continues to shadow Rosanna, and follows her to the apartment of the town villain, Rudolphe Toubert. When she emerges she leads him to a secluded picnic area by the river, where she confides in him that Toubert fathered her child, which was born dead several years ago. In the intimacy of the conversation, she guides Paul's hand to her breast, and suddenly he realizes that love is more than physical desire. Later, when she leaves town abruptly, he continues to feel longing and guilt, even though she has left him an affectionate (and misspelled) note of farewell.

Adelard returns, and Paul is flattered to notice that his uncle seems to seek out his company. One rainy afternoon he finds Paul home alone and takes the opportunity to reveal to him the secret that has passed from uncle to nephew for generations. Adelard can make himself "fade," or become invisible, and Paul also has this ability. Adelard instructs him in the painful transition technique and charges him never to tell a living soul. Dazzled by his new power, Paul begins to experiment with its possibilities. He invisibly watches Pete and his friends on the street corner and then follows a young girl into the back room of Dondier's Market, where he is stunned and repelled to see the elderly grocer pay her to allow him to perform cunnilingus on her skinny adolescent body.

Paul tries to confess this voyeurism and his dalliance

with Rosanna to a priest at St. Jude's, but is unable to ask whether the fade is a sin. He finds that it is beginning to set him apart from the rest of his world—and from God. His uneasiness is confirmed when Adelard, before leaving once more, tells him that the fade has been a burden to him and that he blames it and himself for the long-ago death of his younger brother, Vincent. He warns Paul always to use the power for good and speculates on the terrible possibilities of a future evil fader.

School begins, and Paul and his cousin Jules are plunged into the new world of Silas B. Thornton Junior High School. At first Paul is delighted by the new opportunities, but when a teacher savagely disparages a story he has written, he realizes that these opportunities are not for boys from Frenchtown, the sons of immigrant factory workers. Unexpectedly, he is befriended by cool, wealthy Emerson Winslow, who takes him home after school and introduces him to his twin sister, Page, as "a writer." Paul is entranced by the twins' beauty and sophistication and returns that night in the fade, only to become a shocked and unwilling witness to an incestuous sexual encounter between the pair. When he finds Omer Labatt persecuting a younger boy in an alley and drives him off with unnecessarily vicious invisible kicks and blows, he is appalled to notice that this time the fade has come uninvited and that it has brought no good to his life.

Meanwhile, the workers' growing dissatisfaction with conditions at the comb factory results in a strike. Rudolphe Toubert is instrumental in arranging to have scabs brought in, and with their arrival a fight breaks out on the picket lines. Paul's father is stabbed, and in horror Paul runs away, invites the fade, and goes invisibly to the office of Toubert to avenge his father and his aunt. He picks up a knife. . . .

When he returns home, he learns that his father has survived. Toubert is found dead, but the murder is blamed on Toubert's missing henchman, not Paul. Three weeks later

Paul's younger brother, Bernard, like his uncle Vincent a generation before, dies suddenly in his sleep.

At this point the narrative breaks off, and a new voice begins. The time has shifted to 1988, and Susan Roget, a distant relative of the famous but reclusive writer Paul Roget, explains that she has come to New York to work as an assistant in the office of Paul's former agent, Meredith Martin, and to live with her for the summer in her Greenwich Village apartment. Paul died in 1967, before Susan was born, but his career has been an important influence on her life and her ambition to become a writer. Snooping through Meredith's closets one day when the agent is out, Susan comes upon a hidden manuscript that turns out to be the Frenchtown story we have just read.

Susan is stunned, and when she confesses her find to Meredith, she learns that the older woman is deeply troubled by the possibly autobiographical nature of the narrative. Paul has always given his stories Frenchtown settings, but in this case he has also used actual people and events, named real names. If the rest of the story is real, then so might the fade be—and maybe Paul is also a murderer, although his words are inconclusive on this point.

Meredith is ambivalent, and so sends the manuscript to Jules, Susan's grandfather, for a confidential opinion. She shows Susan the report Jules writes. While trying to deny the autobiographical nature of the narrative and to prove that the story, and the fade, are fiction, Jules inadvertently confirms that the characters and major events are indeed real. Confused and upset, Susan tries to push away the idea that Paul could actually make himself invisible. But Meredith shows her a piece of convincing evidence, a series of three photographs taken secretly by a friend of hers in which Paul is first a blur, and then not there at all. In the morning Susan finds that Meredith has left her a note of apology and a second part of the manuscript, whose existence she has kept a secret from Susan.

Paul's adult voice resumes the tale as Susan reads what he has written. It is now 1963. Paul has become a distinguished novelist, but still lives on the top floor of a Frenchtown three-decker opposite St. Jude's Church. His brothers and sisters have married and had children, and Paul has cultivated the company of his nieces and nephews, watching for the next fader, although thus far he has been unable to detect signs of the fade in any of his nephews. Although he has vowed never to invoke the fade again, it comes on him unexpectedly more and more often, and he lives in dread of detection. This fear has kept him a recluse, afraid to travel, to reap the public rewards of his success, even to seek medical help when he is ill. Like Adelard, he finds that the fade has diminished him over the years. Paul now confesses that he did kill Toubert, describing the events of that night. Bernard's death seems to him to be a retribution for his sin, even though Adelard explained to him at the wake that the fade had little to do with the equivalent death of Vincent. Paul has sought forgiveness from God in vain, and voices torture him with guilt in the night. When his sister Rose confides that she once gave birth to an illegitimate child and left it for adoption in a convent in Maine, he knows that he has found the next fader at last. To go to him and counsel him is Paul's only route to salvation.

Here Ozzie, Rose's abandoned child, takes up the story in the third person. Now thirteen, he has lived a life of neglect and abuse. His alcoholic adoptive mother has died, and his brutal stepfather has beaten him so badly and so often that his nose is now a hideously deformed mass. For a time he ran away to the streets, where his only friend was the wino Old Man Pinder, but now he has been rescued by the nuns and lives in the convent near the town of Ramsey. He is full of rage at the world, and when the fade finds him, he knows just what to do. He goes directly to his stepfather and beats his head to a pulp with a hammer. Delirious with his new power, he goes on an invisible rampage of hitting and breaking, and soon he finds a voice in his head is urging him to do worse things, even to suspect the kindness of the nun who has cared for him. When Old Man Pinder accidentally discovers his secret, the voice tells Ozzie to kill him and then to silence the nun. Ozzie resists temporarily, but when he finds Old Man Pinder has become an informant to Paul, the stranger who has been asking about him, Ozzie beats the old wino's skull in with a rock. The dying man drags himself to Paul to warn him to save the nun. In a midnight courtyard in Ramsey the two faders meet for a showdown. Paul tries to offer compassion and help, but the voice in Ozzie's head understands only suspicion and violence. A knife fight between the two invisibles ends with Paul committing a second, but necessary, murder.

In an epilogue, Susan and Meredith try to convince themselves that the story is fiction. The fade, of course, is obviously impossible, they agree without conviction, and Meredith decides to publish the manuscript. Susan, however, remembers (but doesn't mention to Meredith) a crucial piece of information told her by Jules, one he omitted from his report to Meredith. When he and Paul were boys, one afternoon in the public library Paul disappeared in the stacks and Jules could not find him for an hour. For Susan this is evidence of the reality of the fade, and when she stumbles on a newspaper story about a series of mysterious vandalisms in a nearby state, she begins to realize that there may be a new fader, and her knowledge and her obligation to Paul may have given her a responsibility that terrifies her. The ending of *Fade* recalls the last lines of *Beyond the Chocolate War* and *After the First Death:* like Archie, like Miro, the new fader has served an apprenticeship in evil and is now about to launch unspeakable destruction on the adult world.

The literary style of *Fade,* especially in the first section, is deceptively simple and straightforward. There is none of the complex layering, the brilliant metaphors and allusions that typify most of Cormier's other novels. Only when one attempts to summarize the story does it become clear how intricately linked are the multitude of apparently rambling events. There are thirty-three developed characters (and fifty-five more who are mentioned by name), and each has an essential part in the progress of the plot. Even the seemingly self-indulgent autobiographical details of Frenchtown life are integral in developing the borderless interweave of reality and fiction that makes the novel so disturbing.

Only occasionally is the careful reader aware of Cormier's exercising his stylistic powers. There are a number of pairings, or repeated but contrasted patterns: two illegitimate births (to Rose and to Rosanna), two young brothers suddenly dead (Vincent and Bernard), two bullies (Bull Zimmer and Omer LaBatt), two sets of twins (Yvonne and Yvette, and Emerson and Page), two teenage boys working in grocery stores (Paul and Ozzie), two exiled wanderers (Adelard and Rosanna), and two deaths by knifing (Toubert and Ozzie). Paul himself remarks on some of these: "The endless, unceasing repetitions. The tides of life and living."

Even more striking is the way in which Cormier introduces ideas and words referring to invisibility and secrecy long before he has revealed the fade. The first thing we learn about Adelard is that "he was always disappearing," meaning, in this context, that he was always going away on a journey. "It's hard to see what isn't there," says Paul's father, Louis Moreaux, jokingly. Paul feels different and alienated before he has a reason to, and ironically he longs for a life of drama and mystery. He often behaves as if he were invisible before he can be, searching Rosanna's room and shadowing her in the street. He loves secrets, and prides himself on the ability to hide, which he uses to escape Omer before he finds that there is a better way. And when Adelard comes to the tenement to reveal the secret to Paul on that fateful rainy afternoon, his footsteps cross the piazza and pause at the bottom of the steps as if he were already disembodied.

Adelard is one of the most poignant actors in this intricate drama. Even as a young man his clothes and his eyes are pale and faded; these details hint at the effect the fade is to have on his soul. He knows he is utterly trapped by his destiny, yet there is a wry gallantry about him. "He has a reputation for avoiding straight answers," yet he smiles and changes the subject with gentle humor when questioned too closely on sensitive matters like the mysterious photograph. Later, he takes on a tragic dimension under the burden of the fade, "the lines of weariness enclosing his mouth, the dark pouches like bruises under his eyes." When he confesses to Paul that the fade has driven him to theft and near-rape, he thinks of himself as a monster. But for Paul he will always be "the only person who had the dimensions of a hero, who dared to be different, who wandered the earth."

The other wanderer, Rosanna, is one of Cormier's most endearing feminine creations. Through Paul's eyes, she is that familiar Cormier woman, the utterly desirable and completely unattainable love object. Rosanna is good-hearted, affectionate, but lazy and not too bright. Her fatal flaw is that she is unable to resist the temptation to exercise her one avenue to power. She is seduced by seduction and gets carried away every time she uses her power, even approaching incest with her nephew. But she means well always, and the reader, like Paul, can't help being fond of her.

Before *Frenchtown Summer* Cormier used to say that *Fade* was "probably the most autobiographical novel I've ever written—not the facts of my life but the background . . . I was expanding on my childhood days—sort of reliving my childhood."[7] As we have seen, all of his books are set in the imaginary town of Monument, which is closely modeled on the real towns of Leominster and Fitchburg; significant fictional events in his books often are set in real places, and he used his French Hill childhood in his short stories. But *Fade* goes beyond this limited use of autobiographical material: there are extended passages drawn from Cormier's early memories or cannibalized from his unpublished first novel, "Act of Contrition." The wake, the Rub Room (the awful basement room at the comb factory to which Paul's father is demoted), the chorus of factory whistles, the night sounds in the crowded bedroom—all are part of his past. Moccasin Pond is Fort Pond; Ransom Hill is Rice Hill; Silas B. Thornton Junior High School is May A. Gallagher Junior High School; Ramsey is the hamlet of Ayer near Fort Devens; and the Plymouth Theater actually existed until it was torn down several years ago. Even the mysterious family photograph was real, and the source of the "what if?" for the novel. Devotees of Cormier are apt to feel as Susan did on discovering the Frenchtown manuscript: "I have devoured every piece of material about him and here was new, exciting stuff."

In this seamless blend of autobiography, fiction, and remembered fiction it is important to keep one's bearings by holding firmly to the fact that it is the settings, not the characters or events, that are real. Although Cormier did have a best friend named Pete who lived downstairs, although he did have twin siblings and a brother who died young, none of the *Fade* uncles resembles his own, who, like his father, were gentle men who would never think of rebelling against their employers. And although it is tempting, because of the matching alliteration, to equate Cormier's agent, Marilyn Marlow, with Paul's agent, Meredith Martin, the personalities of the two women are quite different.

Jules speaks of "the tricky mirror of memory—making it difficult to separate the real from the unreal," and Cormier has deliberately used this trick mirror to fuddle our perceptions. Paul says, "I have fictionalized so much of what happened in those days that sometimes, rereading my books and thinking of the past, I'm not sure what's real and what isn't."

Cormier himself had exactly the same problem, he admitted in the essay for *Horn Book* published just before *Fade*[8]. His motives in evoking his childhood so literally were not so much nostalgic, he has explained, as deliberate technique. "I wanted to make something impossible seem possible, by rooting it in autobiography to make it real." The curious trick, the element that makes the reader's head buzz, is that Cormier's autobiography is also Paul's autobiography, and on its reality turns the question of whether the fade is real. Paul Roget was thirteen in Frenchtown in 1938, and so was his creator. Cormier has made Paul as a writer parallel himself as a writer, including such well-known Cormierisms as a devotion to "what if." Like Paul, Cormier follows "his usual method of placing a fictional story against a very real background"—but not always. As Meredith says of Paul, he "has written his most realistic autobiographical novel yet. And if he wrote it that way, then he wanted us to believe what happened in the novel. And we must believe all of it or none of it." And Susan answers dubiously, "Maybe Paul had to create a real world so that the reader would be *forced* to believe the fantasy. But that doesn't mean the fantasy was real." So compelling is this tangled maze of truth and fiction that in the first few months after *Fade*'s publication one friend after another would take Cormier aside confidentially and ask with hesitant intensity, "Bob, *can* you fade?"

The book exerted a compelling force over Cormier, too, during its composition. "It just consumed me," he said, and he let himself go as never before. The first version was six hundred pages long. At this time, Cormier had just ended his publishing association with Pantheon and had signed new agreements with Delacorte Press. He and his new editor, Olga Litowinsky, worked together to edit the giant manuscript down to a workable size. Cormier's affection for the material had led him to write many irrelevant scenes and characters. Even after the manuscript was typeset to galleys he continued to write obsessively—Susan at Jules's funeral, Rosanna as an old lady, and so on.

The most important change involved the structure. The middle section in early versions was entirely in Jules's voice. The stodginess of his personality bothered Cormier, as did an uneasy sense that it just wasn't working. After some thought Litowinsky suggested that a new character might carry the action, perhaps a young woman. Cormier loved the idea, and "Susan was full blown within twenty-four hours." It was also a canny marketing decision on Litowinsky's part to add another teenage voice to what was becoming a rather adult novel.

Another editorial suggestion, but one that Cormier resisted, was the removal of the Winslow twins. Litowinsky felt that they added nothing to the story and was perhaps uncomfortable with the incest scene. But Cormier felt that the characters served several important purposes: the contrast of their life of wealth and ease to Paul's own working-class background showed him the other side of life; Emerson was the first to respect him as a writer; and at the twins' house the fade was again brought into play and again backfired. Cormier justified the incest scene itself, as well as the other sexual scenes in the book, by pointing out that these experiences must shock Paul enough to make him realize that the fade is a curse—and what is shocking to Paul must necessarily be so to the reader. Actually, Paul turns and covers his ears after his realization of what is happening. "I could have written a much more voluptuous scene," Cormier protests with accuracy. "I don't wallow in it. My conscience is clear. I could have made it much more graphic, and I didn't, really."

The fact remains that except for *Tenderness, Fade* is Cormier's most sexually specific novel, but these scenes come directly out of Paul's character. He is a young boy on the verge of exploring adult sexuality, but with a penchant for voyeurism because he is by nature a shy observer. Quite early in the novel we see him setting a pattern of gratification from contemplating what is forbidden, as when he reaches orgasm from staring at Rosanna's breasts. His use of the fade fits into this pattern, and he uses it to satisfy his desire to look all he wants and not be seen. Because he is by nature a sexual spy it is no accident that the fade leads him to "dark and nasty secrets it was better not to know about."

The structure of *Fade* bears some further examination. Zena Sutherland, writing for the *Bulletin of the Center for Children's Books,* said, "*Fade* is brilliant in conception, intricate in structure."[9] From one perspective, it might be described as an unpublished novel interrupted in the middle by a discussion of its reality. From another perspective, Cormier saw it as two disparate halves: a nice, docile ethnic story, and then a sudden turning point that jolts it into another kind of story entirely.[10] (That crucial point, of course, is the moment when Paul turns toward Adelard on the rain-soaked balcony and sees that his uncle has vanished.)

The publisher breaks the book into three sections labeled "Paul," "Susan," and "Ozzie," although the voice in the second section is as much Jules's as Susan's, and the third section is not Ozzie speaking but Paul, writing both in the first and third person. These divisions are useful, however, in getting a grip on the construction of the novel. There are three separate and distinct parts, connected by the plot but each with its own form, style, characters, rhythm, and intention. The Frenchtown idyll is a gentle, nostalgic coming-of-age story. The "Susan" section is a contemplative but brittle essay-with-dialogue on the expediency of reality. The last section is a horror fantasy tale that plunges along to a classic shootout. These three are linked only by the events of the story, and by the central concept of the fade. It is a measure of Cormier's skill that he has pulled them smoothly together into one unified narrative.

In addition to the three formal divisions in the novel

there is a sequence of several voices, each distinctive and clearly differentiated from the others. First there is Paul as a naïve teenager in 1938, but the actual speaker is Paul the writer remembering his own young self. Then we hear Susan's bright, contemporary speech and Jules's stodgy and authoritative cadences. Next is the contrasting voice of Paul as a depressed adult, and then Ozzie's inarticulate and angry thoughts, but filtered through Paul's mind and pen. These two switch back and forth with increasing frequency as the climax approaches, but there is never any doubt as to which is which. And last we return to an older and more responsible Susan. Technically, Cormier has pulled this off brilliantly, but for the reader, establishing so many new orientations to so many changes of speaker can be jarring—perhaps intentionally so. Zena Sutherland remarked, "The shifting of voice is not as successful here as in *I Am the Cheese,* seeming more obtrusively a literary device."[11]

The sheer number of people in Paul's big family can make it difficult for the reader to keep track of identities and relationships, but when the players are laid out in order a startling fact emerges. There can be no next fader because the line ends with Ozzie. The succession has always been from uncle to nephew. Since a nephew is the son of one's sibling, and Ozzie has no siblings, he can be no one's uncle, even if he were to live—unless Rose has another child, who could then bear a son who would be the fader's nephew. Paul has written that Rose dies childless—but then, he didn't know about the first baby until she told him.

But for the fade to end with Ozzie was not Cormier's intention, as can be seen from the argument he presented in a letter to me, saying:

```
This weekend I gave some thought
to the fade succession from un-
cle to nephew in the novel and
```

realized I had developed a blind
spot when we were discussing it.
The end of the line does not come
with Ozzie, simply because the
passage of the fade does not proceed directly from the fader (uncle). . . . Just as Adelard in
his generation did not know who
the fader would be and Paul in his
generation did not know who the
fader would be, then Ozzie, had he
lived, would not have known. But
this does not mean that the line
of succession stopped with Ozzie.
The fade continues from any of
the other nephews in the coming
generation.[12]

Another intriguing point revolves around the telling of
Ozzie's story in the third person. How does Paul, who is the
real speaker in this part, know what goes on in Ozzie's life
and thoughts when he is not with him? Isn't it proof that he
made up the whole thing, if he made up *some* things? At one
point, Cormier had Susan raise this point hopefully yet in-
conclusively with Meredith, but the passage was lost in subsequent cuts.

The struggles of Susan, Meredith, and Jules to believe,
or not believe, in the truth of Paul's manuscript are cleverly
designed to draw the reader into the same dilemma. Each has
a very good reason for not wanting to accept the story as
autobiography, aside from the disorienting prospect of invisibility as a real state. For Meredith, this potentially very
profitable manuscript will be unpublishable unless she can
convince herself it is fiction, because otherwise she will be
in the position of besmirching the reputation of a respected

writer and a dear friend (thus she sends only the first, least damaging section to Jules for corroboration). For Jules, accepting the truth of the story is unthinkable (even though he holds a key piece of evidence) because then it will be known that the family has produced a murderer. For Susan (who is withholding the same piece of evidence) there is a desperate need to think of the story as fantasy, because if it is true, it is she who must find and subdue the next fader.

Embedded in this section is a crafty piece of misdirection. When Susan begins to poke about in Meredith's apartment she tells us that she is "a terrible snoop." Aha, does she share Paul's love of secrecy and spying, and has the fade made a gender jump? Later, Meredith looks her straight in the eye and says, "Fade." We think it is a command, just for one heartbeat, and so does Susan. Has Meredith suspected, and is she testing her? But no, with her next words we know it has all been a typical Cormier trick, and Meredith has only been asking her to consider the unreality of the term when it is presented in isolation.

A last question that must be pondered in analyzing this complex novel is the meaning of the fade. Clearly Cormier is speaking about something much more portentous than a fantasy technique for becoming invisible. At one point, Delacorte had suggested that the book be called *The Fader,* a more concrete term that by contrast throws into relief the many subtle resonances of the actual title. "Fade" as a verb means not only to vanish, disappear, become unseen and to lose color, but also to lose freshness, wither; to lose strength or vitality; to decline in energy; to wane. In the movies it means to dissolve into the next scene. The fade has an effect on its possessors that goes beyond the uses to which it is put. It consumes their personalities, their souls, even their bodies. "Like color gone from an old piece of cloth," says Adelard. It sets them apart from the rest of the world, even from those they love. It leads them into temptation and delivers them to evil.

At first, Paul, like everyone, thinks invisibility brings unlimited power. "I can do anything, go anywhere, cross oceans, reach mountaintops," he exults. But almost at once he finds that the fade's promise of freedom is an illusion. Being invisible is only good for doing things you don't want anybody to see. In other words, bad things. The fade is useful solely for evil purposes, and so is inherently evil. And inherently linked to guilt, he finds. For young Paul guilt means sex, and the fade is linked immediately to his incipient voyeuristic tendencies, as with Ozzie it connects with his potential for violence. There is a corrective function in being watched, and without it Paul has lost his moral compass. Soon he is a murderer and finds that the fade has separated him even from the eyes of God. At the end, under the burden of being invisible to his Savior, he writes in despair, "Hell would not be anger but indifference."

The fade has its own purposes, its own voice that speaks in Paul's head and with Ozzie's mouth. The fade is an Other, as Paul understands when it throttles him with Ozzie's hands—"a deadly enemy, ageless, and mad." And implacable. The futile but redeeming act for Paul is a compassionate murder, as it was to have been for Barney in *The Bumblebee Flies Anyway.* The real redemption from the curse of the fade comes from reaching out to teach and comfort the next one—as Adelard knew and Susan is soon to learn.

Critics were almost unanimous in judging that this novel had joined the triumvirate of Cormier's greatest works—*The Chocolate War, I Am the Cheese,* and *After the First Death.* Several reviewers even proposed that this was Robert Cormier's best novel yet. "Cormier has once again produced a profoundly disturbing, finely crafted gem that's hard, cold, and brilliant," said *Kirkus Reviews.*[13] "There is a sense of terror in daily life, the alien stranger loose out there and also lurking within, the fading of hope and trust," wrote Hazel Rochman in *Booklist.*[14] Cathi MacRae, in the *Wilson Library*

Bulletin, called *Fade* "a paradigm for our use and abuse of power."[15] "Disturbing" was the most frequent verdict, and the one that best pinpointed the feelings of many readers who found that after turning the last page of *Fade,* it was impossible to keep from glancing nervously behind their chairs.

Notes

1. Cormier, Robert, "Creating *Fade,*" *The Horn Book Magazine,* March/April 1989, 166.

2. King, Stephen, letter to the editors of Delacorte Press, May 10, 1987.

3. Wells, H. G., *The Invisible Man,* in *Seven Science Fiction Novels of H. G. Wells,* Dover, 1934.

4. Cormier, Robert, "A Boy Who Possesses Animal Magnetism," *Los Angeles Times,* December 6, 1986, Section 5, 14.

5. "Creating *Fade,*" 166.

6. King, letter.

7. R.D., "A Look at the Creative Process," *Publishers Weekly,* July 29, 1988, 134.

8. "Creating *Fade,*" 166.

9. Sutherland, Zena, *The Bulletin of the Center for Children's Books,* November 1988, 68.

10. "Creating *Fade,*" 166.

11. Sutherland, 68.

12. Cormier, Robert, letter to the author, September 12, 1988.

13. *Kirkus Reviews,* August 1, 1988, 1147.

14. Rochman, Hazel, *Booklist,* September 1, 1988, 67.

15. MacRae, Cathi, *Wilson Library Bulletin,* February 1989, 86.

Chapter Eleven

The Younger Novellas: *Other Bells for Us to Ring,*

Tunes for Bears to Dance To, and *Heroes*

After the critical, if not the popular, success of *Fade* in the adult literary world, devotees speculated that Cormier would go on to write other novels in that larger sphere. But his work was never predictable. In his next book he pulled back from the large excesses of *Fade* to write a small story, a novella, the first of three books for younger readers that he was to write in the next few years. Although they are too different to form a set, all three of these smaller works are set in the 1940s and indirectly show the painful aftermath of World War II layered on the crimes of individual humanity. They are the most overtly religious of his novels, as we see the characters wrestling with moral problems and praying for guidance and forgiveness. And—unusual for Cormier—all three end happily, or as happily as is possible in a world that C. S. Lewis described as "enemy-occupied territory."[1]

Other Bells for Us to Ring
　　Other Bells for Us to Ring is the least known of

Cormier's novels for teens, and the most openly Catholic. In its gentleness it is reminiscent of the style of his early short stories, but while those pieces occasionally teetered on the brink of sentimentality, here the sweetness is balanced and given depth by the shadowing of his dark vision. Perhaps in recognition of the story's message of the hope to be found in faith, Cormier often referred to this book as his "Christmas novella," although he admitted that the holiday was only incidental to the plot.[2]

The story had its beginnings in Cormier's mind when Connie, who was working as a volunteer for the blind, came home one day with an amusing anecdote. On one of her home visits to blind shut-ins, an elderly lady had told her a story about her confusion and terror as a Protestant child when her best friend sprinkled her with holy water and declared her a Catholic. Bob tucked the incident away but never forgot it, and two years later when he and Connie moved into their new summer home on a nearby lake, Bob had a beautiful office room looking over the water. "Now I'm really going to write something nice here," he thought, and out of the peacefulness and happiness of that situation came *Other Bells for Us to Ring*. The book is dedicated to the memory of Hazel Tedford Heald, "who was sprinkled with holy water a long time ago," and who lived to be 104, long enough to know about the story she had inspired.

The novella was different from Cormier's previous books, and in ways beyond its short length and young audience. Among Cormier's very few female lead characters— Kate the bus driver, mad Lulu, and the voluptuous Lori—only Darcy Webster follows the usual pattern of Cormier's *male* protagonists in being internal, shy, and fearful. She is also the youngest, at eleven, and her personality is important enough to the story that Cormier's original title was *Darcy*. Although there are dark shadows, the story as a whole is "suffused with light," as one reviewer commented.[3]

This lightness and especially the touches of humor are quite unique in Cormier's somber canon.

The setting, however, is pure Cormier. Darcy and her mother live in Monument, of course, in a Frenchtown tenement. They shop at Lucier's Meat Market and go to movies at the Plymouth, and Darcy's father is in training at Fort Delta, that same Fort Delta from which General Marchand led the attack on the terrorists in *After the First Death*. And looming over the town, and the story, is the spire of St. Jude's Catholic Church. The time is 1943, a decade later than *Frenchtown Summer* and about three years earlier than *Heroes* and *Tunes,* and a year in which Cormier would have been sixteen and everybody was singing "Praise the Lord and Pass the Ammunition" and "Mairzy Doats" to keep their spirits up. From the first paragraph he colors in the World War II home front with remembered details: ration stamps, War Bonds, banners in front windows with their blue or gold stars, Shirley Temple and Jane Withers in the movies, scrap metal and paper drives.

Darcy perceives Monument as a lonesome place. She and her parents have just moved there, to a three-decker on Second Street, and in this French Catholic neighborhood Protestant Darcy feels very much an outsider. So when red-headed Kathleen Mary O'Hara chooses her to be an ally against the "Canucks" that surround them, Darcy is delighted to have a best friend and fascinated by the exotic details of Kathleen Mary's Irish Catholicism. She willingly tags along on adventures like spying on the wretched miracle seekers who come to the courtyard of St. Jude's Convent to visit ancient Sister Angela in hope of cure, and she reluctantly gives her Shirley Temple doll, a treasured confidante, to the Salvation Army because Kathleen Mary has decreed that they should help the war effort by giving up childish things. The two girls are perfectly matched: daring Kathleen Mary with her flair for dramatic exaggeration and sudden speeches, shy Darcy with her fearful gullibility. They are leader and follower, performer and audience, and one of them has a terrible secret—a pair not unlike Adam and Amy in *I Am the Cheese.*

But Kathleen Mary's Catholicism seems foreign and spooky to Darcy. Here Cormier has achieved the difficult feat of stepping outside the practices of his religion to show them as they might appear to a naïve outsider. "Everything about Kathleen Mary's Catholicism fascinated me," Darcy thinks, "as if Catholics were a different tribe of people who had somehow found their way to earth." Kathleen Mary, always eager to put on a good show, holds her friend wide-eyed with colorful explanations of unfamiliar rules and rituals: confession, Communion, purgatory, cardinal and venial sin—and the story of the man who ate meat on Friday and "choked to death. On the spot. Turned black and blue." So when the redhead lures her into the vestibule of St. Brendan's church, sprinkles her with holy water, and declares her a Catholic, Darcy runs home appalled. The scenes in which the panicky Darcy examines herself for "Catholic symptoms" are amusing but at the same time a bit sad. When Darcy suddenly remembers it is Friday and so is afraid to eat her favorite meal—"hamburg" (Cormier uses the New England dialect term), bought with her mother's precious ration stamps—we smile, but at the same time we feel pity. Humor needs distance from the object of laughter, and Cormier brings us into the hearts of his characters.

Later in the story, after Kathleen Mary's family has suddenly moved away without farewell or explanation, lonely Darcy explores St. Jude's cathedral on her own, and again Cormier gives us an outsider's half-understood view of what is most sacred to him. His picture of the interior of the fictional St. Jude's evokes the real St. Cecilia's cathedral (although some of the details are different), where Cormier said confession and prayed at Mass for seventy-five years.

But here we see through the eyes of a curious Protestant child, who compares the altar to "a huge white bedroom bureau," and the orange and gold stained-glass windows to "standing inside an exploding orange"—as contrasted with Cormier's own more spiritual childhood analogy for those windows, "like being inside the sun."

When Darcy's father is shipped out, and later reported missing in action, she finds in her desperate attempts at prayer that her casual Unitarian churchgoing has given her little useful information about the mechanics of faith. Her mother finally gives in to her persistent questioning and takes her to church, where the sermon comforts and lulls Darcy, but leaves her still asking, "How do you get God to listen to an eleven-year-old girl?" The glimpses of faith Darcy carried away from spying on Sister Angela's healing prayers have been shattered by her witnessing the suicide of a young woman who went to see the nun that day. But then Darcy encounters the child whom she saw brought to Sister Angela an invalid in leg braces, and finds her healed and happy—a miracle, the child's mother insists. "Why does God answer some prayers and not others?" Darcy wonders. Overcoming her fears, she braves the maze of hedges leading to the courtyard where Sister Angela sits, and confesses her fears and worries about Catholicism and her father's safety to the elderly nun. In a quiet scene suffused with afternoon sunlight and peace, Sister Angela helps Darcy to realize that loving and trusting God is all that matters, in spite of the hard truth that miracles sometimes happen and sometimes are denied.

" 'God comes first, you see,' Sister Angela said. 'Not whether you are this or that, Protestant or Catholic, young or old.' " Darcy is reminded of the words she has heard from Unitarian Reverend Weems: "God takes care of us all, whether you know it or not. . . . And if you pray to him he will listen." Sister Angela evokes Michelangelo's image of the creation of Adam: "Prayer is reaching out, like a hand stretched out to God and the hand can reach across eternity." It is significant that both these wise counselors are very old and frail, as if Cormier is saying that it takes a lifetime of spiritual seeking to wear away sectarian rules and doctrines and reveal the essential core of belief.

In true Hollywood fashion, Darcy's father is wounded and sent home to recover and to be with his family on Christmas Eve. And in true Cormier fashion, Darcy is accosted that evening on the porch of the three-decker by Kathleen Mary's older brother, who has come to tell Darcy that his sister has been dead for months, killed by a speeding car as she fled her father's drunken abuse. In her grief, Darcy remembers that earlier that night she heard the bells of St. Jude ringing, although the church has sworn that their music will not be heard until the war has ended. When she finds that she alone has heard the bells, she realizes she has witnessed a miracle, a message from Kathleen Mary. As she finds comfort in remembering her friend's promise that the two of them would find "other bells" to ring together, she says goodbye to her lost childhood innocence through the tiny Shirley Temple doll that has been brought to her by Kathleen Mary's brother.

At least one critic, Janice del Negro in a review for *School Library Journal,* found that the ringing of the bells misfired as a climactic plot device, saying, "The news of Kathleen Mary's death and the miracle of the bells that accompanies it have no spiritual resonance."[4] It is true that the metaphor *is* obscure, both in the Kenneth Patchen poem from which it is drawn, "At the New Year," and in Cormier's use of it. In the original it seems to express a longing for surcease of the world's misery, perhaps through human agency. However, Cormier is quoting Kathleen Mary as well as Kenneth Patchen, and we have seen, in her interpretation of "The Man with the Hoe," how spectacularly askew her understanding of a poem can be. Darcy, too, is puzzled when her friend tells her, "We'll find other bells to ring." She thinks, "I could not imagine what those other bells would be." Nor can we, other than some general sense of validation of the friendship. A far more resonant symbol is the Shirley Temple doll that Darcy gives up. Her sacrifice of the toy that has become almost a religious icon, a patient listener to all Darcy's worries and dreams, is far more human and moving than the miraculous bells, and the posthumous gift of the tiny replica rounds out the symbol perfectly.

Critics also puzzled over the intended readership for the novella, as Cormier himself had. Hazel Rochman in *Booklist* mused, "It's hard to define the audience for this novel, and the publisher says it's Cormier's first children's book, but the narrator is an adult looking back."[5] The details of the forties setting—the Orphan Annie mug, for instance—are evocative only for those who lived them, and the many movie cliches on which Cormier plays have little meaning for readers too young to have seen these films. Darcy's consciousness, like Cormier's, is steeped in these movies; she often feels "as if we were acting out a scene in a movie at the Plymouth." On the other hand, the style of the novella is much more straightforward than previous Cormier works. The story is told simply, lacking the tension that results from a gradual revelation of plot secrets, and with a minimum of the second levels and psychological complexity that are characteristic of his other writing. Delacorte chose to use a large typeface and wide margins as well as illustrations to indicate a younger readership, and chose to market the book as a Christmas gift purchase; nevertheless, the book has never become identified as a story for children. The confusion over readership has perhaps been a factor in making this, undeservedly, Cormier's forgotten book. As Mary Burns in her glowing *Horn Book* review observed, *Other Bells* is "a transcendent, multilayered story that defies simplistic categorization by the age of the audience."[6]

Tunes for Bears to Dance To

Tunes for Bears to Dance To was published two years later, in 1992, after an interlude for the YA novel *We All Fall Down.* Cormier was to come to regret the odd title, drawn from Gustave Flaubert's *Madame Bovary*: "Human language is like a cracked kettle on which we beat out tunes for bears to dance to, when all the time we are longing to move the stars to pity."[7] In answer to the continual queries about the meaning of this passage, he explained in an e-mail message to me, "What the quotation expresses, for me, is the frequent inability of people to reach out and touch each other, the inability to communicate our longings and our heartbreaks when that is really what being human is all about, this yearning to connect."[8] An explanation that seems inexplicably at variance with the theme of the book, until clarified by Cormier's modestly self-revealing further words: "As I wrote the novel the story changed (as mine often do) and the application of the quotation became a little distant (or maybe a lot)."[9] Later, in a correspondence with the translator of the Japanese edition of the book, Masaru Harada, Cormier suggested changing the title to *Henry* or *A Boy Caught In-Between.*[10] However, the title that was finally chosen for that edition caught his fancy strongly, and in a letter to Harada, he wrote, "I truly love your title *[The Voice from the Darkness of My Heart]* and may ask permission to use it for a book that I may write someday that would reflect that title."[11]

The second epigraph—"Deliver us from evil"—in its stark simplicity sums up the novel more accurately. *Tunes,* despite its small size, is an intense examination of the inner workings of evil, the purposes and methods of wickedness and its ultimate vulnerability to simple goodness. The malevolent grocer Mr. Hairston is Cormier's most purely evil villain, so much so that by the end of the story he has almost ceased to be human and has become a metaphor for the

Dark Presence. Henry Cassavant is his antithesis in his innocence and unselfish goodness, but still enough of a real boy to be tempted by Hairston's wiles. And over all is the shadow of the Nazi Holocaust, both as a horrifying historical event and as its reenactment in the destruction of the model village.

Eleven-year-old Henry Cassavant and his mother and father have moved from Monument to nearby Wickburg, hoping to escape their grief over the death of Henry's older brother, Eddie. The move hasn't helped. His parents, Henry says, spend their days "walking wearily and sorrowfully through the hours," remembering that day less than a year ago when Eddie was hit by a car, "his neck broken like a chicken bone snapped apart to make a wish." Temporarily housebound by a cast on his knee, and desperate for diversion from the atmosphere of grief, Henry watches the mental hospital next door and sees an old man leave every day with a black bag in hand. His curiosity grows (as does ours), and when the cast is finally off, Henry follows the old man to a seedy part of town (a kind of neighborhood we would never find in Monument). There, a kindly giant of a man, George Graham, welcomes him into a city-sponsored workshop for the arts, where he discovers that the old man, Mr. Levine, is a master woodcarver finding solace in creating a model of his childhood village before it was destroyed by the Nazis.

In parallel scenes, we see Henry at his after-school job at the Corner Market, where he sweeps up and stocks shelves for the scowling grocer Mr. Hairston. A bigot and a racist, Hairston's greatest pleasure is to stand by the window commenting cruelly on the "polacks" and "irishers" and "kikes" passing by. He is utterly without compassion, as Henry discovers when he tries to explain that the widowed Mrs. Karminski is lonely. "A disgrace," growls Hairston, "making a spectacle of herself crying in public." Yet when customers come into the store, his hypocritical smiles and nods are somehow even more unclean than his hatred. His smile is like his scowl turned inside out, thinks Henry, touching on the ancient idea that evil is good reversed. Hairston looks back on the shortages of the war years fondly because they gave him the power to keep people waiting in line. "I *was* a dictator. Because I had control over them," he crows, unconsciously emulating that World War II dictator who had life-and-death power over millions.

An apposition of good and evil begins to emerge between the portrait of Hairston's malevolence and Henry's innocence. Although Henry is the usual Cormier protagonist, shy and quiet, with a long list of fears, he is also naturally good and unselfish. When his knee injury keeps him home, out of concern for Mr. Hairston he recommends a friend to take his place, although he doesn't want to lose his job. He puts up with the grocer's ill humor patiently and tries to do a good job. In his prayers, he asks for his father to start gambling again, thinking that that interest will bring back his parent's zest for life, difficult as it might be for Henry and his mother. Ironically, he ends his prayer with an afterthought that is more appropriate than he knows: "And deliver us from evil."

Henry and his mother regularly ride the bus back to Frenchtown to visit Eddie's grave. The flowers they bring strike Henry as incongruous: "He had never heard Eddie say that he liked flowers. What boy did?" Instead, he imagines just the right shape for his brother's headstone—a bat and ball to celebrate Eddie's skill at baseball. The idea fires his imagination, although he knows his family could never afford such a monument in Monument. Because he knows no other adult, he makes a serious mistake. He asks Mr. Hairston for advice, and under the grocer's sudden bright-eyed interest, he reveals his dream, unwittingly putting a weapon into the hands of the enemy. When Mr. Hairston offers to help Henry, we know it cannot be out of goodness. But what evil purpose of his own might he have in mind?

Meanwhile, through his growing friendship with Mr. Levine and his admiration for the man's woodcarving skill, Henry grows to understand the healing power of the model and how for the old man it is "bringing his village, and the people who lived there, to life again."

Cormier raises the emotional ante yet again when Henry goes to the workshop and finds a celebration in progress for the delighted old man because he has won a prize for his work; his model will be exhibited at City Hall. George Graham gives a speech about the broader meaning of the village that also explains how this symbol functions in the novel. "This village will be a reminder to everybody about what happened during the war. But also about survival. And how good can overcome evil."

On the day that the old man passes by and draws Mr. Hairston's attention, these two parts of the story come together with an ominous click. Mr. Hairston questions Henry closely about exactly how much love is invested in the creation of the village. For him the malicious equation is how much harm he can do. Henry in his innocence tells the grocer everything he knows about the woodcarver, but he feels uneasy as he resumes work, as if somehow he has betrayed the old man. When he discovers that Hairston is abusing his daughter, Doris, he finally begins to have some sense of the depth of the man's depravity and the extent to which he himself is in danger. That danger begins to surface as the grocer promises Henry a gift of the monument he yearns for, and then withdraws the offer without explanation and suddenly fires him, playing the boy like a hooked fish. Goodness is handicapped by its straightforwardness, its lack of comprehension of the deviousness of evil, and Henry wonders "why Mr. Hairston would do a thing like that."

He soon knows. The revelation of Hairston's plan for

him to destroy the village has a visceral impact, for both Henry and the reader. "Henry recoiled as if Mr. Hairston had struck him in the stomach, taking his breath away." The grocer knows the generous spirit of his young victim well. The incentives—and the punishments—he offers are all for others, not for Henry himself. The monument for Eddie, the better job for Henry's mother at the Wickburg Diner—even Henry's own job, which helps his family survive. Hairston's threats, too, are for people Henry loves, and, like those of Archie Costello in *The Chocolate War,* are "made all the more horrible by his tender, gentle voice." Even worse is the perversity of evil's rationalizing itself as he, like Trent in *The Rag and Bone Shop,* gives his victim reasons to give in: "Listen, it will do him good. . . ."

Henry's instant reaction is "I can't do that." But as the grocer persists, he becomes confused and flees. The next chapter opens with a device Cormier used once before, in *Beyond the Chocolate War,* to startling effect. The bad thing that we fear is indeed happening—in this case, the destruction of the village—but then it dissolves into a bad dream. When Henry's mother comes to comfort him, he longs to tell her about the decision he must make. And if he does? Here again Cormier makes the point that is a constant in his moral universe, that intervention in the name of love could make the difference.

As Hairston backs Henry into a corner with more persuasion and more threats, our understanding of the extent of his moral corruption grows. When he reveals that he has loaned money to the owner of the Wickburg Diner to have another pawn indebted to him and forced to carry out his will, we see how his entire life is a web of schemes. Finally he issues an ultimatum to Henry, sending the boy away with his week's pay in his shirt pocket and orders to smash the village that night or never come back. "Why did Mr. Hairston want the old man's village destroyed?" Henry wonders fearfully. And why has he chosen Henry to do it? Two questions with answers that Henry is not ready to face.

Henry struggles with the terrible dilemma, telling himself he won't do it when all the while his feet are carrying him to the workshop. He unwillingly spots a convenient wooden mallet and finds the perfect hiding place in the storeroom closet, coincidences that make him wonder if he is destined to carry out this dreadful mission. He plans to wrestle with his conscience for the two hours he must wait until closing, but like the disciples in the Garden of Gethsemane, he falls asleep, and when he wakes, the rustling of a rat propels him out into the workroom, where he lifts the mallet over the village and stands paralyzed by indecision. And then an exquisitely ironic touch, and one that Cormier and his editor, Craig Virden, debated in an exchange of letters: a rat runs across the table, and Henry, startled, drops the heavy mallet on the table, crushing the village.

Henry has not done Hairston's will—but he has, as he learns when he runs out into the street and finds the man waiting for him, his eyes bright with anticipation. Although he is consumed with remorse, Henry is still the innocent. He tells Hairston exactly what has happened, never stopping to consider that the truth may jeopardize his reward. "Whether you wanted to or not, you did it," Hairston gloats. But Henry desperately needs to know why it was so important, why the grocer hates the old man so much. The answer is breathtaking in its terrible simplicity and historical resonance: "He's a Jew." And then the other question—why not "hire some wise guys to do it?" Why has he chosen Henry? Another simple and horrifying answer: because corrupting innocence makes the evil deed sweeter. Henry suddenly realizes the central purpose in all these events: "He didn't want me to be good anymore." Hairston acknowledges the revelation with "a ghastly smile, like the smile on a Halloween mask"—and we, like Henry, shiver because we know at last what this man is.

But for once good wins out in the end. Henry staunchly refuses the rewards that will confirm his guilt, and Hairston panics, pleading pathetically as Henry runs off through the rain, "It's not complete unless you accept the rewards. Otherwise the smashing means nothing. . . ." But evil *does* mean nothing, is essentially meaningless, and Henry's refusal forces Hairston to see this. Later Henry shares the precious key with Doris for her own salvation: "The important thing is that I stood up to him. . . . And there was nothing he could do about it. Nothing." The evil grocer with his merciless eyes has seemed implacable, but he is defeated by the one right irrational gesture.

In a conclusion that is the closest Cormier ever came to a happy ending, we see Mr. Levine contentedly at work restoring the ruined village, Henry's family returned to their home in Frenchtown, and Henry at prayer, generously asking for forgiveness for Hairston—and for himself.

But Doris still drifts like a wraith though her life, unable to find the courage to confront her father.

In its one hundred pages this little book takes on some very big ideas. The novel is essentially a morality play with only two characters, a structure that Cormier was to use again to more subtle effect in *The Rag and Bone Shop*. It must always be remembered that Cormier's perception of evil is theological, not psychological, and so he presents Hairston as an abstraction of pure wickedness. He is utterly despicable, without one saving aspect or interest, not one detail to humanize him. While it is a fascinating intellectual exercise to look at evil bare, it is not very useful for moral growth. The lesson we need to draw from contemplating evil (the Nazi Holocaust, for instance) is that we are all capable of it, to one degree or another, and we must recognize and root out this potential in ourselves. No such lesson emerges from the portrait of Hairston. He is too extreme, too pure in his evildoing, something which is not true of Cormier's more complex villains. Archie's bitter grace, Artkin's love of country, even Eric Poole's charisma give them a flesh-and-blood believability that Mr. Hairston lacks, chilling though he is.

But the story has great impact, with its tight, controlled plot and devastating climax, and it has proven appeal for young teens. Teachers have found that it brings a unique contribution to Holocaust studies. Cormier was happy to hear praise from Jewish schools where *Tunes* was welcomed into the curriculum and was also pleased when the little novel won the Catholic Book of the Year Award in Germany.

Heroes

Just what are the qualities or actions that make us regard some people as heroes? In this ironically titled novella about heroes who are perhaps not heroes, Cormier probes that question mercilessly as it is reflected in the shattered life of a young returned soldier whose terrible guilt has led him to an act of unwilling heroism and a burning desire for revenge. This third novella has more substance and significance, is more abstruse in theme and more complex in style than the other two short books we have just examined. Cormier's penetrating analysis of the nature of heroism is not beyond the comprehension of junior high students, and the additional themes of hidden identity, forgiveness, and vengeance fueled by guilt make *Heroes* a rich and rewarding classroom study, as well as an engrossing private read for all ages. Cormier's editor, Karen Wojtyla, regarded *Heroes* as his Hemingway novel, and critics concurred. "Emulating the sparse, sturdy prose of Francis' literary idol, Ernest Hemingway, Cormier sketches the dark underbelly of a brief historic time in shadows that will follow the reader long after the story has ended," said Leslie Rogers in *Booklist*.[12] Other reviewers were equally emphatic in their praise for the novella's strength.

Cormier explained the genesis of the book in an e-mail: "I wanted to write *Heroes* to express how I feel about heroism. The impetus came from two areas—the fiftieth anniversary of D-Day, which recalled those war years, and the obituaries in the local paper of men and women who had fought World War II. The obits told of what they did in that war, stuff that surprised me even with people I had known. There was one really heroic guy—his daughter went to school with one of my daughters. I'd see him at PTA meetings, etc., and I never knew what heroics he'd performed until I read about it. He ran an auto service garage and never in all the time I knew him talked about the war."[13]

It seems strange to hear Robert Cormier, a writer who referred to the parachutes over Fort Devens as "evil flowers" and compared extreme patriotism to terrorism in *After the First Death,* honoring military glory. But it must be remembered that while Cormier's poor eyesight kept him out of the army during World War II, he, like many people of that generation, recalls that huge conflict as the last, or perhaps the only moral war. His further explanation is closer to the understanding he reached in the novel, and is a sentiment that suffuses all of his writing: "My heroes are the ordinary, everyday persons who do their duty quietly, without fanfare, whether it's fighting a war or going to work every day. I feel that we are surrounded by heroes and saints in our daily lives."[14]

The sentence that opens the book is masterfully crafted in its four-part rhythm, its compact conveyance of information, and its final phrase like a blow to the gut. "My name is Francis Joseph Cassavant and I have just returned to Frenchtown in Monument and the war is over and I have no face."[15] Here in one sentence we learn who and where and when— but not yet why—and arrows point to tantalizing questions. Which war—Civil, World War I or II, Vietnam, Iraq, or perhaps even a future war yet to be fought? And why has he come back? Most of all, what does Francis Joseph Cassavant mean by those chilling words: "I have no face"? Is this metaphorical? Or actual? And if the latter, how could such a thing have happened?

Characteristically, in this first section Cormier answers none of the tantalizing questions he has raised. Instead, with a shocking lack of emotion Francis describes his not-face in excruciating detail, not his appearance to others, but what it *feels like* to be inside such a ruin. He can see and hear, but his ears are "bits of dangling flesh" that brush his neck; his nose has been reduced to two gaping holes, constantly running— like tears—or clogged, so that his throat is dry and his voice is hoarse; his thighs sting where skin has been taken to be grafted onto his cheeks, and his gums have shrunk so that his dentures click when he talks and roll around inside his mouth. Cormier leaves us to picture such ghastly deformity for ourselves.

The opening passages also subtly begin to reveal Francis's character—his lack of self-pity, his gentle sweetness, and his obsessive singleness of purpose about his secret mission. His response to Dr. Abrams's grotesque jokes about his wounds is not anger at the man's cruel insensitivity, but inward-turning shame at what he perceives to be his own lack of a sense of humor. When people turn away from him in the street, he sympathizes with their revulsion. He is pleased that Mrs. Belander, a childhood friend, doesn't recognize him when he rents a room in her house because anonymity is important to him—for a reason we don't yet know. His romantic nature shows in his hopes that the white scarf covering his face flows behind him as he walks, like that of some flying ace, but he is realistic enough to realize that it probably doesn't.

And he is religious. His second act, after finding a place to live, is to go to church, to light a candle at St. Jude's. There, amid the "odors of forgiveness" of old incense and burning wax, he prays, in a passage that is striking in the economy of its exposition, for his wounded friend Enrico, for his dead father and mother, for the uncle who housed him, for Nicole Renard, and for Larry LaSalle. From hints and clues we begin to learn Francis's history and his future mission and its main players. In an intriguing ironic twist, he prays for God's forgiveness for Larry LaSalle and then is consumed with shame for that prayer because he is not willing to forgive the man himself, to let go of his determination to kill him. But why not pray for forgiveness for himself, for the sin of omission that weighs so heavily on his heart? Pragmatically, because this question only arises on a second reading; Cormier hasn't yet told us about this sin. But another, more important reason is that as a writer Cormier understands that on some level Francis knows that to find forgiveness from God at this point would derail his mission, his consuming need to wipe out his own sin by killing the person who indirectly caused it.

Francis's courtship of Nicole Renard follows the typical Cormier pattern—the girl assured, cheerful, assertive; the boy yearning but immobilized by shyness. Francis's passive but obsessive nature leads him to lurk for days on the piazza of the tenement, hoping that Nicole will pass by and notice him. When she finally speaks to him as he perches on the railing, it is only to tease: "Don't fall off, Francis." But he has already fallen—hard—in love with her, and in the future he will be a fallen hero. Other resonances of language, not quite puns, abound under the surface of the narrative around the word *face*. Francis has "lost face" with Nicole; he "faces up" to his mission to "face down" Larry LaSalle, etc. Another Cormier pattern we have seen before is to use a term slightly out of tone with the narration, for which both the primary and secondary dictionary definitions apply—Francis's oddly stilted word "mission," for example, which means "a self-imposed duty," but also can be understood here in a military sense ("a combat operation assigned to an individual or unit") or a religious one ("sent to do religious work in a foreign land").[16]

Although Cormier keeps us on his hook by withholding until later two crucial bits of information—the reason Francis wants to kill Larry and the story of how he lost his face—the book now moves on to begin to explore the theme of heroism in war. "Everybody wanted to go to war in those days to defeat the Japs and the Germans," remembers Francis. But then he contrasts this patriotic sentiment with a scene from the real war, in a passage that phases seamlessly from reality to dream and back again. As Francis's platoon, wary of snipers, enters a ruined village, one of the terrified men blurts out, "What the hell are we doing here anyway?" The veterans who congregate at the St. Jude Club after the war talk about their hopes and plans, but not their battle experiences. Only when he is drunk does Arthur Rivier confess, "We weren't heroes. We were only there." Why do heroes so seldom seem heroic to themselves? In an interview Cormier cast his answer as a question: "Who are the real heroes? The one who does a spectacular feat or that everyday soldier who was just there, homesick, probably had diarrhea, and was not particularly brave, but stayed and did the job?"[17]

In the later part of the novel, Larry LaSalle has returned as one of those heroes. Like Francis, he has been awarded the Silver Star for bravery. When he first appeared in Monument two years earlier, Larry, with his wide shoulders and narrow hips, his skill as an athlete and a dancer, and his easy charm, is a charismatic figure of glamour; there is something magical about him to Francis and the other young people of the town. He is larger than life, like a movie star. And mysterious—dark rumors suggest that he has left show business and come back to little Monument because he has "gotten into trouble" in New York City. The young people of Monument flock around him as he creates a place for them in the dilapidated recreation center and, with what seems like genuine concern, sets about building their self-confidence with sports and shows.

But the names of those songs and dances have a dark edge: "Autumn Leaves," "The Dying Cowboy," and especially Nicole's solo, "Dancing in the Dark," which foreshadows the scene of LaSalle's betrayal. The recreation center, too, has an ominous nickname—the Wreck Center—that reflects not only the murder-suicide that took place there years ago at a wedding, but also its central role as the center of the wrecks of the lives of the three main characters by the end of the story. When Larry sees that Francis is good at table tennis, he gives him a way to shine by elevating the sport to sudden importance with a tournament. The final match is between the two of them, and during the game Francis realizes that while the spectators think he is playing brilliantly, Larry is letting him win, in such a way that only he knows it. His victory is spoiled, even though he wins the tournament and with it Nicole's admiration. This subtle cruelty reveals a new side of Larry, and when Francis looks into "his narrowed eyes," they are "suddenly inscrutable, mysterious." Much later, the parents of Monument remember LaSalle as "a bright pied piper for their children." A compliment? Only if you don't recall that the little ones who followed that magical leader were led into an opening in a mountain that closed around them.

Larry leaves for the front, and two years later he is welcomed back to Monument as "one of the great heroes of Pacific action" and "the town's first big war hero." After a gala celebration and dance at City Hall, which the young people observe from the balcony, Larry leads them in a long conga line down the street to the Wreck Center for their own party. "Larry was our war hero, yes, but he had been a hero long before he went to war," thinks Francis. His hero worship dies with shattering suddenness that night, when Larry asks Nicole to stay for a last dance alone with him, and uses his almost hypnotic power to persuade a reluctant Francis to leave. But Nicole has entreated him to stay, and something about the situation makes Francis uneasy, and so, instead of confronting Larry, he waits furtively in the foyer.

Here again we see Cormier's fascination with hiddenness and concealed identity and its effect on action. As we have seen, the idea occurs over and over again in his work, most strikingly in the invisibility of the fade, but also in Barney Snow's artificially constructed past, Adam's false identity under the Witness Relocation Program, Miro's fascination with the mask, and many other guises. In his last years Cormier took great delight in lurking anonymously on young adult literature Listservs on the Internet, observing what people said about his books when they didn't know he was listening. "I really believe that most people hide who they really are," he once told me. "And I think we all have hidden lives."[18] In Francis he has created a character in whom an inherent compulsion to hide is made visible in his facelessness and his concealing bandages. "He is really in disguise," Cormier told an interviewer. "But he is in disguise for two reasons: because he is going to commit this act of revenge and doesn't want people to know who he is. But he is also hiding from his real identity, too, and from something that he did in his past. I have two kinds of identity involved here, which I love to do."[19]

In Francis the tendency to passive observation from concealment becomes a fatal flaw that leads to a terrible sin of omission, a facet of spiritual trespass that Cormier always found more blameworthy than active sins of commission. As Francis listens to the muffled sounds from the other room, he knows what is going on but is paralyzed to intervene, or even to comfort Nicole when she rushes past in her torn blouse, flashing him a glance that is dark with his betrayal. He stays on in hiding as Larry leaves whistling a casual tune, his responsibility for committing the rape resting far more easily on his soul than Francis's guilt for not preventing it. By suggesting the rape only indirectly, through Francis's suspicions and Nicole's dishevelment, Cormier neatly bypassed the censor's red flag of graphic sexuality, but the subtlety of the scene has its drawbacks. Some more literal teens have missed the point, thinking that Larry has merely groped and rumpled Nicole, so that Francis's burning mission for vengeance seems an overreaction. Such a misunderstanding destroys the impact of this key scene, the revelation at last of why Francis has returned to Monument, why he wants to stay anonymous, why he wants revenge so badly.

Earlier, one of the veterans at the St. Jude Club has recognized Francis and revealed to us that he was wounded by throwing himself on a grenade, thereby saving the lives of the others in his platoon. But only Francis knows that this "heroic" act is also tainted by his passive nature. Larry has returned to the war immediately after the attack. Francis again lurks, this time outside Nicole's house, for days until she emerges to accuse and reject him. Then he, too, leaves to join the army, not for patriotic reasons, but because rather than suffering a disgraceful death by leaping from the steeple of St. Jude's, the war, a battle, seems an easy way to end his life, and thus his guilt. So the grenade is only the implementation of that desire for escape. In not facing his sin, he has lost his face.

At the very beginning of the story, Francis tells us that he has a gun in his duffel bag. Now, as Francis goes to confront Larry LaSalle at last, the time has come when, for the sake of the structure of the novel, the gun must be fired. "The gun is like a tumor on my thigh as I walk through the morning streets," he thinks. But in an exquisitely constructed interchange like a graceful and surprising dance, Cormier brings his themes together as Francis remembers how this man was a hero to all of them, and a weak and diminished but still charismatic Larry confesses his attraction to young girls, but then asks the profound question that haunted Cormier and robs Francis of his revenge: "Does that one sin of mine wipe away all the good things?" As Francis faces Larry down with his trembling gun, the older man pulls out his own pistol, not to threaten his former pupil but to say, "One gun is enough for what has to be done." And as Francis goes down the stairs, he hears a shot from above as Larry ends his own life. *A* gun, but not *the* gun, has been fired.

The mission has been completed, but not by Francis. He finds Nicole at a convent school and receives her forgiveness as she asks him in return to absolve her of her guilt for rejecting him. In the railroad station, as he waits for the train that will take him away for good, Francis remembers what he said to Nicole about not knowing who the real heroes are, and he thinks of his old platoon: "Scared kids, not born to fight and kill. Who were not only there but who stayed, did not run away, fought the good war. And don't talk about it now. And didn't receive a Silver Star. But heroes, anyway. The real heroes." He considers buying a typewriter and getting started on their story, tracking down Dr. Abrams for the promised plastic surgery. . . . And then he glances at his duffel bag, picks it up, and heads for the next train.

A happy ending? Perhaps. When questioned about this, Cormier was anxious that his readers not settle for easy outcomes. "Well, a hopeful ending, anyway?" I persisted. He smiled. "Well, maybe. I don't know. That ending when he looks down at the duffel bag—"

"And you remember what's *in* the duffel bag," I interrupted.

He smiled, and after a moment he said, "Well, I really love ambiguity."[20]

1. Lewis, C. S., *Mere Christianity,* Touchstone edition, Simon & Schuster, 1996, 51.

2. Cormier, Robert, letter to the author, February 3, 1990.

3. Perren, Susan, *Quill and Quire,* February 1991, 25.

4. Del Negro, Janice, *School Library Journal,* review of *Other Bells for Us to Ring,* November 1990, 137.

5. Rochman, Hazel, *Booklist,* October 1, 1990, 325.

6. Burns, Mary M., *The Horn Book Magazine,* November/December 1990, 742.

7. Flaubert, Gustave, *Madame Bovary,* 1857, part II, chapter 12.

8. Cormier, Robert, e-mail to the author, April 7, 1999.

9. Ibid.

10. Cormier, Robert, fax to Masaru Harada in care of Rei Uemura, November 28, 1996.

11. Cormier, Robert, letter to Masaru Harada, March 23, 1997.

12. Rogers, Leslie, review of *Heroes, Booklist,* June 1, 1998, 1745.

13. Cormier, Robert, e-mail to the author, July 14, 1998.

14. Ibid.

15. The duplication of last names with Henry Cassavant of *Tunes for Bears to Dance To* is total coincidence. Cormier gives no hints that there might be a relationship.

16. *American Heritage Dictionary of the English Language,* College edition, William Morris, ed., Houghton Mifflin, 1975.

17. Zitlow, Connie S., and Tobie R. Sanders, "Conversations with Robert Cormier and Sue Ellen Bridgers: Their Life and Work as Writers," *Ohio Journal of the English Language Arts,* Winter/Spring 1999, 36.

18. Campbell, Patty, "Conversing with Robert Cormier," Amazon.com, http://www.amazon.com /exec/obidos/tg/feature/-/5191.

19. Zitlow, 37.

20. Campbell, Patty, "Conversing with Robert Cormier," Amazon.com.

Chapter Twelve

The Middle Novels: *We All Fall Down* and

In the Middle of the Night

During the publication period of the three novellas for younger readers we have just examined, Connie Cormier compiled and edited a collection of her husband's earlier newspaper columns, most of them written under the pseudonym John Fitch IV. Titled *I Have Words to Spend: Reflections of a Small-Town Editor,* the book, like the 1980 short-story collection *Eight Plus One,* had little teen appeal but was of great interest to Cormier aficionados for the light these earlier short pieces shed on the author's life and work.

Meanwhile, during this period Cormier also wrote two novels for older readers that are typical of his style and themes, but have not achieved the highest places in the ranks of his work, although they are respected and admired. They are regarded rather as middle books that fill out the Cormier panoply of ideas and genres. Both are psychological thrillers, novels of social conscience, neither is set in Monument; both depend for their denouements on extravagantly deranged characters; and one—surprisingly—is a love story.

The first of these, *We All Fall Down,* opens with an extraordinary passage that describes the ugly details of a house-trashing by four teenage boys. The content is shocking, certainly, and this first page and a half has drawn censors to the book like flies. But what makes this passage so remarkable is not so much what it says, but how it says it. The fine craftsmanship that shapes the telling is worthy of a closer look.

Janis D. Flint-Ferguson, in an article written for the *Ohio Journal of the English Language Arts* in 1999, describes how she drew on the Cormier archives at Fitchburg State College to ferret out original drafts of this and other Cormier manuscripts in order to use them as the basis for a classroom study on the writing process.[1]

Flint-Ferguson found eight progressive versions of the opening of *We All Fall Down.* The earliest drafts begin, "They were in the house exactly forty-eight minutes. . . ." Later, a date and time are added, although not the hour or the ironic April Fools' eve that made it to the finished book: "They entered the house at exactly 9:12 p.m., on a clear and chilly evening, the last Thursday of April." Many small changes and adjustments show the writer perfecting his work. More vigorous verbs are substituted ("slashed" for "tore," for example), and events are rearranged for more impact. Word order is shifted for better sound ("plates and cups and saucers" becomes "china cups and saucers and plates"), and more visual and aural images are added ("assorted crystal," "magnificent hutch"). Most of all, there is a tightening and a shifting so that a rhythm emerges. Compare, for instance, the taut final rendering of the opening sentence—"They entered the house at 9:02 p.m. on the evening of April Fools' Day"—with the more wandering earlier example above.[2]

Beyond Flint-Ferguson's article, a startling fact gradually

becomes apparent to a perceptive critic: Cormier, with the blunt, powerful words of this meticulously structured passage, is foreshadowing the realization of the unconscious poesy in many sections of his work that was not generally acknowledged until the publication of the verse novel *Frenchtown Summer*.

This becomes clear if the passage is recast in poetic format and separated into stanzas. The groups of triple repetition are like the verses of a song, and the variation of "They spray-painted the walls orange" is like a gasp breaking into a description of horror. There are two sections, each beginning with a statement of the hour, separated by a shift into prose describing Karen's homecoming. The concluding stanza uses only seventeen words to create an unforgettably pitiful picture of the young girl's broken body:

"They entered the house at 9:02 p.m. on the evening of April Fools' Day."

```
In the next forty-nine minutes,
     They shit on the floors
     And pissed on the walls
     And trashed their way through the seven-
     room Cape Cod cottage.

They overturned furniture,
     Smashed the picture tubes in three
     television sets,
     Tore two VCRs from their sockets
     And crashed them to the floor.

They spray-painted the walls orange.

They flooded the bathrooms,
     Both upstairs and down,
     And flushed face towels
     Down the toilet bowls.
```

They broke every mirror in the place
    And toppled a magnificent hutch to the
    floor,
    Sending china cups
        and saucers
            and plates
                and assorted crystal
                through the air.

In the second-floor bedrooms, they pulled
out dresser drawers,
    Spilled their contents on the floor,
    Yanked clothing from the closets
    And slashed the mattresses.

In the downstairs den,
    They performed a special job on the
    spinet,
    Smashing the keys with a hammer,
    The noise like a crazy soundtrack to
    the sounds of plunder. . . .

At 9:51 p.m., the invaders left the house,

Abandoning the place as suddenly as they
had arrived,
    Slamming the doors,
    Rattling the windows,
    Sending shudders along the walls and
    ceilings.

They left behind
    Twenty-three beer cans,
    Two empty vodka bottles,

```
And damage later estimated at twenty
thousand dollars.

And, worst of all,
    Karen Jerome,
    Bruised and broken
    Where she lay sprawled
        on
            the
                cellar
                    floor.
```

After we have plummeted into the story with this stunning opening, the narrative unfolds cinematically, scene by
scene, without chapter breaks. Initially, the viewpoint shifts
from the omniscient camera to the mysterious watcher
named the Avenger, then to Jane Jerome's stunned reaction
to the invasion and its aftermath, and finally we are back at
the time of the trashing, in Buddy's mind as he desecrates
Jane's second-floor bedroom by breaking the mirror and
vomiting on the floor.

As the other three howl and destroy downstairs, it soon
becomes clear that Buddy Walker is on a different level,
both figuratively and literally. This is not your typical shy
and bookish Cormier protagonist. Buddy has been a star
athlete, and his sister is "dismayed by his lackadaisical
ways, his lack of ambition, the way he bumped into things."
Unlike Harry Flowers and his amoral sidekicks, Buddy is a
decent kid, but he's drunk—and hurting. His family is coming apart, and he and his sister, Addy, have become "two
kids whose parents were divorcing, living in a house where
nobody loved anybody else anymore." In his pain Buddy
has let Harry Flowers introduce him to the sweet release of
alcohol, and in a few weeks he has become enslaved to its
power to soothe the hate and the ache. Now he feels "like he

is floating, his feet barely touching the floor . . . letting himself go, carried along by this terrific feeling of drift, thinking: the hell with everything and everybody. Especially home." An odd detail in this scene dramatizes how Buddy is different from the out-of-control vandals downstairs. When he breaks the mirror, he cuts himself on a shard. Quite calmly he finds a box of Band-Aids in the bathroom, wipes away the blood, and applies the bandage, stowing a second one in his pocket for later.

Suddenly he becomes aware of a silence from below. As he descends the stairway he sees that fourteen-year-old Karen Jerome has made the mistake of arriving home unexpectedly and the vandals are attempting to rape her. When she breaks loose, Harry pushes her down the cellar stairs in frustration, and in sudden panic, they all flee the scene. In *From Romance to Realism: 50 Years of Growth and Change in Young Adult Literature,* Michael Cart comments that "their unmotivated, violent behavior makes no sense to reasonable readers, and most people would find equally incomprehensible their complete lack of remorse for what they have done. After the trashing and the assault . . . , they adjourn to a nearby restaurant and argue—not about the immorality of what they have done, but about the relative merits of ketchup and mustard as condiments."[3]

"The leader of the self-appointed wrecking crew," continues Cart, "is a high-school senior named Harry Flowers, an upper-middle-class son of privilege whose father is a famous architect."[4] In the lineup of Cormier villains, Harry is a smaller and cruder version of Archie Costello, but without the grace and elegance that Archie brings to his evil tricks. Harry's malevolence is spiteful and pointless, like holding his car's speed to a crawl to frustrate drivers behind him, and while he delights in corrupting Buddy's innocence, he seems more a sociopath than a demonic presence. For one moment he even engages our pity, as he brags to Buddy that when the police apprehended him, he took all the blame and his father helped him out. "My father loves me. He wrote the check and asked no questions." "But love is more than writing a check and looking the other way," Michael Cart says, "and though Harry doesn't, the reader implicitly understands how ironic that statement 'he loves me' is intended to be."[5]

The Avenger, on the other hand, is clearly psychotic in his delusions of revenge, a mysterious, faceless personage who watches and schemes from hiding. Who is he? Cormier enjoys laying out the puzzle here by presenting two candidates—the book-toting fifth grader Amos Dalton and the slow-witted handyman Mickey Looney—and the red herring that the Avenger regards himself as eleven years old. He tells us about two murders he has committed: that of a neighborhood bully (how Cormier relishes getting even with these bullies who appear so often in his work!) and that of his own grandfather when the old man began to suspect something. Right up to the end the misdirection keeps us guessing, and the addition of the Avenger's menace also adds an otherworldly dimension to the domestic tragedy and builds suspense into the narrative. And, as Cart perceives, "this character also provides a kind of psychic relief. Since he is clearly insane, his actions become more comprehensible and less disturbing than the equally violent—but morally incomprehensible—actions performed by the superficially 'normal' kids."[6]

Jane Jerome's voice is a welcome note of sanity in this four-part chorus of a madman, a sociopath, an alcoholic, and a nice suburban girl. Jane grieves after the trashing, for the violation of her home and for Karen, still in a coma in the hospital. She struggles with guilt over her last words to her sister, said in the heat of a sibling quarrel: "Will you please go have an accident?" The love and support of her family is a bulwark to her, until Harry plants the poisonous suspicion with the police that it was Jane who gave the trashers the key to her house. Alienated from her family, she also loses her two best friends, who have no understanding of what she is going through. She feels "empty, dead inside. Like a vessel waiting to be filled." Soon Buddy's love fills that vacuum. Obsessed with this girl he has harmed, he begins to follow her, and eventually they meet accidentally at the mall, when Buddy (in a neat symbolic reference to the title) falls down, and Jane tries to ease his embarrassment by lying that on the first day of school, she, too, fell down. From these first words they are in love, "instantly and irrevocably."

Cormier had always wanted to write a sweet love story, and he had thought that *After the First Death* might be the one, but it turned out otherwise. When *We All Fall Down* began to move in that direction, he was apprehensive "because I was applying my memories of what it would be like. . . . I know today there's all this knowledge kids are supposed to have about sex, but I think there's still a kind of an innocence there. When boy and girl get together, they're still fumbling. . . . And so I just followed my instincts about what I thought it would be like." Those instincts were dependable guides. The passages describing the love of Buddy and Jane are lyrical in their sweetness, but honest and recognizable to anyone who has ever suffered that divine madness, as when Buddy looks at Jane "as if he was listening not only to her voice but to some sweet music coming from somewhere. And the somewhere was her." But still, Cormier told me, he worried. "Is it really working? Is a kid going to think that this isn't really the way it happens? But, gee, I got some wonderful letters—I got a letter from a girl who said that she rereads that last part . . . 'over and over and it still breaks my heart. . . . I want it so much not to be that way, and I'm always drawn to it.' "

Because, of course, a love story has to have a sad ending to have that yearning quality that is so entrancing. But this love affair was doomed from the beginning, as Cormier admitted, and this is what makes it so fascinating to watch. We know that Jane will find out Buddy's secret sooner or later, if not from Harry or a misguided attempt by Buddy to clear his conscience, then from Karen when she wakes from her coma. And when Jane learns that Buddy was the one who desecrated and contaminated her bedroom, it will all be over. So as their love grows, we desperately want to warn them away from the abyss, but there is no way to avoid it. When Jane finally does learn the truth from the Avenger, a possibility we hadn't anticipated, her love dies, and with it the possibility of Buddy's redemption. Yet we, like Buddy, continue to hope that somehow she will find it in her heart to forgive him. "In the haunting last scene of the book," says Cart, "Jane and Buddy meet, once again by accident, in the mall. Buddy is now a lost soul, drinking again and lying about it, lying about and denying the reality of his life."[7] Jane turns away from him, steps on the escalator, and slowly ascends, not looking back, leaving him down below. "It is obviously no exaggeration to equate 'down below' with Buddy's personal hell, and Jane's ascension with—not heaven, exactly, but the possibility of a happy future. For her, at least, it is a cautiously optimistic ending. For Buddy . . . well, Buddy is fatally flawed, incapable of making the moral choice, and so he is destroyed."[8]

This wrenching scene is the true emotional catharsis of the story, but preceding it is another climax that winds up the Avenger plot thread. Jane is accosted on the street by Amos Dalton, who implores her to come with him because of some nameless emergency. Things have been going well for Jane—Karen has emerged from her coma and is healing; her parents are recovering their balance; her love affair with Buddy is blooming. But now, nervously suspecting another catastrophe, she follows Amos. (Aha! we think. The Avenger!) Cormier here obliquely acknowledges his debt for the impending episode in the books Amos is carrying: "Stephen King kind of books with gruesome covers plus a copy of *The Adventures of Tom Sawyer*" (Cormier's childhood favorite). But we have been misled once again. The Avenger turns out to be not Amos, but Mickey Looney, who has paid Amos to bring Jane to him and who has delusions that he is still the eleven-year-old who killed the bully and his grandfather. In a messy scene saturated with blood and vomit, Jane uses her wits to save herself, and Mickey Looney commits suicide—but only after revealing Buddy's guilt.

The clue to the beginning of understanding for any Cormier book lies in the title. About halfway through the book, Buddy notices that Harry delights "in finding the rotten side of anything." Watching a group of children playing ring-around-the-rosy, he tells Buddy that the song with its refrain of "we all fall down" refers to the Black Plague. Michael Cart goes further to find a theme for all Cormier's writing here, in that "his work is informed by an overarching, personal vision . . . summarized by . . . the very title of the book we have been discussing. . . . The plague, thus, provides the symbolic underpinning for this book about the death—not of the body but of the spirit."[9] Because, as Harry sneers, "We all fall down, don't we?"

In the Middle of the Night

In 1995, just after the publication of *In the Middle of the Night*, Cormier shared with me a terrible story about the book's background.

> About three years ago, one summer, we were up at our place at the lake, and I thought I woke up early in the morning—it was light out. And the most terrifying thing in the world happened to me. I went blank. Utterly and completely blank. But

I *knew* I had gone blank. It was terrifying—awareness without content. It lasted probably about thirty seconds; I don't think it was a minute. But I can hardly describe it. All I could see or hear was like snow on a television set. I mean, when you fall asleep and don't dream, there's no awareness, but when you *realize* "My brain isn't working," it's awful.

I'm not saying it was a near-death experience, because I don't know what it was. You know, you hear a lot about near-death experiences, but all you hear is the light at the end of the tunnel. The most terrifying thing about this was waiting for it to happen again.

Was it a minor stroke, one of my neurons exploded? Because when I finally told Connie about it—I didn't tell her until a year and a half, two years later, when I knew I was going to use it in this novel—she wanted me to go to the doctor for a brain scan or something. I did do some research on it, and I thought, "Well, if it happens again, I'll go." But even now, if snow comes on the television it gives me a jolt.[10]

Ever the craftsman, Cormier decided to use his own terror to explain Lulu's transformation. "I couldn't use it right away," he said. "In fact, I hated to even talk about it in case that would bring it back." But three years later, he was writing about Lulu and wondering about the source of her bitterness. "I knew there would be something psychological about her, and suddenly that whole section of the book just clicked when I realized I could use that terrifying experience I had had. But there was a reluctance to even write about it." Yet Lulu's words evoke his—and her—terror vividly: "Unable to think and yet aware, knowing that I was a cipher and a zero. And, worst of all, my brain not working, only my awareness alive. That was the horror—knowing that I would be like this forever, for an eternity."[11]

Lulu is convinced that she has had a taste of what death will be like. But did Cormier himself believe this horrifying idea as a result of his own taste of nothingness? He denied it emphatically: "It's one of my characters speaking, not me. (That's a problem I often have.) No, it would go against everything. I go to church every Sunday; I say my prayers every day—yet there's no proof. It's strictly faith—you *hope* that there's something there."[12]

In the Middle of the Night returns to one of Cormier's favorite themes—guilt, and especially guilt from sins of omission. The event that inspired the book was the Boston Coconut Grove fire of 1942, in which 490 people were burned to death in an overcrowded nightclub. At first a young busboy was blamed—he had been sent to the basement to change a lightbulb, and lit a match—but he was later exonerated. As Cormier watched the newspaper re-creations of this disaster each year on its anniversary, he wondered: What if that boy had grown up and had a son? How would the annual orgies of finger-pointing and the assumption of guilt affect their lives? And what if it had been not a nightclub full of adults, but a theater full of children? What if the balcony collapsed on them just before the fire broke out? What if a young usher had been sent up to the balcony without his flashlight to investigate the strange creaking noises and had lit a match, burned his fingers, and dropped the matchbook just as the balcony lurched and made a screeching groan like a ship pulling away from the dock before it crashed down on the children below?

But Cormier is too subtle to make the disaster the center of his novel. Although the story of the catastrophe is told three times— once in a prologue, by two children, Dave and Lulu; once by John Paul Colbert, the young usher; and once, briefly, many years later, by John Paul's wife—it is the far more penetrating drama of John Paul's guilt that holds center stage. The torturing nature of this guilt is its ambiguity: "Am I to blame?" he asks himself in the hospital afterward. "Did I do something wrong?" And although it is obvious that the fire did not cause the collapse, and a court clears him of culpability almost immediately, he continues to probe his conscience.

Cormier is always most interested in sins of omission, and so John Paul almost eagerly seeks guilt by wondering if he should have overcome his fear of the rats and spiders to explore the strange noises in the balcony earlier; if he should have pressured the owner to do something to repair it. The public, too, is eager to blame him, even though he has been officially cleared, and after the theater owner's suicide, there is no scapegoat left but John Paul. Year after year, there are hate letters and anonymous phone calls, no matter how often the family moves, and eventually he comes to accept them as his penance.

Denny, John Paul's son, has grown up against this background of silent guilt, often seeing his father listening quietly to hate phone calls in the middle of the night. At school he is uninvolved, both because the family has moved so often and because he fears taunts about his father's supposed crime. One day, in a scene that recalls Emile's attack on a nonresistant Jerry in *Beyond the Chocolate War,* John Paul sees a boy being pushed around by three others and accepting their blows with complete passivity. Later, the boy explains, "I didn't figure I was the victim that day. They were." Denny has the key to his father's behavior, and when he confronts him, John Paul's explanation reveals the Christlike nature of his suffering: "The pain stays, and it has to go someplace. It comes to me. . . . So. Let them use the telephone, let them write me letters. Let them accuse me. . . . It makes them feel better. I offer myself up to them."

The question, of course, is whether John Paul is a positive or a negative example. Guilt must be accepted to exist, and there is something unhealthy in his pursuit of it in the face of facts. In a life spent drenched in guilt, the sins of the father have been visited upon the son: their family life is hidden and silent, and Denny has learned not to reach out or intervene. He respects his father's commitment to nonviolence and says, "No comment," to the reporter who wishes to clear the record. Yet part of him yearns to take action, to "do *something.*" When he meets Dawn (a name that means "sunrise, full of hope" to Denny), she encourages his impulses for positive action, but in the end he rejects her for the imaginary seductiveness of another woman, Lulu, as his father has rejected life for the seductiveness of imaginary guilt. Here Cormier returns to the theme of the stifled potential of individual action against evil, a theme that he explored so effectively in *The Chocolate War* and attempted to resolve with Jerry's pacifism in *Beyond the Chocolate War.*

A second level of the story focuses on Dave and his sister, Lulu, who are victims of the disaster. Lulu nearly dies, and she returns to life disabled and bitter. She and Dave grow up twisted around each other like stunted and malformed plants, and she becomes the malevolent presence who seduces Denny on the phone and finally tries to kill him as revenge for the theater catastrophe. Lulu is one of

Cormier's strangest creations. The name—and as we have seen, names are often the source of secrets in his work—evokes the nineteenth-century avant-garde: artists' models, modistes, the feverish excesses of the demimonde. For much of the book she is seen obliquely through Dave's eyes as an avenging fury skulking in the night, or through Denny's ears as a voluptuous voice on the telephone. In a classic case of Cormier misdirection, we are led to suppose (cleverly, we think) that Lulu has actually died and has become a voice in Dave's head, a voice that makes him disguise his own voice on the phone to entice Denny. When Lulu finally does appear in the flesh as an old, crippled harpy, we mourn the loss of the illusion along with Denny.

The relationship between Dave and Lulu is claustrophobic, almost incestuous, and reminiscent of other pairs of too-close brothers and sisters in *Fade* and *The Bumblebee Flies Anyway*. Lulu calls Dave "Baby," and as children they re-enact a scene from *Wuthering Heights,* Heathcliff carrying a dying Cathy to the window. Dave is in remission from cancer, and the wig and false teeth he wears are symbols of the false personality he presents to everyone but Lulu. She has taken care of him in his "dark days" of cancer, and he takes care of her in "her own darkness" of spirit. Dave grieves that Lulu has been changed by her "death," become cold and withdrawn. She refuses to talk about her experience in the beyond until the final scenes, when she reveals the "glimpse of horror" that has frozen her soul and driven her mad with the desire for revenge.

The novel is tightly constructed and the language is clipped and spare, but occasionally Cormier allows himself one of those gorgeous metaphors that gladden readers' hearts: "Small and dark and energetic, she was like a hummingbird, going sixty miles an hour while standing still." The structure, which seems quite straightforward at first, proves complex on analysis. As in many Cormier stories, there are three narrators: Dave, who speaks in the first-person present tense, and Denny and John Paul, who both speak in the third-person past tense. Each chapter has only one voice, but it is immediately clear from internal clues who is speaking. The action shifts back and forth from 1993 to 1968, but again, the transitions are obvious to the observant reader.

The book is Cormieresque not only in style and content, but in the many characteristic markers and references to the author's life and other works. Although the story is not set in Monument, that town is just offstage, and the actual setting, the city of Wickburg (based on Worcester, Massachusetts), we know from the novel just before this one, *Tunes for Bears to Dance To.* There is that familiar young man who meets the girl of his dreams at the bus stop. There are young lovers who tryst at the public library, a familiar place of comfort and refuge in times of distress. There are nurses gliding in silent hospital corridors as in *Bumblebee,* and a Jewish girl who expands Denny's horizons, a direct excerpt from Cormier's own life. There is even a sly reference to Trinity High School, when Denny sees "guys who want to take over, pushing people around, intimidating young kids. It happens at other schools, too."

But most of all there are the references to old films, so ubiquitous in Cormier's work. The disaster occurs in his place of ultimate childhood happiness—a movie theater. In it is an ornate chandelier drawn directly from the original version of *The Phantom of the Opera,* a lighting fixture that is the cause of Dave and Lulu's ironic change of seats from under its imagined danger to under the balcony's real danger. Denny names the rowdy little kids at the bus stop Frankenstein and Dracula. Dave and Lulu drive up to capture Denny in "an old car, four doors, black, like a car in an old gangster movie." In their house is an empty interrogation room with "an unshaded bulb in the ceiling filling the place with naked light." And the melodramatic climax recalls a half-dozen old movies with the last-minute struggle over a poisoned hypodermic needle.

And of course, there is the ending. Cormier could not allow us the luxury of a cheerful conclusion even if he had set it up himself. In this case, several friends and editors pleaded with him to let Denny and Dawn go off happily together, but he held firm. "Life's just not like that," he insisted. After trying several variations, he still felt that his original version was the most natural. After the deadly turmoil with Lulu and Dave, Denny returns to his ordinary life and the daily routine of the school bus. But when he sits down beside Dawn he finds he no longer has anything to say to her. His memories of his fantasy of Lulu have filled his mind. After all, he thinks, "How do you learn to say goodbye to someone who never existed?"

Reviews were favorable but not ecstatic. Joel Shoemaker, writing for *School Library Journal,* called the novel a "sophisticated psychological thriller,"[13] and Roger Sutton, then of the *Bulletin of the Center for Children's Books,* said, "Relatively speaking, . . . it's easy Cormier, and kids . . . should have no trouble following the plot and its suspenseful turns."[14] Generally the critics then, and since, have regarded this novel as good standard Cormier, craftsmanlike but not a masterpiece. While "taut" and "suspenseful" are accurate judgments, it must be admitted that the novel is thrown out of balance by the histrionics surrounding Lulu, a character we don't believe for one minute, and by the horror scene with the hypodermic needle. However, this fault is almost balanced out by the poignance of Denny's situation in a novel that is typical, if not great, Cormier.

Notes

1. Flint-Ferguson, Janis D., "Being and Becoming a Real Writer Through Reading the Manu-

scripts of Robert Cormier," *Ohio Journal of the English Language Arts,* Winter/Spring 1999, 14.

2. Ibid.

3. Cart, Michael, *From Romance to Realism: 50 Years of Growth and Change in Young Adult Literature,* HarperCollins, 1996, 179.

4. Ibid., 182.

5. Ibid., 182, 186.

6. Ibid., 181.

7. Ibid., 183.

8. Ibid., 184.

9. Ibid., 186.

10. Cormier, Robert, audiorecording of telephone conversation with the author, February 8, 1995.

11. Ibid.

12. Ibid.

13. Shoemaker, Joel, *School Library Journal,* May 1995, 118.

14. Sutton, Roger, *The Bulletin of the Center for Children's Books,* May 1995, 302.

Chapter Thirteen

Tenderness

In 1997 Robert Cormier reached the apex of his career with the publication of *Tenderness,* the last of his five dark masterworks. Each is superb in its own way: *The Chocolate War* for its power to evoke a passionate reaction in the reader; *I Am the Cheese* for its masterful structure and turn-around ending; *After the First Death* for its challenging difficulties of voice and political relevance; *Fade* for its profoundly upsetting blend of fiction and reality; and *Tenderness* for the restraint of its shocking, and ultimately sympathetic, portrayal of the mind of a killer.

Tenderness is a novel drenched in irony. Each of the three main characters achieves his or her heart's desire, but loses it at exactly the same time and from exactly the same events. Not only these main story arcs, but also many small turns of dialogue and plot, and even the title, have ironic twists. The word "tenderness," as the pair of epigrams show, can have opposite meanings, point to pleasure or pain. The American Heritage dictionary gives a whole constellation of definitions for the term, all of which apply to the novel: The quality of being "easily crushed or bruised; soft, fragile; young and vulnerable; easily hurt, sensitive; painful, sore;" as well as "gentle and solicitous; expressing gentle emotions, loving; given to sympathy or sentimentality; considerate and protective."[1]

Cormier gave credit to two "what if's" for the genesis of the novel. The first was the phrase from Kahlil Gibran's *The Prophet*: "to know the pain of too much tenderness." These words had haunted him for many years. Then one night on the evening news he saw a story about a young boy who had committed a murder and been tried as a juvenile and incarcerated at a juvenile facility, but who was now being released because he had turned eighteen. Should some young offenders be tried as adults? asked the reporter. The question was causing political turmoil, and many states were changing their laws to allow serious juvenile offenders to be brought to adult justice. What if, wondered Cormier, a kid who had admitted to killing his parents was let loose on the world scot-free? Would he kill again? And did he have other dark secrets? In a writing exercise, Cormier had been playing with the idea of a sexy but naïve young girl who was running away. What if the two of them met? he mused. And *Tenderness* began.

The book centers entirely on the three main characters: Eric Poole, Lori Cranston, and Jake Proctor. The events of the story emerge inexorably from who they are, both individually and in collision with each other. The three voices are subtly different, and while Lori speaks for herself in the present tense, Eric and Jake are portrayed from the omniscient third-person perspective in the past tense. Blocks of narrative focus on each character, and as the story progresses and tension rises, the point of view shifts back and forth at shorter and shorter intervals—a technique Cormier later also used to great effect in *The Rag and Bone Shop*. The structure is comparatively simple as he builds our understanding of each character, then brings them together and lets them move each other to the inevitably tragic ending.

In the first three chapters we meet Lori, whose full name is Lorelei, a character who embodies Cormier's love of paradox. "A voluptuous innocent" was his most frequent description of her. Lori is both lovable and despicable, and we see both qualities immediately in the opening pages. "A technical virgin"—another contradiction—she is both naïve and experienced about sexuality, and uses it to her own advantage, as when she "cops a CD" by posing for the lecherous music store manager in the back room. She is even a bit prudish in the way she refers to her large breasts as her "good figure" or her "top," but at the same time she is aware that these are her most useful attributes. Cool unattainability is the quality most characteristic of Cormier's female characters, but Lori, like Rosanna in *Fade,* is eminently attainable—if she thinks tenderness might be involved. Like the Rhine maidens she is named for, she seduces men to their destruction, but often without intention. She dignifies her crush on Throb with the psychological term "fixation" ("to attach oneself to a person or thing in an immature or neurotic fashion"[2]) but talks about it with childish naïvete. She enjoys the contrast as she listens on earphones to his depraved howls about violence and death in the safe, ordinary comfort of the public library. On the other hand, Lori is good-hearted and generous in her concern for her mother's feelings, and forgiving of her parental shortcomings. She even has pity for the longing in the eyes of the men she arouses—although that pity doesn't stop her from stealing their wallets while they are distracted by her sexual favors. But it does make her feel a bit sorry afterward.

When we first see Lori she is in the throes of her obsession with Throb, a rock singer, whose name carries those sly connotations Cormier did so well. It all adds up to a repulsive picture, and here Cormier touched on an insight about the cult of celebrity that is so ubiquitous in our culture. A person need not be outstandingly beautiful, or intelligent, or good, or have done great deeds to become a celebrity among us. Simply to be often seen and heard can make one a celebrity. In these times the media, and especially TV, have created a class of people who are famous for being famous, not for having been or done anything valuable for humanity. Indeed, there is often an element of perversity, of strangeness or ugliness, that adds to their popular appeal. Throb is a particularly loathsome example, with his missing front tooth, "his spiky hair the color of salmon, his freckles and that terrible clown outfit: baggy pants and green plaid suspenders and no shirt, his nipples like old pennies stuck on his chest." Yet Lori adores him, and yearns to put her tongue in that hole in his mouth.

What is it that makes some people especially vulnerable to this cult of celebrity? In Lori's case it is a yawning void where love should be. Her mother, cheerful and good-natured though she may be, has raised Lori "on the run," following—or fleeing—one man and then another, leaving the teenager with massive confusion about the different natures of lust and love, sex and tenderness. The older woman has modeled for her daughter a pattern of expecting good from a man who is obviously bad, of "following somebody she met who makes promises that are always broken" and shrugging off the unhappy results by blaming her "bad luck with men." Her mother's bad luck has been Lori's, too, as she experiences physical and sexual abuse from a string of "stepfathers," leaving her with a yearning for tenderness at any cost. But when Gary, her mother's latest man, corners her and begins to stroke her breast, she first thinks, "His hand feels good, tender . . . ," but then, without the least hesitation, her generosity takes over, and she knows she must leave for her mother's sake. And not for the first time.

Her fixation on Throb, and her conviction that she can end it by kissing him, gives her a destination, and so with childish directness she tracks him down in nearby Wickburg, waits for him by the side door of his hotel in an alley appropriately malodorous with decaying garbage, and achieves her goal. She has hitchhiked to get here, and as she rejects a dangerous ride offer, we see that Lori *does* have good sense about handling a "sicko," when her perceptions are not blurred by a fixation. The driver she chooses to accept is gentle. "I know that I can handle him," she thinks, at the same time that she hopes, as always, that gentleness will transform into tenderness. Soon she succumbs to his obvious desire and offers to let him fondle her for twenty dollars. The scene is remarkable for its nonspecific eroticism, in which the reader's mind fills in the details, perhaps to more intense effect than descriptive words on the page. In the aftermath Lori lifts the man's wallet and later is overcome by compassion, promising herself to mail back his photos and credit cards, while she pockets the money. "Sometimes I'm such a bitch," she thinks, accurately.

Now that we have gotten acquainted with Lori, Cormier begins to introduce the much more complex character of Eric, but still through Lori's eyes. In a café she sees television news coverage of Eric's imminent release from prison on his eighteenth birthday. "Thus a murderer will be loose among us," says the reporter ominously. But Lori sees only his winning smile, and remembers that she met him several years ago and he wished her a happy birthday on that day when everyone else had forgotten her. Helplessly, she realizes she is fixated again.

In the reaction of two other women in the café Cormier carries the cult of celebrity to its perverse extreme.

"I wouldn't mind being incarcerated with him," the blonde in the next booth says.

"But he's a murderer," the dark-eyed girl says.

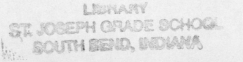

217

"What a way to die," the first one responds.

It is a peculiar truth that men in prison for grisly murders are often the target of feminine adoration, hordes of groupies, and piles of fan mail. What is the explanation of this spectacularly illogical behavior? Why are killers attractive to some women? Eric contemptuously dismisses the kids who see him as a martyr or a victim, and the girls who send him gifts and letters as "skinheads, neo-Nazis, grotesques, and freaks." Psychologists are at a loss to explain this well-documented phenomenon, but in Lori's needs and yearnings Cormier gives us glimpses of understanding. Her dream, she tells us prophetically, is "a great-looking guy stopping and picking me up . . . he's also kind and gentle . . . and we drive all over the USA." Soon she will be shaping her perception of reality to fit the dream.

And now we meet Eric Poole, in a passage that tests the reader's mettle by its sheer nastiness. Eric, like most serial murderers, begins his pattern of killing with animals—kittens, in his case. He describes their fragile bones and how they snap under too much pressure. And then a terrible sentence: "Which he did, of course, impossible to resist." The horror here lies in that wide-eyed "of course," as if Eric assumes that anybody would find the temptation to crush the kitten irresistible. The perversity increases as he deplores, but doesn't describe, the higher level of violence necessary to kill adult cats, and the problem of what to do with them afterward. He finds virtue in his actions, congratulating himself for "cleaning up the neighborhood" of felines and getting healthy exercise by digging their graves. This and the pleasant, everyday tone of the passage make it even more chilling in its way than the descriptions to come of Eric's fatal encounters with young women. In these early killings Eric has already begun to justify his actions to himself. As Mary Wollstonecraft wrote, "No man chooses evil because it is evil; he only mistakes it for happiness, the good he seeks."[3] This delusion of innocence allows Eric to go on without guilt to commit much worse crimes.

Eric Poole is atypical of Cormier's purely theologically evil villains in that he fits a recognized pattern of psychological pathology, that of the sociopath or psychopath. One diagnostic feature of this personality disorder is a pervasive pattern of disregard for and violation of the rights of others that begins in childhood or early adolescence and continues into adulthood. The disorder is characterized by a lack of empathy and a callous, cynical, and contemptuous attitude toward the feelings of others. Although such individuals may show a superficial charm, they are deceitful and manipulative and have little remorse for the consequences of their acts. Psychopathy is much more common among males than females, and some of the predisposing conditions may be parental neglect, or physical or sexual abuse.[4] But Eric goes far beyond this pattern in his cold alienation, his lack of emotion, his utter selfishness, and the crossed wires of his necrophilia. Jake Proctor says to him, "You're a psychopath, Eric." And then he adds, "A monster."

Indeed, in early versions of the novel Eric was nameless, and Cormier referred to him as the Monster. But his editor, Craig Virden, thought he should have a name. "I felt that giving him a moniker like that distanced Eric from the story and made him probably more stereotypical than he needed to be, and really stacked the deck against this guy," Virden remembers. "I felt that if Bob put a more human— seems an odd word for this kid—but put a more human face on him, it gives the reader an opportunity to make the decision for him or herself, exactly how good or bad this kid is at the end." Cormier found the suggestion valuable. "So I started rewriting," he said, "and giving him a name changed Eric completely."[5]

To the world Eric seems charming, intelligent, polite, well behaved, good-looking. But we are party to his chilling

219

thoughts, as he remembers secretly killing his aunt Phoebe's canary and being amused at her grief, and as he prowls the mall, looking for more exciting prey. In short, truncated sentence fragments, Cormier gives us the disjointed processes of Eric's mind, and brings us to a peak of suspense as Eric spots just the right girl and hastens breathlessly after her as she leaves the mall. But suddenly it is three years later, and Eric, on the brink of being released, is being visited for the last time in prison by Jake Proctor. We learn that Eric is in jail because he admitted to killing his mother and his stepfather, claiming abuse. The conversation is twice interrupted by Eric's memories; first, at the mention of "pain," he remembers deliberately burning his skin with a cigarette and coolly contemplating breaking his arm—to have evidence of abuse, we realize later.

And when Jake accuses him of lack of feeling, we are suddenly back at the mall parking lot, in a hidden grove of trees, and Eric holds in his arms the dead body of Laura Andersun, the girl he has just killed and presumably raped. Later Eric carries out four more murders, but Cormier never shows us the actual killings, and only in this one instance does he confront us with the grisly details of the aftermath. Eric's depraved emotions as he cradles the dead girl and feels an overwhelming wave of tenderness, his significant compulsion to trail his lips along the moist flesh of her arm, and his grisly curiosity as he opens her mouth and counts her fillings make this one of the most powerful and also one of the most horror-filled scenes in all of Cormier's writings.

The ghastliness of this one scene shows how much more horrific he could have made the book if he had not chosen to exercise restraint. When questioned on this point, he defended his intentions: "When you're dealing with a serial killer and a sexually precocious girl, it's easy to let the blood flow and the sex roll. The harder part is to contain it and suggest it."[6] Even so, in the original draft of this scene there was one sentence, as Cormier says, that upset everybody—his wife, Connie; his daughter; and his editors. Not only did Eric say "I waited to get dry," but the scene ended with his necrophiliac remark: "I held her until the change in the texture of her flesh told me it was time to go." Cormier loved the line, but "if it bothers that many people, out it comes," he resolved, not wanting the reaction to one line to skew the reaction to the book as a whole.

Nor should this passage taken alone influence the critical judgment of the novel as a whole. It is necessary for Cormier to show us as much as we can bear of Eric's depravity—once. But he is not writing horror, although he enjoyed the genre and was attracted to it. His purposes are far more subtle in taking us into the intimate aftermath of Eric's murders. Once we have glimpsed the intensity of the killer's need for tenderness as he follows it to its conclusion, that intensity can be evoked again indirectly without being described. A word, a phrase, a hint are enough to let us fill in the details as Eric goes on to other victims, and to give us the beginnings of understanding, even eventually of compassion.

Jacob Proctor is the third member of this unholy triad. The tired old cop who suspects more than he can prove is a standard character in crime fiction, and the detective who for years pursues a particular criminal obsessively has his prototype in Javert of Victor Hugo's *Les Miserables*. With the help of these literary antecedents, Cormier in just three sentences presents Jake full-blown to our imagination: "He was an old man, crevices in his face, sorrowful blue eyes, wispy gray hair. He smoked endless cigarettes, the ashes falling indiscriminately on his shirt or tie. His jacket never matched his trousers." We recognize Jake, and we feel sad for him, but even though he is the Good Guy, somehow we don't like him as much as we feel we ought to. Like both Lori and Eric, Jake is driven by a force beyond his control, his guilt over his failure to prove the culpability of another serial killer, a boy barely eighteen who, Jake was sure, had strangled five little girls. These murders happened twenty years ago on the other side of the continent, in Oregon, but Jake is still pursued by memories of them in dreams, and especially since he put the handcuffs on Eric's wrists three years ago. Somehow, he feels, he will atone for his earlier failure if he can bring *this* serial killer to justice.

But as things stand, Jake cannot convict Eric, even if he could prove that Eric is responsible not only for his parents' deaths, but also for those of two girls. Only Eric knows that there was a third girl, Alicia Hunt. All three had long dark hair and have been found strangled and sexually assaulted after death. These hidden and shared certainties and suspicions link detective and suspect in an uneasy alliance as Jake needles Eric in the last of the visits he has felt compelled to make every three months while Eric has been in the prison. "You're my hobby, Eric," the old cop tells him. "Like you're the broken watch and I'm the repairman." Eric is annoyed at the suggestion that he is "broken" and needs fixing, and even more annoyed when Jake calls him a monster, but he keeps a cool mien as he fences verbally with the detective and secretly gloats over his coming freedom—and what he knows and Jake doesn't. Eric has long-range plans. One of the reasons he killed his parents, more important to him than the insurance money, is that by choosing three years of jail he has quite deliberately, before the laws about the prosecution of minors could be changed, given himself a time protected from temptation. When he is released he can move in the world as an adult, free to pursue tenderness on his own terms.

But Jake, too, has his plans and secrets, hinted at in a brief conversation between the detective and his "legs," a young rookie named Jimmy Pickett. He has laid traps to keep Eric in prison or to get him transferred to an adult facility.

When a boy Eric has never seen before kicks him flat in the cafeteria line, Eric doesn't rise to the provocation because he has been warned by another prisoner. He looks up at his assailant and thinks, "Like a hired hit man," and we know who is behind the attack. A second trap also fails, as Eric is warned not to get involved with a lunchtime riot, and feigns illness so that he is in the infirmary when the violence erupts. But there is a third trap, one that we recognize as such only on a second reading. A beautiful dark-haired young woman shows herself to Eric in the mess hall, and later sends him a note with her name—Maria Valdez—and a phone number where she can be contacted after her—and his—imminent release. All his long-suppressed yearnings for tenderness rise up in him at this, and give him an immediate goal for his first months of freedom.

These scenes in the juvenile detention facility in some ways reflect not current prison realities, but recall, as Cormier so often does, the movies of the thirties: the Irish guard, the secret bully, the Distributor who carries messages, the mess hall riot. But two other seemingly insignificant incidents in this section are important in building our understanding of Eric. He comes to expect the visits of a mouse to his cell, and when the tiny creature fails to appear one day, he, for the first time in his life, experiences the emotion of loneliness, although he eventually suffocates the little animal in search of a fleeting moment of that emotion he calls tenderness. Under the compulsion of the same motivation, he tries to kill the bully, but realizes in time that such a murder will not bring him the ecstasy he so desperately seeks.

The next section opens with a passage in Lori's voice recounting the full story of her first encounter with Eric, an episode that becomes heavily ironic on a second reading because by then we have also seen it from Eric's point of view. Lori had been wandering in a lonely place by the railroad tracks when she wistfully envied a couple up ahead—who we later know are Eric and Alicia Hunt—walking hand in hand and kissing. They then disappeared into the woods. Returning later, Lori sees Eric alone and is immediately struck with his dancing blue eyes and his smile. When she lies about her birthday celebration, he sees through her deception at once, and his voice becomes tender in commiseration. Lori feels that he has seen into her soul, and she is pleased by the way he looks at her, even when he seems angry that she is here alone. When a gang of bikers appears, he protects her by facing them down, an act that on first reading seems out of character. In her mind Lori calls him "gallant" and "brave," and when he sends her away "before something else happens," she asks innocently, "What else could happen?" and wants to add *I'm safe with you. How could anything else happen?* She runs home crying, completely forgetting to ask about the girl she had seen earlier. Later, after Eric has seen Lori's picture in the newspaper as one of the watchers outside Aunt Phoebe's house, he remembers the episode. He had been fresh from Alicia Hunt's death, and as he talked with Lori he was fighting with himself over the possibility of risking a second blissful session of tenderness, excited by her youth even though he recognized that blond Lori was not his type. Only the intervention of the bikers saved her from him, not the other way around. After his release from prison, Lori's presence outside Aunt Phoebe's worries Eric, because if she remembers the girl he was with, he tells himself, she represents a serious threat to his safety.

The action shifts to a time of preparation before the trajectories of the three move into direct collision. Lori lies her way into the safe base of a home for pregnant girls called Harmony House and spends her days standing vigil with all the other fans outside the house where Eric is living with his aunt Phoebe, awaiting his driver's license, while Jake waits patiently for the lures he has set out to take effect. The reporter who takes Lori's picture reveals to her that Eric is suspected of two more murders, but she denies the possibility. Jimmy Pickett, who has also seen Lori in the newspaper, suggests to Jake that perhaps they could use her, but Jake, with exquisite irony, declines, saying, "Let's not put her in jeopardy." Eric gets his license and buys a van; he plans to set out early the next morning. Lori is forced to leave Harmony House with only ten dollars when another girl steals her money and sets her up for the theft of the matron's registry, and early the next day Jimmy Pickett reports to Jake that Eric is driving west on Route Two.

After this preparatory lull, the story flares into high action as the encounter we have awaited for so many pages finally happens. But in typical Cormier fashion, it comes at us sideways. As Eric drives along the highway, exulting in his freedom but alert for signs that he is being followed, he hears ominous noises from the backseat that tell him he is not alone in the car. Pulling off the highway to an abandoned gas station, he is astonished (and so are we) to find the stowaway is a sopping wet Lori, who has taken refuge from the rain in his van.

"Hello," she says.

"You," he responds.

The rest of the novel is both a love idyll and a death dance, as the two travel in what to Lori seems like a romantic ramble but to Eric is a purposeful evasion of Jake and pursuit of Maria Valdez. As they drive, she finds herself falling in love with him, but he only tolerates her presence because he doesn't dare to let her go, and plans to kill her soon. With her knowledge of his link to Alicia Hunt, she is a danger to him that cannot be allowed to continue, he thinks, while he postpones the moment of her death—to find out who she is and what she's up to, he tells himself. To his surprise, he finds her naïvete and odd little ways beguiling, although to Lori's puzzlement her voluptuous body tempts him very little. The tensions between them shift and change from line to line as their strange attraction twines around Eric's murderous intentions and Lori's dawning realization of them, a tension that makes their most ordinary exchanges electric with our apprehension. Gradually we begin to see tiny flickers of humanity in Eric, as he buys her fancy clothes just to see her pleasure in them, although he still plans to kill her.

In an incident that foreshadows what is to come, Eric spots a lovely girl with long dark hair, and Lori sees the naked need in his eyes. With sudden insight, she shivers at the look, which makes her think of "those horror movies . . . where a man turns into a werewolf before your eyes." Nevertheless, with generosity of spirit she urges him to approach the girl. In spite of this evidence of her selfless devotion, that night in a motel he waits until she is asleep, then raises a pillow to smother her. But Lori wakes and sighs, "Go ahead, then. Do it," in a childlike total surrender that is both admirable and pathological. As Eric finds he cannot kill her and Lori declares her love once again, there are no longer any deceptions between them. He turns away in bewilderment at himself, and as he falls asleep, she knows she should, and could, run away to save herself, but doesn't.

The next morning he is puzzled that she is still there, since he knows she understands what he might do. At breakfast he watches her lick jelly off her cheek and has an astounding epiphany. He wonders what it would be like "to kiss the jelly off that cheek, to feel her body close to him, not like with the others, but stopping before the act was completed. Maybe there would be tenderness in all that." So immersed have we become in Eric's thinking that the chilling phrase "before the act was completed" seems almost a logical consideration in judging whether he can love Lori. At once he is astonished at himself. But a moment later when Lori asks him to be "tender," this key word triggers an unexpected excitement in him.

Lori has released something human in Eric, and with it comes a repressed memory of intimate, too intimate, moments with his mother when he was a child. Here at last we have the final piece to the puzzle of why Eric murdered his parents—the mother who took away the tenderness that he thought was his and gave it to a hated stepfather. The incest is conveyed subtly in one sentence—"He remembered dark nights, her long black hair enveloping him, her lips trailing across his flesh. . . ." So subtly, in fact, that many readers argued that incest was not Cormier's intention. But clearly it is the explanation for Eric's obsession with dark-haired women and tenderness, and Cormier himself confirmed this when asked directly.

Now the story moves quickly to its conclusion. Eric makes an appointment to meet Maria Valdez at a nearby amusement park, and Lori nods and smiles, encouraging him, even as they arrive at the park and Eric and Maria walk away into the woods to the accompaniment of the tinny carnival music. Like a little girl left to amuse herself while her daddy goes off on business, she buys a ride on the Ferris wheel, trying not to imagine what Eric and Maria are doing. But from the top of the wheel she spots the surveillance van and Jake Proctor and three detectives heading for the woods. Instantly she understands the trap, and races to warn Eric. He is about to give himself up to the tenderness he has missed for so long when Lori crashes into the glade, followed by the detectives. Maria escapes, but not before Eric sees that she is a dupe, and Jake is left with no crime to prosecute. And, amazingly, we are pleased at this outcome; we are rooting for Eric at this point, and Jake has become the enemy.

Afterward, Eric says "Thank you" to Lori, the first time he has ever said those words and meant them. That night they sleep by a lake, and when Lori is afraid in the night, he finds that he wants to be gentle with her, to protect her.

"What is wrong with me?" he thinks at this flood of normal human emotions. The next day he rents a canoe to fulfill her dream of drifting on the lake. Overcome with happiness, she stands up in the boat—and falls into the water. Desperately he tries to save her, as she gasps, "Love me, Eric," and then slips out of his arms. He dives for her repeatedly, and then much later, paddles toward the shore and the waiting police, knowing what is in store.

In the end Lori finds the love from Eric she yearns for, but only by dying; Eric finds the tenderness without death he has glimpsed, but only through Lori's death; and Jake has finally brought Eric to prison, but for a crime he *didn't* commit. In prison, Eric finds moisture on his cheek as he thinks of Lori's last words, and wonders if this is what crying is like. "Later, in the deepest heart of the night, the monster also cried." And so Robert Cormier, who began his career with a worldview seemingly based on a vision of the opposing duality of God and Evil, in this last magnificent book finds God even at the bottom of the pit that is Eric Poole's soul. As the psalmist avows, "If I ascend to heaven, thou art there! If I make my bed in Sheol, thou art there!"[7] We feel compassion for Eric not because he is a victim of society or because he is mentally ill, but because he, like us, is human, and we, like him, are capable of evil.

Notes

1. *American Heritage Dictionary of the English Language,* College edition, William Morris, ed., Houghton Mifflin, 1975.

2. Ibid.

3. Wollstonecraft, Mary, *A Vindication of the Rights of Men,* 1790.

4. *Diagnostic and Statistical Manual,* American Psychiatric Association, 1994, 86, 648.

5. Zitlow, Connie S., and Tobie R. Sanders, "Conversations with Robert Cormier and Sue Ellen Bridgers: Their Life and Work as Writers," *Ohio Journal of the English Language Arts,* Winter/Spring 1999, 39.

6. Gardner, Lynn, "Robert Cormier," *Guardian Review,* November 6, 2000, www.guardian.co.uk/obituaries/story/0,,393224,00.html.

7. Holy Bible, Revised Standard Version, Thos. Nelson, 1953, Psalm 139:8, 655.

Chapter Fourteen

Last Words: *Frenchtown Summer* and

The Rag and Bone Shop

In the summer of 1998, after the publication of *Tenderness* and the completion of the manuscript for *Heroes,* Robert Cormier turned, as he had a decade earlier, from grim subjects to a smaller work of gentle nostalgia. As *Fade* had been followed by *Other Bells for Us to Ring,* so *Tenderness* and *Heroes* were succeeded by *Frenchtown Summer.* Recovered from the broken back he had sustained in a fall the year before, he was at peace at his lake house, and again in a mood of playful remembrance, he reached into his own childhood years for a work that was entirely unlike what had come before.

Frenchtown Summer

Cormier's original concept for *Frenchtown Summer* was quite different from the final form of the work. Karen Wojtyla, his editor at the time, recalls that he sent her, much to her surprise, a long poem that he visualized as having many illustrations, almost a picture book. The poem was what became the final chapter of *Frenchtown Summer,* the piece titled "The Airplane." Read alone, without the rest of the book that later came to precede it, this poem is perfect in its encapsulation of a moment in a boy's life. From these few brief words we *know* this boy Eugene, his bookishness and timidity, his ambivalent relationship with his swaggering older brother and his cronies in the neighborhood, and, most of all, his yearning love toward his father. After Eugene has had a day of humiliation because an amazing airplane he spotted in a tenement backyard was no longer there when he led the other kids to see it, the adults sit talking on the piazza as the young people toss a ball desultorily in the gathering dusk. Then, in an exquisite preparatory image, the father flicks his cigarette butt into the air—"we watched it spiral like a small comet to the sidewalk"—and with breathtaking tact and grace speaks the simple words that restore the son's social standing and validate the father's love for him. "Funny thing, I saw an airplane this morning on the way to the shop, in the backyard of three-deckers on Fifth Street. But it was gone when I looked again on the way home. Eugene saw it, too." His son's boundless gratitude is expressed visually as he looks at his father and sees that "smoke circled his head like a halo." But the human heart is never simple for Cormier; as always, he leaves us with a question. Did the father really see the airplane? Or has he, in his kind wisdom, seen his son's need and risen to it with a loving lie? Can a lie be a blessing? And, in the end, does it really matter whether he saw the airplane or not?

While it is intriguing to speculate on this book-that-never-was, and to wonder what it might have looked like, what the critical reaction might have been, and who would have been perceived as the audience, the book that was published went far beyond this initial concept. Cormier traced the genesis of this first lovely poem and his feelings about what came next in an e-mail in 1998:

Last spring while driving to the Lunenburg Library, I saw, of all things, an airplane in the backyard of a house. A World War One biplane, like the ones in those war movies I saw as a kid. It was like a vision. No place for it to land or take off. What was it doing there? . . . Then I remembered that there had been an air show at the local airport earlier and figured that the plane must have been a part of that, probably taken to that site on a flat-bed truck or something. But the image remained with me and I began a what-if kind of thing. . . . As I began to write it seemed to cry out for verse. I tried writing it in prose but it didn't work, so I let it go its own way. It turned out to be a thirteen-page verse which, in a mad moment, I sent off to Karen and Marilyn. I was mysteriously moved by what I had written.[1]

So were editor in chief Craig Virden, agent Marilyn Marlow, and editor Karen Wojtyla. But they "all agreed it was only the beginning of something. Craig said," Cormier remembered, that "he envisioned a *Winesburg, Ohio* kind of thing, with darkness in it." That set him off. "Late spring and during the summer, I did some of the most enjoyable writing I've ever done. Dug deep into my memories (and probably my psyche) and came up with stuff I didn't even know was there."[2] For a while he toyed with the idea of making it an autobiographical memoir. "I was very much aware as I wrote this free-verse story," he told the *English Journal,* "that I was drawing on my own boyhood—people I know, stories I had heard, legends that had fascinated me throughout my life. I instinctively disguised characters and events as I wrote, but I was constantly aware of the autobiographical elements. The thought occurred to me: should I begin all over again and make it strictly autobiographical, actually a memoir?"[3] The moment of decision came when he faced the naming of his main character. Should it be Bobby, which is what he was called as a child? Or a thinly disguised Robbie? Finally he settled on Eugene, which took the book in the direction of fiction, a name drawn, he later realized, from Thomas Wolfe's protagonist in *Look Homeward, Angel.* "At that moment, there ceased to be any doubt about what *Frenchtown Summer* would be," he declared.[4]

Soon it became a novel, a coherent story with a plot, and Cormier was surprised to find himself writing it entirely in free verse. Later, when the book was published, readers, too, were surprised. At first. Then critics began to notice, as we have said, that many passages in his previous books could be read as poetry—the opening bicycle ride of *I Am the Cheese,* the transition to the *Fade* and the flight of the *Bumblebee,* the ending of *Tenderness,* and—as we have seen—the beginning of *We All Fall Down,* just to name a few. Cormier eschewed for himself the label "poetry" for *Frenchtown Summer,* however, as somewhat high-flown, preferring the more modest term "verse."

To make *Frenchtown Summer* a verse novel—a form that was coming to be recognized in young adult literature—Cormier expanded the story backward from "The Airplane" to include several other plot threads and more on Eugene's vulnerability and agonizing need for his silent father's approval, as well as some lyrical passages that are simply evocations of the smell and taste and feel of small-town New England during the Depression. Other poems come more directly from his own childhood memories.

An example of this last type is "The Confessional," which almost exactly follows Cormier's earlier description of a recurring psychological trauma that he endured as a child (see chapter 2) but reveals more about the secret source of the young boy's sexual guilt. Other images and incidents have their origins in memory: the paper route beset with dogs, the lovely Irish mother, the tragic loss of a baby brother, his impossible love for a beautiful young nun, his joy in seeing clearly for the first time with new glasses. And always there is the bully. In "The Goggles" Cormier indulges himself, as he often did in his other novels, in imagining a just vengeance for his boyhood suffering at the hands of bullies, a vengeance that restores to him the power usurped by their intimidation.

Other images seem, in their sensuality, to be unquestionably based on childhood pleasures—or pains—recalled. Vivid taste sensations leap from "The Birthday" ("the cake, my favorite, golden, with butter frosting, ice cream a dripping rainbow of vanilla, chocolate and strawberry"), or "A Sliver of Ice" ("The ice, stingingly cold, burned my lips and fingers but at the same time brought delicious tingling to my tongue.") Others are equally vivid but not so happy, as in "My Father at Work" ("The smell of celluloid, sweet and acid at the same time, lanced my eyeballs and long before had penetrated my father's pores"), or the description of a universal women's injury in the thirties in "The Dark Dance" (". . . her wrist bruised purple from the times she'd caught her arm in the wringer. All Frenchtown women wore those purple badges").

Other passages, often tinged with melancholy, dramatize Eugene's sensitive, fearful nature or show him growing into adult understanding by pondering hard truths in this summer "when I knew my name but did not know who I was." The poem "The Bald Spot" is one of several that touchingly picture Eugene's yearning for the validation of his father's love. In "My Father at Work" Eugene delivers lunch to the noisy factory "up the wooden stairs to the second floor, where my father worked at the shaking machine, which rained bristles down into celluloid shells that would later become hairbrushes" and begins to understand his parent's hard life. In "My Father's Pilgrimage," the father, in spite of his wife's resistance, goes with dignity to pay his respects at the funeral of the owner of the Monument Comb Shop, a skinflint who has exploited his workers. Most poignant is "My Father at Night," a quiet nocturne in which Eugene wakes in the middle of the night to find his father sitting at the kitchen table, smoking his Chesterfields, guarding his family, and staring out the window at nothing.

But the father remains "a silhouette, as if obscured by a light shining behind him." "He was unknowable as a foreign language," Eugene concludes—the central mystery in a town he sees as full of mysteries and unanswered questions. Some of these vignettes of secrecy are darkly ironic, as in the anecdote "My Silent Uncle," which tells of a father who prayed for his son's deliverance from military service, a prayer that was granted when a pile of crates fell and crippled the young man, earning the father his son's lifelong enmity.

But the dark thread that ties all these remembrances together and parallels Eugene's search for his father's love is his suspicion, born of hidden clues and whispers, that his beloved uncle Med was somehow implicated in the murder of Marielle LeMoyne, a young woman whose strangled body was long ago found in the woods, "a yellow necktie with black stripes coiled like a snake around her neck." Eugene is haunted by the identity of the murderer, and unwillingly finds significance in small hints, such as Uncle Med's preference for crisply laundered white shirts, but never a tie. After his suicide Eugene finds a box of unused tie clips in his uncle's closet and buries it, along with his unanswered questions, in the backyard.

Cormier, like Eugene, was also haunted by just such a killing, as he described to Leonard Marcus in the interview that accompanies the audiotape version of the book. "There was a young woman murdered in a secluded area just next to that neighborhood where I grew up, and the murder has been unsolved all these years. It was a very emotional thing, the knowledge that the murderer could be walking the streets of Frenchtown. I wanted to use that, and even try to solve it in the book. I saw it as a chance to bring it to a kind of a closure. But even then, I left the door open that it might not have been Uncle Med . . . after all."[5]

These shadows give depth to the memoir, but it is Eugene's search for his father's love that suffuses it with a rosy haze of reminiscence as, in the end, the boy and his father fade from our view walking "home together in the tender sunlight of a Frenchtown summer." The book occupied a special place in Cormier's affections. "I feel toward this book as I have no other book—maybe the closest was *Now and at the Hour*" (significantly, another story about his father). "It was such a delight to write," he said in an e-mail, "to tinker with, to refine, play with like a toy that had the power to please me and touch me and move me."[6] Critics were also pleased and touched and moved, although some questioned whether this nostalgic memoir was truly a book for teens. However, such questions of readership were transcended by the book's quality when *Frenchtown Summer,* much to Cormier's gratification, won the prestigious Los Angeles Times Book Award for best young adult novel of the year.

Then, at the peak of his powers, this world-famous and highly acclaimed author turned away from literary and commercial success for several months to research and write, as a gift to the church, the text for a pictorial history of St. Cecilia's Parish, a striking depiction of the continuity of a church community made largely of people who have spent all their lives in this one town.[7] And yet Leominster's most distinguished citizen, the humble author of this booklet, appears in a note of thanks from the current priest only as "Robert Cormier, a parishioner"—an attribution that was probably the modest author's own choice.

The Rag and Bone Shop

Cormier had an almost superstitious fear of talking away a book, so I learned never to ask about a work in progress, but occasionally he would share a hint about the incident or idea that had triggered the story taking shape in his mind. In April 2000, when he and Connie came to Southern California to accept the Los Angeles Times Book Prize for *Frenchtown Summer,* he confided that he was working on a book he called "The Interrogator."

"You mean like Brint?" I asked, thinking of Adam's sinister questioner from *I Am the Cheese.*

"It *is* Brint," he said, grinning mischievously at the red herring he had just handed me.

Later there was an interim title, "Down Where All the Ladders Start," drawn, like the final version, from the last stanza of a poem by William Butler Yeats, "The Circus Animals' Desertion."

```
I must lie down where all the
    ladders start,
In the foul rag-and-bone shop
    of the heart.
```

Strangely enough, the passage illustrates not only the state of mind of the soul-weary interrogator, Trent, and that of the aging poet, but also perhaps that of Cormier himself in its insistence on the artist's painful need to commune with the dark places of the heart and the weariness that comes from long acquaintance with humanity's foul castoffs.[8] Cormier's last novel is utterly characteristic in this communication with darkness, and in its themes of innocence corrupted, political authority misused, sin and confession and forgiveness and guilt—with an undergirding of religious faith and glimmers of hope just offstage. With the mastery of a literary lifetime in the rag-and-bone shop, Cormier lays out these themes, then twists them and turns them inside out, shows us their ragged undersides, and leaves us with an uneasy handful of questions that we must answer ourselves. As his editor, Karen Wojtyla, wrote, "It's a slim volume, deliberately attenuated in order to take the cat-and-mouse tension he was so adept at to its barest bones: two protagonists facing each other in a bare room. And in that room, in a confrontation that uses only words as weapons, he manages to create such suspense that readers may squirm as they turn the pages."[9]

The story centers on the long, excruciatingly intense interrogation of twelve-year-old murder suspect Jason by the cynical detective Trent. This tension-filled passage stretches taut over a third of the book, with a brief break—much needed by both the characters and the reader—during which Jason almost escapes, but is cleverly dissuaded by Trent. The first section of the book sets the stage for the interrogation. In the opening pages we see Trent at work extracting a confession of a hideous triple murder from a seventeen-year-old boy. The detective is cold, ambitious, fiercely devoted to his skill at questioning. "You are what you do," his dead wife said, with an edge of accusation, and he accepts the judgment willingly. Soon afterward we confront another hideous murder, as the body of seven-year-old Alicia is found battered in the woods.

But in between is a typically Cormieresque contrast, a lovely lyrical interlude in which Jason, a shy and sweet-natured seventh grader, wakes to contemplate happily the delicious freedom of the first day of summer vacation—a passage that turns ironic on a second reading, with our knowledge of what actually does happen on that day. On that afternoon, Jason has ostensibly gone to visit a classmate, Brad, but his actual friend at that house is Brad's little sister, Alicia, who amuses the lonely boy with her grandmotherly ways. Alicia has been furious with her brother for some secret reason, so that he soon leaves with his two buddies, and Jason then becomes the last person to see the little girl alive— or "almost the last person," as he desperately insists later.

When Alicia's murder is discovered, there are no clues, no evidence, no suspects. The police are under heavy political pressure from the media, the district attorney, even a senator, to find the killer, and so they send for Trent, a man who, it is rumored, "can get blood out of a stone." His assignment: a confession from Jason, the only suspect, because Alicia's brother has an alibi. The boy is brought to a waiting room in the police station, and he comes with innocent willingness because he wants to help, although he wonders "if it was a mistake to come here" because he can recall nothing suspicious. By the end of the waiting period that phrase has turned ominous, as he begins to sense his peril.

Trent carefully sets the stage—a small, cluttered room, hot and crowded, with two chairs of different heights—and the curtain goes up on the interrogation. The unequal contest has the horrid fascination of a weaving, hypnotic encounter between a boa constrictor and a mouse, and its outcome is as inevitable. (In an evocative image, Jason notices Trent's "eyes like black marbles.") These chapters are thrilling in their intricate construction and elegance, the delicate perversity of their progression toward the unthinkable. Each one of Trent's questions changes the situation ever so slightly, moving Jason cleverly toward the confession the detective must have. At just the right moment, Trent shifts from opponent to advocate, in a hideous parody of compassion. And with each question, Jason becomes more and more uneasy, blunders a bit further in the direction Trent has led, until suddenly the cage door clangs shut, and Jason realizes he is caught. His protests of innocence only trap him more deeply, as Trent points out with implacable illogic that his denial only proves his guilt, and offers the seductive poison of a false confession.

In these brilliant passages, the point of view snaps back and forth, showing us the emotional thrust and parry of the two participants in the unholy game. Layered under the tension as the questioning proceeds is a second conflict, when Trent comes to "a blazing realization" that Jason is innocent, but that his job is to get a confession nevertheless. Like a medieval executioner, his goal is not truth, but an admission, and if the victim is destroyed in the process, that only confirms his guilt. Trent's twisted logic as he frantically tries to talk himself out of the impulse toward good parallels the twists that have turned lies into truth as Jason desperately denies his guilt but finally begins to believe in it, to be tempted by the sweetness of forgiveness even without sin.

Questions of faith are inherent in the novels of Robert Cormier, especially the nature of good and evil and their relationship to guilt and forgiveness, but often he shows us the light by focusing ironically on the shadow. In *The Rag and Bone Shop* he has structured these ideas into the very fabric of the narrative with a comparison of Trent's unholy work to that of a priest, but one who hears confessions and grants not absolution but indictment. The forgiveness he offers is an illusion, and the peace it grants is short-lived. Like a priest, he is weary with all the terrible deeds he has heard, "the unending litany of confessions," but he can find no peace for himself, nor remission for his own sin of betrayal. When Jason emerges from the interrogation room he looks "broken, as if just lifted down from the cross," yet his ordeal leads not to redemption, but further sin, as in the end he tries to bring reality back into focus by making the lie of the false confession true with a second murder.

Once again we have a provocative and uncomfortable

ending from Robert Cormier. But perhaps the key lies in the fact that the novel has *two* points of climax, two resolutions of tension, and in the second one we find that potential for goodness, that "if only" that always lies at the heart of Cormier's ethical statement. The first resolution comes with Jason's admission of having committed the crime, a scene that, significantly enough, takes place offstage. The second, again seen indirectly, in a flashback, is the true confession, that of Alicia's brother. Trent, triumphant with Jason's taped confession in hand, and Jason, wan and abject, have just emerged from the interrogation room when they get the news. Suddenly everything is— or could have been— different. Trent could have felt a cleansing shame that might have led to his transformation. Jason could have felt released, vindicated, restored to life. But neither happens. Trent continues in the conviction that "you are what you do," even if he can no longer do the work he has been born to do. Jason continues to be haunted and soiled by Trent's manipulations, trying with another murder to make sense of his disturbed universe.

And so we come to the last sentence in the last book by Robert Cormier. As Jason heads for the kitchen to get that butcher knife, we yearn for an easy answer, a neat and comfortable conclusion. But at the same time, we know that the answer would be "What do *you* think?" because Robert Cormier always hands it back to us.

Will Jason actually use that butcher knife on Bobo? And is he guilty of Alicia's death? Cormier has left the first question entirely open, but I prefer to think that Jason's inherent goodness will prevail, and that he will find through his inability to use the knife that he is not capable of murder after all. The answer to the second question— did Jason kill Alicia?— depends somewhat on the answer to the first. It was hotly debated after the book's publication, and critic Jonathan Hunt stoutly maintained that *The Rag and Bone Shop* was a much lesser book if read from the point of view that Jason was innocent all along.[10] The contention of literary complexity may be true, but it seems to me that a wrench from Cormier's clear intention is required in order to prove Jason's culpability. There are no subtle hints about his guilt, nor are there any indications of a motive. Jason is quite simple, and we see no hidden depths of violence in his mind. The episode in which he attacks Bobo in the cafeteria seems to him a clear-cut case of stopping a bad guy. And a second argument for Jason's innocence is that to regard him as guilty violates Cormier's established pattern of innocence corrupted by an evil person in power. And, finally, if Jason has already killed, why does he feel he has to prove himself with the butcher knife?

Also there is no reason to doubt Brad's confession, since it was freely given, not coerced by Trent. But why, then, did *Brad* kill his sister? Cormier—wisely—chose not to explore the nature of this relationship, because it would add complications to the story that would shift it away from the intense focus on the confrontation between interrogator and victim.

Another set of questions centered on the legality of the interrogation of a minor without the permission or presence of parents or an attorney. Could such a violation of our system of justice possibly happen? The answer is an unequivocal yes. There have been a number of recorded instances of such breaches of legal procedure. For example, the television show *60 Minutes* aired a story on July 7, 2002, about the Pioneer Hotel fire in Tucson, Arizona, in 1971. Following the disaster, the police, pressured to find a suspect, interrogated sixteen-year-old Louis Taylor all night without a guardian or legal counsel, and he was convicted on the basis of that night's testimony.[11] A more spectacular miscarriage of justice happened in Escondido, a town near San Diego, in 1998, when twelve-year-old Stephanie Crowe was found stabbed to death on her bedroom floor. The police settled on Stephanie's fourteen-year-old brother Michael as the prime suspect. After two sessions of ten hours of questioning he finally admitted that he had probably killed his sister, although he continued to maintain that he didn't remember any details. DNA testing later led to the conviction of a transient who had been seen and reported near the Crowe house the night of the killing.[12]

Always, Cormier's interest lies in Trent—his struggle with ambition and morality, his inability to forgive himself for his previous victims, and the paradox of the false confession that he is unable to stop himself from extracting and the true confession that confirms his self-loathing. The rejection by his wife, Lottie, and his potential girlfriend, Sarah, only reinforces the verdict, and they exist in the story only for this purpose. *The Rag and Bone Shop* is a two-person show, even essentially a one-man show, and perhaps Cormier's original intention to call it "The Interrogator" was on target. The implacable, remote, and bloodless Brint has evolved into the still implacable, but suffering, flesh-and-blood Trent.

A final question revolves around whether the book was finished before Cormier's death in November 2000. Rumors flew about the degree of completion of the manuscript, the implication being that the book was somehow not quite as excellent as it might have been. Most of these tales were fueled by a misunderstanding of one sentence in Joel Shoemaker's review in the *School Library Journal*: "Cormier revisits familiar psychological and temporal territory in this memorable novella that was finished, but unpolished, at the time of his death."[13]

The truth was explained by Connie Cormier in "A Personal Remembrance," which prefaced the publisher's advance reading copy. Her words came as no surprise to those acquainted with Cormier's working methods. In a graceful and touching essay about her husband, she not only clarified this point, but went on to remind us all of the writer and human being we had lost. It seems fitting to let her have the last words in this book. She wrote:

This is Bob's last book. He always hated to see his books end, and he loved to tinker with them after they were finished—to ponder, to search for the perfect word, the perfect phrase. Tragically, he died . . . before he was able to do that with *The Rag and Bone Shop.*

He often said that he was a man without regrets. He loved life, loved his family, and loved his hometown of Leominster, Massachusetts. He sat down every day to do what he enjoyed most—to write.

Bob also loved books, of course. He sometimes visited several libraries in one day and never walked out empty-handed. He delighted in meeting old friends and schoolmates as he did errands downtown. He enjoyed all kinds of movies and music, and had a weakness for old jokes. He was a perennial optimist, always hopeful, always able to see the humor in a situation. He made life so much fun.

He often said that he was indebted to teachers and librarians for introducing students to his books. He loved meeting them and talking with them at conferences and workshops. He would come home energized and excited and eager to head back to the typewriter. Had he

been here to dedicate this last
novel, I believe he would have
gratefully acknowledged all those
who read his books and supported
his writing through the years. His
legacy lives on in his writing,
and we are thankful for that, but
we will always miss the man behind
the words. We know that his readers
will too.

Notes

1. Cormier, Robert, e-mail to the author, December 2, 1998.
2. Ibid.
3. Cormier, Robert, "A Character by Any Other Name," *English Journal,* January 2001, 31.
4. Ibid.
5. Marcus, Leonard, *Frenchtown Summer,* Listening Library, 2000 (audiobook plus interview).
6. E-mail, December 2, 1998.
7. Cormier, Robert, *Portrait of a Parish,* St. Cecilia's Parish, Leominster, Massachusetts, 2000.
8. A "rag-and-bone shop" was probably a precursor to the contemporary thrift shop, a store where society's unwanted leftovers were sold. My impression that this is true comes from childhood memories of the "rag-and-bone man," who used to come down the alley behind our house on Sunset Boulevard in Hollywood with an old wagon and a horse. He would cry out, "Any rags, any bones, any bottles today?" Housewives would come out and give him whatever they had for a bit of money, and he evidently resold it in some unimaginable pocket of poverty.

9. Wojtyla, Karen, letter to members of the Assembly for Adolescent Literature of the National Council of Teachers of English, August 21, 2001.

10. Hunt, Jonathan, e-mail to adbooks listserv, November 26, 2001.

11. *60 Minutes,* "Pioneer Hotel Fire," April 7, 2002.

12. Sauer, Mark, and John Wilkens, "Haunting Questions: The Stephanie Crowe Murder Case," *San Diego Union Tribune,* May 11–16, 1999, www.union trib.com/news/reports/crowe.

13. Shoemaker, Joel, *School Library Journal,* September 2001, 223.

SELECTED BIBLIOGRAPHY

PRIMARY WORKS

Novels

After the First Death. Pantheon, 1979. Pbks Avon, 1980; Avon Flare, 1982; Laurel-Leaf, 1991. Audiobook Random House/Miller Brody, 1982.

Beyond the Chocolate War. Knopf, 1985; Peter Smith, 2001. Pbk Laurel-Leaf, 1986, 1991.

The Bumblebee Flies Anyway. Pantheon, 1983. Pbk Laurel-Leaf, 1984, 1991.

The Chocolate War. Pantheon, 1974; Random House, 1986; Knopf, 1997. Pbks Laurel-Leaf, 1975, 1986, 2000; Knopf Readers Circle, 2004. Audiobook Listening Library, Random House/Miller Brody, 1982.

Fade. Delacorte, 1988. Pbks Laurel-Leaf, 1991; Delacorte Press, 2004.

Frenchtown Summer. Delacorte Press, 1999. Pbk Laurel-Leaf, 2001. Audiobook Listening Library, 2000.

Heroes. Delacorte Press, 1998. Large print Thorndike, 2000. Pbk Laurel-Leaf, 2000.

I Am the Cheese. Pantheon, 1977; Random House, 1994, 1997; Knopf, 1999. Pbk Laurel-Leaf, 1991, 1999. Audiobook Random House/Miller Brody, 1982.

In the Middle of the Night. Delacorte Press, 1995. Pbk Laurel-Leaf, 1997.

A Little Raw on Monday Mornings. Sheed & Ward, 1963. Pbk Avon, 1980.

Now and at the Hour. Coward McCann, 1960. Pbk Avon, 1980.

Other Bells for Us to Ring. Delacorte Press, 1990. Pbk Laurel-Leaf, 2000.

The Rag and Bone Shop. Delacorte Press, 2001. Large print Thorndike, 2002. Pbks Laurel-Leaf, 2003; Knopf Readers Circle, 2004. Audiobook Recorded Books, 2002.

Take Me Where the Good Times Are. Macmillan, 1965. Pbk Avon, 1981.

Tenderness. Delacorte Press, 1997. Pbk Laurel-Leaf, 1998.

Tunes for Bears to Dance To. Delacorte Press, 1992. Pbk Laurel-Leaf, 1994.

We All Fall Down. Delacorte Press, 1991. Large print Thorndike, 1993. Pbk Laurel-Leaf, 1993.

Short Stories

"And All Our Yesterdays . . ." *Savior's Call,* February 1945.

"Anniversary." *Sign,* September 1954.

"Anniversary." *Toronto Star Weekly,* June 8, 1955.

"Another of Mike's Girls." *McCall's,* November 1973; also in *Eight Plus One,* Pantheon, 1980.

"A Bad Time for Fathers." *Woman's Day,* October 1970.

"A Bad Time for Fathers." *Woman's Own,* July 3, 1971; also in *Eight Plus One,* Pantheon, 1980.

"Between the Darkness and the Daylight." *Sign,* January 1968.

"Bunny Berigan—Wasn't He a Musician or Something?" *Redbook,* January 1966. Reprinted in *Women's Mirror,* January 1967; also in *Eight Plus One,* Pantheon, 1980.

"The Busted Heart." *Sign,* April 1951.

"Charlie Mitchell, You Rat, Be Kind to My Little Girl." *McCall's,* April 1969.

"Color Scheme." *Sign,* September 1947.

"The Crush." *Sign,* August 1966.

"The Day of Fire Engines." *St. Anthony's Messenger,* January 1971.

Eight Plus One. Pantheon, 1980; Econo-Clad, 1999. Pbk Laurel-Leaf, 1991.

"An Elegy for Edgar." *Sign,* January 1949.

"Eye of the Beholder." *Sign,* March 1957.

"First Chance." *Sign,* January 1957.

"The First Day." *Sign,* November 1953.

"The Flutter as of Wings." *Sign,* December 1955.

"Full Count." *Sign,* July 1957.

"The Gesture." *Sign,* January 1952.

"The Gift." *Sign,* November 1949.

"Goodbye, Little Girl." *Woman's Own,* July 5, 1969.

"Guess What? I Almost Kissed My Father Goodnight." *Saturday Evening Post,* Winter 1971; also in *Eight Plus One,* Pantheon, 1980.

"The Heart of Mrs. Bonville." *Sign,* December 1952.

"In the Heat." In *Sixteen.* Donald Gallo, ed. New York: Delacorte Press, 1984. Audiocassette Listening Library, 1987.

"Let's Try for a Happy Ending Anyway." *St. Anthony's Messenger,* September 1967.

"The Little Things That Count." *Sign,* May 1944.

"The May Basket." *Sign,* December 1947.

"The Mill." *Sign,* May 1954.

"Mine on Thursdays." *Woman's Day,* October 1968.

"A Moment of Wisdom." *New York Telegram,* April 16, 1955.

"The Moustache." *Woman's Day,* November 1975. Reprinted in *Scholastic Voice,* October 31, 1980; also in *Eight Plus One,* Pantheon, 1980.

"My Father's Gamble." *Sign,* April 1961.

"My First Negro." *Sign,* March 1969; also in *Eight Plus One,* Pantheon, 1980.

"No Time to Be Far from Embraces." *Extension,* November 1967.

"The Other Side of the Mountain." *Sign,* January 1954.

"President Cleveland, Where Are You?" *Redbook,* May 1965; also in *Eight Plus One,* Pantheon, 1980.

"Pretend, A Verb: To Make Believe . . ." *St. Anthony's Messenger,* April 1967.

"Protestants Cry Too." *St. Anthony's Messenger,* January 1967; also in *Eight Plus One,* Pantheon, 1980.

"The Soldier." *Sign,* July 1945.

"Spoiled Girl." *Sign,* June 1958.

"Spring Will Come Again." *Sign,* March 1946.

"The Tenderness." *Sign,* December 1947.

"Uncle Jay's Last Christmas." *Sign,* December 1949.

Nonfiction

"1177 Main Street" [columns]. *St. Anthony's Messenger,* 1967–80.

"A Book Is Not a House: The Human Side of Censorship." In *Authors' Insights: Turning Teenagers into Readers and Writers,* edited by Donald Gallo. Portsmouth, NH: Boynton/Cooke-Heinemann, 1992.

"Books Remembered." *The Calendar of the Children's Book Council,* June/December 1986.

"A Character by Any Other Name." *English Journal,* January 2001.

Fitchburg Sentinel [articles], 1955–78.

"Creating *Fade.*" *The Horn Book Magazine,* March/April 1989.

Fitch, John IV [Robert Cormier]. *Fitchburg Sentinel* [columns], 1966–78. *Fitchburg-Leominster Sentinel and Enterprise* [occasional columns], 1978–83.

"Forever Pedaling on the Road to Realism." In *Celebrating Children's Books: Essays on Children's Literature in Honor of Zena Sutherland,* edited by Betsy Hearne and Marilyn Kaye. New York: Lothrop, Lee & Shepard, 1981.

"The Gradual Education of a YA Novelist." Introduction to

Twentieth-Century Young Adult Writers, edited by Laura Standley Berger, Farmington Hills, MI: St. James Press, 1994.

I Have Words to Spend: Reflections of a Small-Town Editor, edited and with an introduction by Constance Senay Cormier. New York: Delacorte Press, 1991.

"Introduction." In *I Am the Cheese,* Twentieth Anniversary Edition. New York: Knopf, 1997.

"Introduction." In *Images of America: Leominster.* Leominster Historical Society, 1994?

LeVert, John. "A Boy Who Possesses Animal Magnetism." Review of *The Flight of the Cassowary. Los Angeles Times,* December 6, 1986.

"Looking Back While Going Forward." In *The Phoenix Award of the Children's Literature Association, 1995–1999,* edited by Alethea Helbig and Agnes Perkins. Lanham, MD: Scarecrow Press, 2001.

"My Best Teacher." *London Times Educational Supplement,* September 2000.

"On Telling Movies." In *Literature for Today's Young Adults,* by Alleen Pace Nilsen and Kenneth L. Donelson. 4th ed. New York: HarperCollins, 1993.

"On Writing: A Mystery." In *Literature for Today's Young Adults,* by Alleen Pace Nilsen and Kenneth L. Donelson. 6th ed. Boston: Pearson, 2001.

"The Pleasures and Pains of Writing a Sequel." *ALAN Review,* Winter 1985.

Portrait of a Parish. Leominster, MA, 2000.

"Robert Cormier." In *Speaking for Ourselves: Autobiographical Sketches by Notable Authors of Books for Young Adults,* compiled and edited by Donald R. Gallo. Urbana, IL, National Council of Teachers of English, 1990.

St. Cecilia's Church. Worcester, MA: Commonwealth Press, 1984.

"Sentinel Bookman." *Fitchburg Sentinel* [columns], 1964–78.

"Stephen King and the Monsters Within," review of *It. Washington Post Book World,* August 24, 1986.

"Waxing Creative." *Publishers Weekly,* July 17, 1995.

Speeches

"The Cormier Novels: The Cheerful Side of Controversy." Speech given at the Cervantes Convention and Exhibit Center, sponsored by the Children's Libraries Section of the Catholic Library Association, March 29, 1978. *Catholic Library World,* July 1978.

"Margaret A. Edwards Acceptance Speech." *Journal of Youth Services in Libraries,* Fall 1991.

"Probing the Dark Cellars of a Young Adult Writer's Heart." Frances Clark Sayers Lecture, May 17, 1998, University of California, Los Angeles, 1999.

SECONDARY WORKS

Books, Theses, and Parts of Books

Bjerk, Kristine M. "Journey to Understanding: Defending *I Am the Cheese.*" In *Censored Books II: Critical Viewpoints, 1985–2000,* edited by Nicholas J. Karolides. Lanham, MD: Scarecrow Press, 2002.

Campbell, Patricia J. *Presenting Robert Cormier.* Boston: Twayne Publishers, 1975, 1989; New York: Dell, 1990.

Campbell, Patty. "Robert Cormier." In *Writers for Young Adults,* edited by Ted Hipple. New York: Charles Scribner's Sons, 1997.

Cart, Michael. *From Romance to Realism: 50 Years of Growth and Change in Young Adult Literature.* New York: HarperCollins, 1996.

Contemporary Authors Online. Farmington Hills, MI: Gale Group. http://web7.infotrac.galegroup.com. Accessed April 17, 2002.

Dresang, Eliza T. *Radical Change: Books for Youth in a Digital Age.* New York: H. W. Wilson, 1999.

Fraustino, Lisa Rowe. "The Age of Cheese: Readers Respond to Cormier." In *The Phoenix Award of the Children's Literature Association, 1995–1999,* edited by Alethea Helbig and Agnes Perkins. Lanham, MD: Scarecrow Press, 2001.

Gallo, Donald R. "Reality and Responsibility: The Continuing Controversy over Robert Cormier's Books for Young Adults." In *The VOYA Reader,* edited by Dorothy Broderick. Lanham, MD: Scarecrow Press, 1990.

Garrett, Agnes, and Helga P. McCue, eds. *Authors and Artists for Young Adults,* vol. 3. Detroit: Gale Research, 1987.

Helbig, Alethea. "Peace, Justice, and Liberation Theology in *After the First Death.*" In *The Phoenix Award of the Children's Literature Association, 1995–1999,* edited by Alethea Helbig and Agnes Perkins. Lanham, MD: Scarecrow Press, 2001.

Hendrickson, Linnea. "Truth, Fiction, and the Impossible in Robert Cormier's *The Bumblebee Flies Anyway* and *Fade.*" In *The Phoenix Award of the Children's Literature Association, 1995–1999,* edited by Alethea Helbig and Agnes Perkins. Lanham, MD: Scarecrow Press, 2001.

Iskander, Sylvia Patterson. In *Concise Dictionary of American Literary Biography: Broadening Views, 1968–1988.* Farmington Hills, MI: Gale Group, 1989.

Iskander, Sylvia Patterson. "Readers, Realism, and Robert Cormier." In *Annual of the Modern Language Association, Division on Children's Literature and the Children's Literature Association,* vol. 15. New York: MLA, 1987.

Kertzer, Adrienne. *"Tunes for Bears to Dance To:* Prayers and Silence."* In *The Phoenix Award of the Children's Literature Association, 1995–1999,* edited by Alethea Helbig and Agnes Perkins. Lanham, MD: Scarecrow Press, 2001.

LeBlanc, Robert. *Postmodern Elements in the Work of Robert Cormier.* M.A. thesis, Fitchburg State College, Fitchburg, MA, 2005.

Lesesne, Teri S., and Rosemary Chance. "Robert Cormier, *The Chocolate War."* In *Hit List for Young Adults 2: Frequently Challenged Books.* Chicago: American Library Association, 2002.

Lundin, Anne. "A Stranger in a World Unmade: Landscape in Robert Cormier's Chocolate War Novels." In *The Phoenix Award of the Children's Literature Association, 1995–1999,* edited by Alethea Helbig and Agnes Perkins. Lanham, MD: Scarecrow Press, 2001.

MacLeod, Anne Scott. "Ice Axes: Robert Cormier and the Adolescent Novel." In *American Childhood: Essays on Children's Literature of the Nineteenth and Twentieth Centuries.* Athens, GA: University of Georgia Press, 1994.

Myszor, Frank. "The See-Saw and the Bridge in Robert Cormier's *After the First Death."* In *Children's Literature,* 16, edited by Margaret R. Higonnet and Barbara Rosen. New Haven, CT: Yale University Press, 1988.

Nilsen, Alleen Pace, and Kenneth L. Donelson. *"The Chocolate War* as a Problem Novel." In *Literature for Today's Young Adults,* 6th ed. Boston: Pearson, 2001.

Nodelman, Perry. "Robert Cormier's *The Chocolate War*: Paranoia and Paradox." In *Stories and Society: Children's Literature in Its Social Context,* edited by Dennis Butts. London: Palgrave Macmillan, 1992.

Oneal, Zibby. " 'They Tell You to Do Your Own Thing, but They Don't Mean It': Censorship and *The Chocolate*

War." In *Censored Books: Critical Viewpoints,* edited by Nicholas J. Karolides, Lee Burress, and John M. Kean. Lanham, MD: Scarecrow Press, 1993.

Rees, David. "The Sadness of Compromise: Robert Cormier and Jill Chaney." *The Marble in the Water: Essays on Contemporary Writers of Fiction for Children and Young Adults.* Boston: Horn Book, 1980.

"Robert Cormier." In *Children's Literature Review,* vol. 55, edited by Deborah J. Morad. Farmington Hills, MI: Gale Group, 1999.

"Robert Cormier." In *St. James Guide to Young Adult Writers,* 2nd ed., edited by Tom and Sara Pendergast. Farmington Hills, MI: Gale Group, 1998.

"Robert Cormier." In *Something About the Author,* vol. 93, edited by Alan Hedblad. Farmington Hills, MI: Gale Group, 1997.

Simmons, John S. "The Avenger Strikes Again: *We All Fall Down.*" In *Censored Books II: Critical Viewpoints, 1985–2000,* edited by Nicholas J. Karolides. Lanham, MD: Scarecrow Press, 2002.

Stines, Joe. "Robert Cormier." In *Dictionary of Literary Biography: American Writers for Children Since 1960: Fiction.* Farmington Hills, MI: Gale Group, 1986.

Straub, Deborah A. *Contemporary Authors New Revision Series,* vol. 23. Farmington Hills, MI: Gale Group, 1988.

Sweeney, Joyce. "The Invisible Adolescent: Robert Cormier's *Fade.*" In *Censored Books II: Critical Viewpoints, 1985–2000,* edited by Nicholas J. Karolides. Lanham, MD: Scarecrow Press, 2002.

Tarr, C. Anita "The Absence of Moral Agency in Robert Cormier's *The Chocolate War.*" In *Children's Literature,* vol. 30, edited by Elizabeth Lennox Keyser and Julie Pfeiffer. New Haven, CT: Yale University Press, 2002.

Trites, Roberta Seelinger. *Disturbing the Universe: Power and Repression in Adolescent Literature.* Iowa City: University of Iowa Press, 2000.

Yoshida, Junko. "The Quest for Masculinity in *The Chocolate War*: Changing Conceptions of Masculinity in the 1970s." In *Children's Literature,* vol. 26. New Haven, CT: Yale University Press, 1998.

Articles and Papers

"Are Cormier's Teen Novels Sending the Wrong Messages?" [letters to the editor] *Los Angeles Times,* June 2, 1998, E2.

Bagnall, Norma. "Realism: How Realistic Is It: A Look at *The Chocolate War.*" *Top of the News,* Winter 1980, 214.

Bell, Amelia M. "Adolescent Initiation in Cormier's *After the First Death.*" *ALAN Review,* Winter 1985, 37.

Bixler, Phyllis. "*I Am the Cheese* and Reader-Response Criticism in the Adolescent Literature Classroom." *Children's Literature Association Quarterly,* 1985, 13.

"The Bob: Robert Cormier Center for Young Adults." *Voice of Youth Advocates,* April 2005, 24.

"A Bouquet for Bob." *Voice of Youth Advocates,* February 2001, 390.

Campbell, Patty. "Hangin' Out with Bob." *Top of the News,* Winter 1986, 135.

Campbell, Patty. "A Loving Farewell to Robert Cormier." *The Horn Book Magazine,* March/April 2001, 245.

Carlson, Peter. "A Chilling Case of Censorship." *The Washington Post Magazine,* January 4, 1987, 10.

Cart, Michael. "A Modern Master." *Booklist,* December 15, 2000, 807.

Carter, Betty, and Karen Harris. "Realism in Adolescent Fiction: In Defense of *The Chocolate War.*" *Top of the News,* Winter 1980, 283.

Cheaney, J. B. "Teen Wars: The Young Adult Fiction of

Robert Cormier." *Book World: Writers and Writing,* December 2001, 254.

Clements, Bruce. "A Second Look: *The Chocolate War.*" *The Horn Book Magazine,* April 1979, 217.

Daly, Jay. "The New Repression." *Top of the News,* Fall 1980, 79.

Davis, William A. "Tough Tales for Teenagers." *Boston Globe Magazine,* November 16, 1980, 17.

De Luca, Geraldine, and Roni Natov. "Taking True Risks: Controversial Issues in New Young Adult Novels." *The Lion and the Unicorn,* Winter 1979–80, 125.

Ellis, W. Geiger. "Cormier and the Pessimistic View." *ALAN Review,* Winter 1985, 10.

Flint-Ferguson, Janis D. "Being and Becoming a Real Writer Through Reading the Manuscripts of Robert Cormier." *Ohio Journal of the English Language Arts,* Winter/Spring 1999, 14.

Gallo, Donald R. "Reality and Responsibility: The Continuing Controversy over Robert Cormier's Books for Young Adults." *Voice of Youth Advocates,* December 1984, 245.

Gallo, Donald R. "Robert Cormier: The Author and the Man." Speech at a reception commemorating the establishment of the Robert Cormier Collection, Fitchburg State College Library, Fitchburg, MA, May 3, 1981. Printed in *ALAN Review,* Fall 1981, 34.

Gardner, Lyn. "Dead Bodies in Suburbia." *Guardian Review,* August 19, 2000. http://books.guardian.co.uk/departments/childrenandteens/story/0,,355908,00.html.

Gerson, Lisa. "Try a Little Tenderness." *Boston Magazine,* December 1997, 168.

Glick, Andrea. "Robert Cormier Dead at 75." *School Library Journal,* December 2000, 24.

Gottlieb, Annie. "A New Cycle in YA Books." *New York Times Book Review,* June 17, 1984, 24.

Green, Bob. "Cormier Mural Depicts Leominster Writer's

Life, Influences." *Sentinel and Enterprise,* Fitchburg, MA: May 10, 2002, A1.

Guilfoy, Christine. "Library Will Name Room for Man Who Would 'Drop By.' " *Telegram and Gazette,* April 2, 2002, B1.

Head, Patricia. "Robert Cormier and the Postmodernist Possibilities of Young Adult Fiction." *Children's Literature Association Quarterly,* Spring 1996, 28.

Headley, Kathy Neal. "Duel at High Noon: A Replay of Cormier's Works." *ALAN Review,* Winter 1994, 34.

Hollingdale, Peter. "The Adolescent Novel of Ideas." *Children's Literature in Education,* vol. 26. November 1995, 83.

Jackson, Joanna. "FSC Students, Staff Pay Tribute to Robert Cormier." *Sentinel and Enterprise*, Fitchburg, MA: December 7, 2001, A2.

Keeling, Kara. " 'The Misfortunes of a Man Like Ourselves': Robert Cormier's *The Chocolate War* as Aristotelian Tragedy." *ALAN Review,* Winter 1999, 9.

Kids @ Random, Author Spotlight: "Robert Cormier." www.randomhouse.com/kids/author/cormier.html.

Kister, Ken. "Censorship in the Sunshine State: Florida Libraries Respond." *Wilson Library Bulletin,* November 1989, 29.

Knudsen, Elizabeth G. "Is There Hope for Young Adult Readers?" *Wilson Library Bulletin,* September 1981, 47.

Lent, ReLeah, and Gloria Pipkin. "We Keep Pedaling." *ALAN Review,* Winter 2001, 9.

Lenz, Millicent. "A Romantic Ironist's Vision of Evil: Robert Cormier's *After the First Death.*" Paper presented at the Eighth Annual Conference of the Children's Literature Association, Minneapolis: March 1981.

Lodge, Sally. "Children's Writers Plumb the Depths of Fear." *Publishers Weekly,* March 27, 1995, 28.

Loer, Stephanie. "Leominster's Inventive Son." *Boston Globe,* January 30, 1989, D9.

Long, Tom, and William A. Davis. " 'Chocolate' and 'Cheese' Author Gave Voice to Adolescent Angst." *Boston Globe,* November 3, 2000, D15.

Lukens, Rebecca. "From Salinger to Cormier: Disillusionment to Despair in Thirty Years." *ALAN Review,* Fall 1981, 38.

Lynch, Chris. "Today's YA Writers: Pulling No Punches." *School Library Journal,* January 1994, 37.

MacLeod, Anne Scott. "Robert Cormier and the Adolescent Novel." *Children's Literature in Education,* Summer 1981, 74.

March-Penny, R. "From Hardback to Paperback: *The Chocolate War,* by Robert Cormier." *Children's Literature in Education,* Summer 1978, 78.

Monseau, Virginia R. "Cormier's Heroines." *ALAN Review,* Fall 1991, 40.

Monseau, Virginia R. "Studying Cormier's Protagonists." *ALAN Review,* Fall 1994, 31.

Nilsen, Alleen Pace. "The Poetry of Naming in Young Adult Books." *ALAN Review,* Spring 1980, 3.

Nodelman, Perry. "Robert Cormier Does a Number." *Children's Literature in Education,* Summer 1983, 94.

Peck, Richard. "The Silver Anniversary of Young Adult Books." *Journal of Youth Services in Libraries,* Fall 1993, 19.

"The People v. Robert Cormier?" *ACLU Freedom Network News.* January 10, 1997. http://www.aclu.org/news/w011097a.html. Accessed April 3, 2003.

Peters, Mike. "*The Chocolate War* and After: The Novels of Robert Cormier." *The School Librarian,* August 1992, 85.

Ritter, John H. "A Reflection upon the Death of Robert Cormier." *ALAN Review,* Winter 2001, 6.

"Robert Cormier Remembered." *Publishers Weekly,* January 1, 2001, 28–33.

Schwartz, Tony. "Teen-agers' Laureate." *Newsweek,* July 17, 1979, 87.

Semon, Craig S. "Library Legacy: Modest Author's Life Celebrated." *Telegram and Gazette,* Worcester, MA: April 8, 2002, B1.

Simmons, John S. "You Dared, Bob; Thank God You Dared." *ALAN Review,* Winter 2001, 8.

Smith, Lynn. "Unhappily Ever After." *Los Angeles Times,* May 26, 1998, E2.

Stewart, Barbara. "Dangerous Books, Dangerous Deeds." *The Orlando Sentinel, Florida Magazine,* July 12, 1987, 9.

Stringer, Sharon. "The Psychological Changes of Adolescence." *ALAN Review,* Fall 1994, 27.

Susina, Jan. "*The Chocolate War* and 'The Sweet Science.' " *Children's Literature in Education,* vol. 22. September 1991, 169.

Sutton, Roger. "The Critical Myth: Realistic YA Novels." *School Library Journal,* November 1982, 33.

Veglahn, Nancy. "The Bland Face of Evil in the Novels of Robert Cormier." *The Lion and the Unicorn,* vol. 12. 1988, 12.

West, Mark. "Censorship in Children's Books: Authors and Editors Provide New Perspectives on the Issue." *Publishers Weekly,* July 24, 1987, 108.

Williamson, Dianne. "Censorship an Endless Challenge." *Telegram and Gazette,* Worcester, MA: June 13, 2000, B1.

Woo, Elaine. "Robert Cormier; Author Gave Dark Touch to Juvenile Fiction." *Los Angeles Times,* November 11, 2000, B6.

Zitterkopf, Deanna. "Robert Cormier." *Children's Literature Association Quarterly,* Spring 1986, 42.

Interviews

"Robert Cormier: London, July 11, 2000." Part 1: www.achuka.co.uk/special/cormier01.htm. Accessed March 15, 2003. Part 2: www.achuka.co.uk/special/ cormier02.htm. Accessed March 15, 2003.

Bugniazet, J. "A Telephone Interview with Robert Cormier." *ALAN Review,* Winter 1985, 14.

Campbell, Patty. "Conversing with Robert Cormier." Amazon.com teen pages. http://www.amazon.com/exec/ obidos/tg/feature/-/5191.

Cohen, John. "An Interview with Robert Cormier." *Reading Time,* February 1993, 7.

De Luca, Geraldine, and Roni Natov. "An Interview with Robert Cormier." *The Lion and the Unicorn,* Fall 1978, 109.

Douglas, Jonathan. "Robert Cormier Meets Melvin Burgess." Achuka, September 11, 2000. www.achuka.co. uk/special/cormburg.htm. Accessed March 15, 2003.

Graeber, Laurel. "PW Interviews: Robert Cormier." *Publishers Weekly,* October 7, 1983, 98.

Grove, Lee. "Robert Cormier Comes of Age." *Boston Magazine,* September 1980, 78.

Hoffman, Laura B. "Beyond the Shadows of Robert Cormier." Writes of Passage. http://www.DAVIDVL.ORG/ 262WebFilesSpring04/w1cg.pdf.

Janeczco, Paul. "An Interview with Robert Cormier." *English Journal,* September 1977, 10.

Kelly, Patricia P. "An Interview with Robert Cormier." *Journal of Youth Services in Libraries,* Fall 1993.

McLaughlin, Frank. *Cheese, Chocolates, and Kids: A Day with Robert Cormier.* Videotape prepared for PBS, n.d. (Robert E. Cormier Collection, Fitchburg State College, Fitchburg, MA).

McLaughlin, Frank. "Robert Cormier: A Profile." *Media and Methods,* May/June 1978, 28.

Marcus, Leonard. *Frenchtown Summer.* Audiobook plus interview. Listening Library, 2000.

Myers, Mitzi. "No Safe Place to Run To." *The Lion and the Unicorn,* September 2000, 445.

"Robert Cormier." Teenreads.com. http://teenreads.com/authors/au-cormier-robert.asp.

Rosenberg, Merri. "Teenagers Face Evil." *New York Times Book Review,* May 5, 1985, 36.

Silvey, Anita. "An Interview with Robert Cormier." *The Horn Book Magazine,* Part 1, March/April 1985, 145; Part 2, May/June 1985, 289.

Sutton, Roger. "Kind of a Funny Dichotomy." *School Library Journal,* June 1991, 28.

West, Mark. In *Trust Your Children: Voices Against Censorship in Children's Literature,* New York: Neal Schuman, 1988, 29.

Zitlow, Connie S., and Tobie R. Sanders. "Conversations with Robert Cormier and Sue Ellen Bridgers: Their Life and Work as Writers." *Ohio Journal of the English Language Arts,* Winter/Spring 1999, 34.

Study Guides

Bushman, Kay Parks, and John H. Bushman. "Dealing with the Abuse of Power in *1984* and *The Chocolate War.*" *Adolescent Literature as a Complement to the Classics,* vol. I, edited by Joan F. Kaywell. Norwood, MA: Christopher-Gordon, 1993.

Campbell, Patricia J. *A Reader's Companion: "Heroes" by Robert Cormier.* Delacorte Press, 1998.

———. *Readers' Companion: The Novels of Robert Cormier.* Delacorte Press, 2000.

———. *A Reader's Companion: "Tenderness," A Novel by Robert Cormier.* Delacorte Press, 1997.

"The Chocolate War" and Related Readings: Literature Connections. Geneva, IL: McDougal Littell, 1998.

Guilliland, Donna. *Critical Reading Activities for the Works of Robert Cormier.* Portland, ME: J. Weston Walch, 2000.

Lucht, Stephan Thorven. "Robert Cormier's World in the High School Literature Classroom." http://www.uiowa.edu/english/profpage/blandon/tlucht/lit-teachingcormier.html. Accessed September 13, 2003.

Poe, Elizabeth Ann. "Alienation from Society in *The Scarlet Letter* and *The Chocolate War.*" In *Adolescent Literature as a Complement to the Classics,* vol. I, edited by Joan F. Kaywell. Norwood MA: Christopher-Gordon, 1993.

Samuels, Barbara G. "The Beast Within: Using and Abusing Power in *Lord of the Flies, The Chocolate War,* and Other Readings." In *Adolescent Literature as a Complement to the Classics,* vol. I, edited by Joan F. Kaywell. Norwood, MA: Christopher-Gordon, 1993.

Stanek, Lou Willett. *A Study Guide to "After the First Death" by Robert Cormier.* New York: Avon, n.d.

———. *A Teacher's Guide to the Paperback Edition of "The Chocolate War" by Robert Cormier.* New York: Dell, 1975.

———. *A Teacher's Guide to the Paperback Edition of "I Am the Cheese" by Robert Cormier.* New York: Dell, 1978.

Selected Book Reviews

After the First Death

Booklist, March 15, 1979, 1141.

The Bulletin of the Center for Children's Books, June 1979, 172.

Campbell, Patty. *Wilson Library Bulletin,* April 1979, 578.

Davis, L. J. *Washington Post Book World,* May 13, 1979, K3.

Ellin, Stanley. "You Can and Can't Go Home Again." *New York Times Book Review,* April 29, 1979, 30.

Harrison, Barbara. *The Horn Book Magazine,* August 1979, 426.

Hibberd, Dominic. "Missing the Bus." [London] *Times Literary Supplement,* December 1979, 125.

Hirsch, Lorraine. *Christian Science Monitor,* June 1, 1979, 22.

Kirkus Reviews, April 1, 1979, 391.

Norsworthy, James A. *Catholic Library World,* November 1979, 182.

Pollack, Pamela. *School Library Journal,* March 1979, 146.

Publishers Weekly, January 29, 1979, 115.

Beyond the Chocolate War

The Bulletin of the Center for Children's Books, April 1985, 143.

Burns, Mary M. *The Horn Book Magazine,* July/August 1985, 451.

Cohen, Marcia. *Seventeen,* August 1985, 184.

Estes, Sally. *Booklist,* March 15, 1985, 1048.

Hayes, Sarah. "One Black Marble." [London] *Times Literary Supplement,* November 29, 1985, 1358.

Keresey, Gayle. *Voice of Youth Advocates,* June 1985, 128.

Nelms, Beth; Ben Nelms; and Linda Horton. *English Journal,* September 1985, 85.

Publishers Weekly, February 15, 1985, 102.

Rochman, Hazel. *The New York Times Book Review,* May 5, 1985, 37.

Silvey, Anita. "An Interview with Robert Cormier." *The Horn Book Magazine,* Part 1, March/April 1985, 145; Part 2, May/June 1985, 289.

Sutton, Roger. *School Library Journal,* April 1985, 96.

The Bumblebee Flies Anyway

Basbanes, Nicholas. "Cormier Launches *Bumblebee*." *Worcester Evening Gazette,* September 14, 1983, A3.

The Bulletin of the Center for Children's Books, September 1983, A3.

Cooper, Ilene. *Booklist,* September 1, 1983, 82.

Disch, Thomas M. "Boys on the Brink." *Washington Post Book World,* November 6, 1983.

Ellis, W. Geiger. *ALAN Review,* Fall 1983, 23.

Estes, Sally. *Booklist,* September 1, 1983, 37.

Hammond, Nancy C. *The Horn Book Magazine,* December 1983, 715.

Horowitz, Anthony. [London] *Times Literary Supplement,* November 25, 1983, 1318.

Knowles, John. "Defiance and Survival." *The New York Times,* November 13, 1983, 40.

Loescher, Judy. "Cormier's *Bumblebee* Stings." *Fitchburg-Leominster Sentinel and Enterprise,* September 8, 1983, 20.

Madden, Susan B. *Voice of Youth Advocates,* December 1983, 278.

Publishers Weekly, August 5, 1983, 92.

Rochman, Hazel. *School Library Journal,* September 1983, 132.

The Chocolate War

The Bulletin of the Center for Children's Books, July 1974, 173.

Chelton, Mary K. *School Library Journal,* May 1974, 62.

Fagg, Martin. "Beasts and Monks." *New Statesman,* May 23, 1975, 694.

Hearne, Betsy. "Whammo, You Lose." *Booklist,* July 1, 1974, 1199.

Hunt, Peter. [London] *Times Literary Supplement,* April 4, 1975, 364.

Kirkus Reviews, April 1, 1974, 371.

Peck, Richard. "Delivering the Goods." *American Libraries,* October 1974, 492.

Pelorus. *Signal,* September 1975, 146.

Publishers Weekly, April 15, 1974, 52.

Weesner, Theodore. *The New York Times,* May 5, 1974, Section VII, 15.

Eight Plus One

The Bulletin of the Center for Children's Books, December 1980, 67.

De Mott, Benjamin. *The New York Times,* November 9, 1980, 55.

Heins, P. L. *The Horn Book Magazine,* October 1980, 524.

Jaffee, Cyrisse. *School Library Journal,* September 1980, 81.

Lenz, Millicent. *Voice of Youth Advocates,* December 1980, 28.

Publishers Weekly, August 29, 1980, 365.

Wilson, R. *Washington Post Book World,* January 11, 1981, 7.

Zvirin, Stephanie. *Booklist,* September 15, 1980, 110.

Fade

Clark, Beverly Lyon. *The New York Times Book Review,* February 12, 1989, 18.

Donelson, Kenneth L., and Alleen Pace Nilsen. *English Journal,* vol. 79, January 1990, 88.

Fakih, Kimberly Olson, and Diane Roback. *Publishers Weekly,* September 30, 1988, 69.

The Horn Book Magazine, March/April 1989, 166.

Kirkus Reviews, August 1, 1988, 1147.

MacRae, Cathi. *Wilson Library Bulletin,* February 1989, 86.

Pickworth, Hannah. *ALAN Review,* Fall 1988, 19.

R. D. "A Look at the Creative Process." *Publishers Weekly,* July 29, 1988, 134.

Rochman, Hazel. *Booklist,* September 1, 1988, 67.

Sutherland, Zena. *The Bulletin of the Center for Children's Books,* November 1988, 68.
Unsworth, Robert. *School Library Journal,* October 1988, 160.

Frenchtown Summer

Anderson, Sheila, and Gwendolyn Davis. *Voice of Youth Advocates,* December 1999, 330.
Bush, Elizabeth. *The Bulletin of the Center for Children's Books,* November 1999, 81.
Campbell, Patty. Review of *Frenchtown Summer.* Amazon.com/books, 1999.
Campbell, Patty. *The Horn Book Magazine,* September/October 1999, 608.
Cart, Michael. *Booklist,* September 15, 1999, 259.
Fisher, Enicia. *Christian Science Monitor,* February 10, 2000, 21.
Sullivan, Edward. *School Library Journal,* September 1999, 221.

Heroes

Bush, Elizabeth. *The Bulletin of the Center for Children's Books,* September 1998, 11.
Campbell, Patty. Review of *Heroes.* Amazon.com/books, 1998.
Fakolt, Jennifer A. *School Library Journal,* August 1998, 160.
Fitzgerald, Carol. Teenreads.com. www.teenreads.com/reviews/0440227690.asp.
Lacey, Paula. *Voice of Youth Advocates,* August 1998, 198.
Rogers, Leslie. *Booklist,* June 1, 1998, 1745.

I Am the Cheese

Booklist, April 1, 1977, 1155.
The Bulletin of the Center for Children's Books, April 1977, 121.

Callendar, Newgate. "Boy on the Couch." *The New York Times Book Review,* May 1, 1977, 26.

Heins, Paul. *The Horn Book Magazine,* August 1977, 427.

Laski, Audrey. "No Laughing Matter." [London] *Times Educational Supplement,* November 18, 1977, 34.

May, Clifford D. "Catchers in the Rye." *Newsweek,* December 19, 1977, 85.

Norsworthy, James A. *Catholic Library World,* December 1977, 234.

Publishers Weekly, March 7, 1977, 100.

Salway, Lance. [London] *Times Literary Supplement,* December 2, 1977, 1415.

School Library Journal, May 1977, 78.

In the Middle of the Night

Campbell, Patty. *Children's Book Review,* Winter 1995, 40.

Campbell, Patty. *The Horn Book Magazine,* May/June 1995, 365.

Hand, Elizabeth. *Washington Post Book World,* May 7, 1995.

Joseph, Gary E. *Voice of Youth Advocates,* June 1995, 92.

Knoth, Maeve Visser. *The Horn Book Magazine,* May/June 1995, 335.

Metzger, Lois. *The New York Times Book Review,* July 16, 1995, 27.

Shoemaker, Joel. *School Library Journal,* May 1995, 118.

Sutton, Roger. *The Bulletin of the Center for Children's Books,* May 1995, 302.

Triner, Jeanne. *Booklist,* April 1, 1995, 1387.

Now and at the Hour

Adams, Phoebe-Lou. *The Atlantic,* September 1960, 118.

Serebnick, Judith. "Triumph in Tragedy." *Library Journal,* June 1, 1960, 2203.

Time, August 1, 1960, 68.

Other Bells for Us to Ring

Burns, Mary M. *The Horn Book Magazine,* November/ December 1990, 742.
Campbell, Patty. *Five Owls Magazine,* September 1990, 4.
Del Negro, Janice. *School Library Journal,* November 1990, 137.
Publishers Weekly, November 16, 1990, 57.
Rochman, Hazel. *Booklist,* October 1, 1990, 325.

The Rag and Bone Shop

Campbell, Patty. "The Last Cormier." *The Horn Book Magazine,* September/October 2001, 624.
Cline, Rob. Teenreads.com. http://aolsvc.teenreads.aol.com/ reviews/0440229715.asp. Accessed October 26, 2005.
Munat, Florence H. *Voice of Youth Advocates,* October 2001, 273.
Oppenheimer, Mark. "Murder in Frenchtown." *The New York Times Book Review,* November 18, 2001, 54.
Shoemaker, Joel. *School Library Journal,* September 2001, 223.
Sutton, Roger. *The Horn Book Magazine,* November/ December 2001, 742.

Tenderness

Del Negro, Janice. *The Bulletin of the Center for Children's Books,* April 1997, 278.
Harrison, Barbara. *The Horn Book Magazine,* March/April 1997, 197.
Munat, Florence M. *Voice of Youth Advocates,* April 1997, 273.
Phillips, Marilyn Payne. *School Library Journal,* March 1997, 184.
Zvirin, Stephanie. *Booklist,* February 1, 1997, 935.

Tunes for Bears to Dance To

Cline, Ruth. *Voice of Youth Advocates,* October 1992, 222.

Publishers Weekly, September 7, 1992, 97.

Rochman, Hazel. *Booklist,* June 15, 1992, 1825.

Scott, Anne. *Washington Post Book World,* December 6, 1992, 20.

Sutton, Roger. *The Bulletin of the Center for Children's Books,* September 1992, 8.

Whitehurst, Lucinda Snyder. *School Library Journal,* September 1992, 274.

We All Fall Down

Cart, Michael. *Los Angeles Times Book Review,* October 27, 1991, 7.

Cart, Michael. *School Library Journal,* September 1991, 277.

Estes, Sally. *Booklist,* September 15, 1991, 137.

Hearne, Betsy. *The Bulletin of the Center for Children's Books,* October 1991, 35.

Hayhoe, Mike. *School Librarian,* August 1992, 112.

Publishers Weekly, October 25, 1991, 69.

Voice of Youth Advocates, December 1991, 308.

Vsilakis, Nancy. *The Horn Book Magazine,* November/December 1991, 742.

APPENDIX I

ROBERT CORMIER'S AWARDS AND HONORS

Personal Awards

Best Human Interest Story of the Year Award, Associated Press in New England, 1959.
Bread Loaf Writers' Conference Fellow, 1968.
Best Human Interest Story of the Year Award, Associated Press in New England, 1973.
Best Newspaper Column, K. R. Thomson Newspapers, 1974.
Honorary Doctorate of Letters, Fitchburg State College, 1977.
Robert E. Cormier Collection established at Fitchburg State College, 1981.
ALAN Award, Assembly on Literature for Adolescents, National Council of Teachers of English, 1982.
Massachusetts Author of the Year, Massachusetts Library Association, 1985.
International Reading Association Commendation, 1985.
Margaret A. Edwards Award, Young Adult Library Services Association, American Library Association/ *School Library Journal,* 1991.

Awards and Honors for Books

Now and at the Hour

A *New York Times* Outstanding Book of the Year, 1960.

The Chocolate War

A *New York Times* Outstanding Book of the Year, 1974.

A Best Book for Young Adults, Young Adult Services Division, American Library Association, 1974.

Included in *Still Alive: The Best of the Best Books for Young Adults, 1960–1974.* Young Adult Services Division, American Library Association, 1974.

Maxi Award, *Media and Methods,* 1976.

Lewis Carroll Shelf Award, 1979.

Included in *Best of the Best Books for Young Adults, 1970–1983.* Young Adult Services Division, American Library Association, 1983.

Included in *Nothin' but the Best: Best of the Best Books for Young Adults, 1966–1986.* Young Adult Services Division, American Library Association, 1986.

Margaret A. Edwards Award, 1991. Young Adult Library Services Association, American Library Association/ *School Library Journal,* 1991.

Included in "100 All-Star Choices for Teens." Young Adult Library Services Association, American Library Association, 2000.

I Am the Cheese

A *New York Times* Outstanding Book of the Year, 1977.

A Best Book for Young Adults, Young Adult Services Division, American Library Association, 1977.

Woodward School Annual Book Award, 1978.

California Young Reader Medal, 1981.

Included in *Best of the Best Books for Young Adults, 1970–1983.* Young Adult Services Division, American Library Association, 1983.

Margaret A. Edwards Award, Young Adult Library

Services Association, American Library Association/ *School Library Journal*, 1991.
Phoenix Award, Children's Literature Association, 1997.

After the First Death

A *New York Times* Outstanding Book of the Year, 1979.
A Best Book for Young Adults, Young Adult Services Division, American Library Association, 1979.
Included in *Nothin' but the Best: Best of the Best Books for Young Adults, 1966–1986*. Young Adult Services Division, American Library Association, 1986.
Included in *Best of the Best Books, 1970–1983*. Young Adult Services Division, American Library Association, 1983.
Margaret A. Edwards Award, Young Adult Library Services Association, American Library Association/*School Library Journal*, 1991.

Eight Plus One

A Notable Children's Trade Book for Young People, National Council for Social Studies and Children's Book Council, 1980.
World of Reading Readers' Choice Award, Silver Burdett & Ginn, for short story "President Cleveland, Where Are You?" 1983.

The Bumblebee Flies Anyway

A Best Book for Young Adults, Young Adult Services Division, American Library Association, 1983.
A *School Library Journal* Best Book of the Year, 1983.
Short-listed for the Carnegie Medal, 1983.

Beyond the Chocolate War

A *New York Times* Notable Book, 1985.
Honor List citation, *The Horn Book Magazine,* 1986.

Fade

A Best Book for Young Adults, Young Adult Services Division, American Library Association, 1988.
World Fantasy Award nomination, 1989.

We All Fall Down

Included in *Top One Hundred Countdown: Best of the Best Books for Young Adults.* Young Adult Library Services Association, American Library Association, 1994.
Winner of the California Young Reader Medal, 1993–94.

Tunes for Bears to Dance To

A Best Book for Young Adults, Young Adult Library Services Association, American Library Association, 1992.
Catholic Book of the Year Award, Germany, 1992.

In the Middle of the Night

A Best Book for Young Adults, Young Adult Library Services Association, American Library Association, 1996.
Edgar Award nominee for Best Young Adult Mystery, Mystery Writers of America, 1996.
Short-listed for the Carnegie Medal, 1996.

Tenderness

A Best Books for Young Adults, Young Adult Library Services Association, American Library Association, 1998. Short-listed for the Carnegie Medal, 1998.

Heroes

A Best Book for Young Adults, Young Adult Library Services Association, American Library Association, 1999. Carnegie Medal "Highly Commended" citation, 1999.

Frenchtown Summer

Los Angeles Times Book Prize for Best Young Adult Fiction, 1999.

The Rag and Bone Shop

A Best Book for Young Adults, Young Adult Library Services Association, American Library Association, 2002.

APPENDIX II

FILMS BASED ON ROBERT CORMIER'S NOVELS

I Am the Cheese—1983

Premiere in Leominster, Massachusetts, April 27, 1983.
Debut at Gemini Theater, New York City, November 10, 1983.
Video distribution by Vestron.

Cast:
Adam—Robert Macnaughton
Brint—Robert Wagner
Adam's father—Don Murray
Adam's mother—Hope Lange
Amy—Cynthia Nixon
Amy's father—Robert Cormier

Director—Robert Jiras
Producers—Robert Jiras and David Lange
Screenplay—Robert Jiras and David Lange
Cinematographer—David Quaid

The Chocolate War—1988

Premiere in Los Angeles and New York, October 28, 1988, as a benefit for Amnesty International.
Video distribution by Forum Home Video.

Cast:
Brother Leon—John Glover

Jerry—Ilan Mitchell-Smith
Archie—Wally Ward
Obie— Doug Hutchinson
Goober—Corey Gunnestad
Emile Janza—Brent Fraser
Brian Cochran—Robert Davenport
Lisa—Jenny Wright
Brother Jacques—Bud Cort
Carter—Adam Baldwin
Caroni— Ethan Sandler
Gregory Bailey—Wayne Young
Frank Bollo—Landon Wine
Coach—Max Dixon
Jerry's father—Roger Tempkins
Jerry's mother—Elizabeth Yoffee
Brother Eugene—Robert Munns

Director—Keith Gordon
Producers—Jonathan D. Krane and Simon Lewis
Screenplay—Keith Gordon
Cinematographer—Tom Richmond
Art director— David Ensley

Lapse of Memory (based on *I Am the Cheese*)—1992

Cast:
Adam's father—John Hurt
Adam's mother—Marthe Keller
Adam—Mathew Mackay
Also with Kathleen Robertson, Marion Peterson, Serge
Dupire

Director—Patrick Dewolf
Screenplay—Patrick Dewolf, Philippe Le Guay, John
Frizzell

The Bumblebee Flies Anyway—2000

Premiere in Fitchburg, Massachusetts, March 29, 2000.

Cast:
Eileen Snow—Janet Paparazzo
Barney Snow—Elijah Wood
Dr. Harriman/Handyman—Janeane Garofalo
Billy—George Gore II
Mazzo—Joe Perrino
Dr. Croft—Roger Rees
Nurse Bascam—Oni Faida Lampley
Allie Roon—Jeffrey Force
Chris Ronson—Christopher Mark Petrizzo
Cassie—Rachael Leigh Cook
Samuel Ronson—Samuel Haft
Willy/Orderly—John E. Mack
Young Barney Snow—Matthew Cavallary
Richard Snow—David France
Woman in Suburbs—Joan Levy

Director—Martin Duffy
Producer—Steven Haft and Shooting Gallery Films
Screenplay—Jennifer Sarja

INDEX

Key:

After the First Death = AFD

Beyond the Chocolate War = BCW

The Bumblebee Flies Anyway = BB

The Chocolate War = CW

Fade = F

Frenchtown Summer = FS

Heroes = H

I Am the Cheese = IAC

In the Middle of the Night = IMN

Other Bells for Us to Ring = OB

The Rag and Bone Shop = RB

Tenderness = T

Tunes for Bears to Dance To = TB

We All Fall Down = WAFD

Note: Characters are listed by first name

Accelerated Reader, 76–77

"Act of Contrition," 22, 159

Adam Farmer (IAC), xii, 12, 42, 99–115, 172, 189

Adelard Roget (F), 151–152, 155, 157–158, 165–166

After the First Death, 28, 37, 40, 119–135, 156, 184, 213

ALAN Award (National Council of Teachers of English), 1, 29

Allusions. *See* Imagery.

Ambiguity, 40, 96, 113–114, 191, 207

Amnesia, 139, 144, 146–147

Amy Hertz (IAC), xii, 13, 102, 108–110, 112

Archie Costello, (CW, BCW), 37, 53–64, 71, 81–95, 134, 156, 180, 183, 200

Artkin (AFD), 44, 120–123, 125–135, 183

"At the New Year" (Kenneth Patchen), 174

Avenger, The (WAFD), 199–204

Awards, 1, 17–18, 23, 29, 30, 183, 237, 238, 273–277

Barney Snow (BB), 86, 137–148, 166, 189

Bay County, Florida (censorship attack), 73–76

Ben Marchand (AFD), 86, 120–126, 129, 130

Beyond the Chocolate War, 28, 42, 81–96, 156, 180, 208

Bible, allusions from, 57–58, 181, 228

Billy the Kidney (BB), 137–140, 146, 148

Black marble, 54–55, 63–64, 90

Brint (IAC), 100, 102–108, 113, 144, 238, 244

Brother Leon (CW, BCW), 54–64, 84, 86–87, 90, 92–93, 95

Buddy Walker (WAFD), 45, 199–204

Bullies, 19, 42, 152–153, 157, 200–201, 223, 235

Bumblebee Flies Anyway, The, 26, 28, 42, 89, 137–148, 166, 210, 234

Film, 281

Cadnum, Michael, 3

Camus, Albert, 26

Cart, Michael, 2, 5, 8, 200–204

Carter (CW, BCW), 55, 62, 64, 84–86, 90–92

Cassie Mazzofono (BB), 26, 89, 138–142, 146–147

Catholic Church. *See* Cormier, Robert— Catholicism

Catcher in the Rye, The (J. D. Salinger), 4, 13

Celebrity, 216–218

Censorship, xiii, 1, 48, 71–78

Characters, 37–38, 44–45, 62, 82, 85, 157

Chelton, Mary K., 68

Chocolate War, The, xi, xii, 2, 3, 5, 8, 27–28, 37–38, 40, 48, 53–78, 81–82, 84–85, 87, 92, 96, 110, 134, 180, 213
  Film, 63, 279–280
Christian symbolism, 58–59, 87, 89, 125–126, 142. *See also* Cormier, Robert—Catholicism, God
"The Circus Animals' Desertion" (William Butler Yeats), 238
Cohen, Fabio, 28
Conlon, Florence, 21
Contender, The (Robert Lipsyte), 4
Cormier archives. *See* Robert E. Cormier Collection, Fitchburg State College
Cormier, Bobbie (Roberta), 12
Cormier, Christine, 13
Cormier, Constance Senay, xii, 12, 21–22, 28–30, 170, 195, 221, 244–246
Cormier, Irma Collins, 14–15
Cormier, Leo, 15, 47, 129, 235
Cormier, Lucien Joseph, 14, 23–24
Cormier, Peter, xii, 13, 27
Cormier, Renee, 13, 126
Cormier, Robert
  Adolescence, 19–20
  And teens, 6–7, 13–14, 49, 202
  As a young adult author, 2, 5–6, 27–28, 48–49, 69, 237
  Catholicism, 16–17, 19, 26, 31, 43–44, 46–47, 58–59, 89, 115, 142, 144–146, 169–170, 172–174, 189, 206, 235, 237–238, 241
  Childhood, 15–17
  Children, 13, 27–29
  Death, 30–31
  Influence on young adult literature, 1–8
  Insomnia, 13
  Libraries, 17–18, 29, 210, 245
  Literary influences, 17–20, 57–58, 221
  Marriage, 14, 21–22
  Newspaper work, 22, 26, 28, 39
  Obituary tributes, 6–7
  Phobias, 12, 19, 43, 110, 115 *See also* Dogs, Elevators
  Radio writing, 21

Crutcher, Chris, 3
Darcy Webster (OB), 44–45, 170–175
Darkness, 2, 8, 47–48, 62, 67–68, 70, 75, 170, 183, 188, 233, 238
Dave (IMN), 207–211
Delacorte Press, 4, 48, 160, 165, 175
Denny Colbert (IMN), 207–211
"Do I dare disturb the universe?" 55–56, 63, 69, 75, 88
Dogs, 12, 19, 42, 92, 104, 108, 112, 235
Eight Plus One, 28, 195
Elevators, 12, 104
Eliot, T. S, 57–58, 63, 143
Emerson Winslow (F), 153, 161
Emile Janza (CW, BCW), 55, 61, 85, 88–90, 95, 134, 207
End of the Affair, The (Graham Greene), 150
Eric Poole (T), 183, 214, 217–228
Eugene (FS), 45, 232–237
Evil, 1, 2, 8, 11, 42–46, 59–64, 67, 70–71, 84–88, 90–91, 94, 105, 107, 111, 114, 126, 131, 133, 144, 156, 165–166, 176–183, 208, 218–219, 228, 241, 243
Fade, 15, 29, 44, 48, 149–167, 169, 213, 215, 234
Farrell, Alyne, 76
Feminist criticism, 41, 70–71
Films, 1, 63, 150, 279–281. *See also* Movies, influence of
Fitchburg, Massachusetts, 158
Fitchburg Sentinel, 22
Fitchburg State College, 14, 21, 29, 41
Flaubert, Gustave, 176
Flight of the Cassowary, The (John LeVert), 150
Flint-Ferguson, Janice D., 35–36, 196
Forever (Judy Blume), 5
Forgiveness, 43, 62, 123, 155, 169, 182, 185–186, 191, 239, 241
Fort Delta, 120, 122, 124, 126, 171
Fort Devens, 127, 159, 184
Frances Clarke Sayers lecture 1999, 47–48, 69
Francis Joseph Cassavant (H), 184–191
French Hill, 14–22, 25, 159

Frenchtown, 151, 153–155, 157, 159–160, 162, 171, 182, 184, 235, 237

Frenchtown Summer, 15, 30, 45, 158, 171, 197, 231–237

From Romance to Realism: 50 Years of Growth and Change in Young Adult Literature (Michael Cart), 200–201

Gallo, Donald, 69, 77

General Marcus Marchand (AFD), 44, 120–125, 129–130, 133–135

Gibran, Kahlil, 214

Giles, Gail, 3

God, 26, 43–44, 153, 155, 166, 173–174, 186, 228

Goober, The (CW, BCW), 54, 59, 64, 85, 88–90, 95

Gordon, Keith, 63, 280

Greene, Graham, 150

Grey (IAC), 106, 109, 113–114

Groton, Massachusetts (censorship attack), 71–72

Guilt, 41, 43, 46, 61, 89–90, 94, 122–124, 130, 133, 149, 152, 155, 166, 183, 190–191, 201, 203, 204, 206–208, 221–222, 235, 241–242

Hairston, Mr. (TB), 43, 45, 176–183

Hall, Leonard, 73–76

Halls, Kelly Milner, 6

Handyman, The (BB), 137–139, 144, 146–147

Harada, Masaru, 176

Harry Flowers (WAFD), 43, 200–204

Hearne, Betsy, 67

Hemingway, Ernest, 19, 183

Henry Cassavant (TBD), 45, 177–182

Heroes, 20, 30, 171, 183–191

Hinton, S. E., 4–5

"Hollow Men, The" (T. S. Eliot), 143

Hunt, Jonathan, 242

I Am the Cheese, xi, 3, 5, 12, 13–14, 28, 39, 73–76, 99–115, 144, 172, 213, 234, 238
Film, 279

Identity, hidden and revealed, 43, 130–134, 141, 147, 183, 189, 209

I Have Words to Spend: Reflections of a Small-Town Editor (Constance Cormier), 195

Imagery, 57–58, 90, 92–93, 112, 145, 175, 179, 186–187, 196, 203, 209, 213

"Implacable force," 24, 41–43, 45, 59, 62–63, 111, 128–129, 146, 166, 182, 241, 244

In the Middle of the Night, 204–211

"In the Midst of Winter," 26, 42, 89

Influence. *See* Cormier, Robert—Influence on young adult literature

Innocence as evil, 61, 125, 127, 130, 132–133, 219

Innocence, corruption of, 43, 107, 126, 181, 200, 239, 241, 243

Interactivity, 40, 63, 71

Invisibility, 124, 149–150, 152, 154, 155–156, 157, 164–166, 189

Invisible Man, The (Ralph Ellison), 150

Invisible Man, The (H. G. Wells), 150
Film, 150

Irony, 2, 64, 84, 103–104, 111, 130, 181, 183, 186, 201, 211, 213, 225, 228, 239, 241

Jake Proctor (T), 214, 220–222, 224–225, 227

Jane Jerome (WAFD), 45, 199, 202–204

Jason (RB), 239–242

Jerry Renault (CW, BCW), xii, 8, 42, 53–64, 70–71, 81–96, 110, 208

"John Fitch IV," 195

Jules Roget (F), 154, 156, 159, 161–165

Karen Jerome (WAFD), 197–199, 202–204

Kate Forrester (AFD), 37, 120–122, 125–134

Kathleen Mary O'Hara (OB) 171–172, 174

Kerr, M. E., 4–6

King, Stephen, 151, 203

Klein, Norma, 5–6

Lake home, Hubbardston, 30, 170, 231

Lancaster, Massachusetts (censorship attack), 78

Larry LaSalle (H), 44, 186–191

Lent, ReLeah, 74–75

Lenz, Millicent, 130

Leominster, Massachusetts, xii, 12, 14, 158, 238, 245

Leominster Public Library, 7, 17–18, 29. *See also* Robert Cormier Center for Young Adults

Leon. *See* Brother Leon

LeVert, John, 150

Lilacs, 92, 105, 145

Lipsyte, Robert, 4

Litowinsky, Olga, 160–161

Little Raw on Monday Mornings, A, 25

"Little Things That Count, The," 21

Look Homeward, Angel (Thomas Wolfe), 234

Lori Cranston (T), 214–218, 223–228

"Love Song of J. Alfred Prufrock, The" (T. S. Eliot), 58, 63

Lulu (IMN), 43–44, 206–207, 208–211

Lynch, Chris, 3

MacRae, Cathi, 166–167

MacLeod, Anne Scott, 132–133

Madame Bovary (Gustave Flaubert), 176

Manter, Connie, 71–72

Marble box. *See* Black marble

Marchand, General Marcus. *See* General Marcus Marchand

Margaret A. Edwards Award (American Library Association), 1, 17–18, 29

Marlow, Marilyn, 23–25, 27–28, 46, 159, 233

Mazer, Harry, 4

Mazer, Norma Fox, 5

Mazzo (BB), 138–140, 142, 146, 148

McCaffrey, Dr Marilyn, 14

Meredith Martin (F), 150, 154, 156, 159–160, 164–165

Metaphors. *See* Imagery

Miro Shantas (AFD), 119–123, 125–133, 156, 189

Misdirection, 92–95, 100–101, 165, 201, 204, 209

Mr. and Mrs. Bo Jo Jones (Ann Head), 5

Monument, Massachusetts, xii, 83–84, 101, 123, 148, 151, 158, 171, 177–178, 184, 187–188, 190, 210

Movies, influence of, 20, 38–39, 56, 84, 91, 150, 175, 210, 223, 233, 245

My Darling, My Hamburger (Paul Zindel), 5

Names, meaning of, 40, 58, 60, 84, 131–132, 137, 209, 215, 234

Nazi Holocaust, 177, 182–183

Nicholson, George, 4

Nicole Renaud (H), 186, 188–191

Nodelman, Perry, 100–101, 103

Now and at the Hour, 24–25, 69, 145, 237

Nuclear holocaust, 143–144

Nuns, 15–16, 19, 26, 46, 92, 146, 155, 173–174, 235

Obie (CW, BCW), 53, 58, 62, 64, 81–87, 90–95

Oppenheimer, Mark, 45

Other Bells for Us to Ring, 44–45, 47, 76, 169–175

Outsiders, The (S. E. Hinton), 4

Ozzie (F), 155–157, 162–164, 166

Pairing, 123, 125, 134, 142, 153, 157, 172, 209. *See also* Twins

Pantheon (publisher), 28, 160

Patchen, Kenneth, 174

Patriotism as fanaticism, 120, 125–126, 130, 132–135

Paul Moreaux/Roget (F), xii, 150–166

Peck, Richard, 4, 5, 68

Pigman, The (Paul Zindel), 4

Pipkin, Gloria, 76

Plot structure, 20, 39–40, 42, 45–46, 81–82, 100–101, 103–105, 122–124, 161–162, 210–211

Poetry, 196–199, 231–236

Point of view, 56, 121–123, 125, 139, 142, 162–163, 201, 210, 214, 223, 241

Postmodernism, 2, 40–41, 70–71

Prophet, The (Kahlil Gibran), 214

Psychopathy, 219–220

Rag and Bone Shop, The, 31, 40, 45, 144, 180, 182, 214, 238–246

Ray Bannister (BCW), 83–84, 92–93, 95

Raymond (AFD), 121, 128–129, 132

Religion. *See* Cormier, Robert— Catholicism, Catholic Church

Ricker, Lillian, 20

Robert Cormier Center for Young Adults, Leominster Public Library, 7–8

Robert E. Cormier Collection, Fitchburg State College (Cormier archive), xii, 29, 35, 196

Rochman, Hazel, 96, 166, 175

Rosanna Roget (F), 152–153, 157–158, 162, 215

Rossellini, Roberto, 45

St. Cecilia's Church, xii, 16–17, 172, 237

St. Jude's Church, xii, 151, 153, 155, 171–172, 174, 185

Salinger, J. D., 4

Sanabria, Diane, 7

Saroyan, William, 19

Sexual references and scenes, 91–92, 152–153, 161–162, 190, 215–217, 220–221, 227, 235

Shakespeare, allusions to, 57–58

Shoemaker, Joel, 244

Short stories, 22, 26, 28, 170, 195

Similes. See Imagery

Sister Angela, 44–45, 171, 173–174

Sister Catherine, 17

Structure. See Plot structure

Style, 2, 39, 46, 56–57, 76–77, 82, 92, 103, 125–126, 156–157, 162, 175, 183, 210, 220, 239–241

Suicide, 86–87, 129, 148, 173, 191, 207, 236

Susan Roget (F), 44, 154–156, 159–166

Sutherland, Zena, 162–163

Sutton, Roger, 43, 96, 211

Symbols. See Imagery

Take Me Where the Good Times Are, 25

Tarr, C. Anita, 70–71

Tenderness, 6–7, 30, 161, 213–228, 234

Terrorism, 119–135, 184. See also Patriotism as fanaticism

Themes, 38, 41–42, 43, 62, 85, 89, 107, 125, 130–135, 144, 176, 183, 191, 204, 206, 208

Thomas, Dylan, 126

Thompson (IAC) See Grey

Throb (T), 215–217

Tom Sawyer, The Adventures of (Mark Twain), 17, 151, 203–204

Trent (RB), 44, 180, 239–244

Tunes for Bears to Dance To, 45, 76, 171, 176–183

Twins, 15, 138, 161. See also Pairing

Verse, verse novel. See Poetry

Viewpoint. See Point of view

Vigils, The, 53–64, 71, 84–86, 90, 93

Virden, Craig, 181, 219, 233

Voice. See Point of view

Waste Land, The (T. S. Eliot), 143

We All Fall Down, 36, 45, 195–204, 234

Wells, H. G., 150

"What if?", 38, 149, 159–160, 206–207, 214, 233

Wizard of Oz, The (L. Frank Baum), 105

Wojtyla, Karen, 45, 183, 231, 233, 239

Wolfe, Thomas, 19–20, 101, 129, 234

Wolff, Virginia Euwer, 3

Worcester, Massachusetts, 93, 210

Worcester Telegram, 22

World War II, 20–21, 169, 171, 178, 184, 187

Writing methods, 12, 29, 35–39, 115, 128, 140–141, 160–161, 196–199, 214, 220–221, 233, 239, 244–245. See also Characters, Imagery, Plot structure, Style, Themes

Wuthering Heights (Emily Brontë), 74, 125, 209

Yeats, William Butler, 238

Zale, Andrew, 72

Zindel, Paul, 4

ABOUT THE AUTHOR

Patty Campbell has been a critic, author, teacher, and librarian in the field of young adult literature for over thirty years. During the formative years of the genre, she was the assistant coordinator of young adult services for the Los Angeles Public Library system, and she has taught adolescent literature at UCLA and Denver University. Her critical writing has appeared in the *New York Times Book Review* and many library journals. Currently she writes "The Sand in the Oyster," a column on controversial issues in books for teens, for *The Horn Book Magazine* and is a young adult editorial reviewer for Amazon.com online bookstore. Campbell is the author of six books, among them *Two Pioneers of Young Adult Library Services* (Scarecrow Press). She has shaped two series of literary criticism as editor: Twayne's Young Adult Authors, and, currently, Scarecrow Studies in Young Adult Literature. She has served on the board of directors of both the Young Adult Library Services Association of the American Library Association and the Assembly on Adolescent Literature of the National Council of Teachers of English, and as the president of the latter organization in 2005. In 1989 she was the recipient of ALA's Grolier Award for distinguished service to young adults and books, and in 2001 she won the NCTE's ALAN Award. Campbell lives on an avocado ranch in California and in her spare time writes and publishes books on motor-home travel abroad with her husband, David Shore.